# Korea's Unborn Future

## UNDERSTANDING LOW-FERTILITY TRENDS

OECD
BETTER POLICIES FOR BETTER LIVES

**Please cite this publication as:**
OECD (2025), *Korea's Unborn Future: Understanding Low-Fertility Trends*, OECD Publishing, Paris, https://doi.org/10.1787/005ce8f7-en.

ISBN 978-92-64-54511-3 (print)
ISBN 978-92-64-35909-3 (PDF)
ISBN 978-92-64-32192-2 (HTML)

**Photo credits:** Cover © Vincent Koen, OECD.

Corrigenda to OECD publications may be found at: https://www.oecd.org/en/publications/support/corrigenda.html.

# Preface

Korea is facing an unprecedented demographic challenge, with the lowest fertility rate in the world. In 2023, the country's total fertility rate was down to 0.72, reflecting a profound shift with far-reaching implications for the economy, labour market, and social structures.

At the heart of Korea's demographic dilemma lies a sharp trade-off preventing both women and men from living balanced lives combining career and family. Korea has made significant strides in family policies over the years. However, they still fail to fully meet the diverse needs of working parents. Moreover, rigid gender norms and entrenched labour market practices further exacerbate these challenges, especially for women, who are often forced to choose between pursuing a career and raising a family. This book highlights that family policies can only reach their full potential when they are paired with efforts to make working hours shorter and more flexible and active promotion of gender equality in the workplace.

In response to this challenge, this book, a joint effort between the Korea Institute for Health and Social Affairs (KIHASA) and the Organisation for Economic Co-operation and Development (OECD), is a go-to reference for anyone trying to understand ultra-low fertility in Korea. It is also a good case study for anyone analysing falling fertility in different country contexts, as the underlying drivers are similar across the OECD and indeed globally.

The findings presented in this book are based on two OECD Economics Department Working Papers, produced jointly by KIHASA and OECD experts: Korea's Unborn Future: Lessons from OECD Experience, and Women's Employment and Fertility in South Korea: A Review of Recent Research. The book also draws on a special chapter in the 2024 OECD Economic Survey of Korea and material from the 2022 OECD Economic Survey of Korea. This collaborative effort represents the combined expertise of KIHASA, which brings deep insight into Korea's demographic and societal challenges, and the OECD, which provides a broad, international perspective on policy solutions. The partnership underscores the value of global cooperation in tackling complex demographic challenges and developing effective policies that can be applied not only to Korea but also to other OECD member countries facing similar issues.

This book aims to promote informed and effective policy measures by identifying the root causes of low fertility in Korea. It advocates a future in which both men and women can achieve their career and family goals without compromise, in a country and a context where the joy of bringing children to the world and see them grow outweighs the costs and sacrifice involved. This should be a primary policy goal in and of itself, while dampening population decline and labour shortages and improving public finances are additional benefits.

**Álvaro Pereira**

Chief Economist, OECD

**Hyekyu Kang**

Vice President, Korea Institute for Health and Social Affairs

# Foreword

This book is the outcome of a collaboration between the Korea Institute for Health and Social Affairs (KIHASA) and the Organisation for Economic Co-operation and Development (OECD). The findings presented in this book are based on two OECD Economics Department Working Papers, produced jointly by KIHASA and OECD experts: *Korea's Unborn Future: Lessons from OECD Experience,* and *Women's Employment and Fertility in South Korea: A Review of Recent Research*. The book also draws on a special chapter in the 2024 OECD Economic Survey of Korea and material from the 2022 OECD Economic Survey of Korea.

The report was prepared by Jon Pareliussen, Yoonyoung Yang, Hyunjeong Hwang, (Economics Department), Sunyoung Choi and Sunyu Ham (Korea Institute for Health and Social Affairs) under the supervision of Vincent Koen (Economics Department). Statistical research assistance was provided by Axel Purwin, administrative and editorial assistance by Sisse Nielsen and communication assistance by François Iglesias (Economics Department). The authors would like to extend warm thanks to the Government of Korea, members of the Economic Development and Review Committee, Luiz de Mello, Isabell Koske, Christophe André and Young-Hyun Shin (Economics Department), Willem Adema (Directorate for Employment, Labour and Social Affairs) and Randall Jones (Korea Economic Institute), for giving invaluable comments and facilitating the production of this book and its background material.

# Table of contents



## FIGURES

## TABLES

# Executive Summary

Birth rates are falling across the world and nowhere more so than in Korea, where fertility has imploded to unprecedented lows. As a consequence, the Korean population is expected to halve over the next six decades and the elderly (aged 65 or older) will account for around 58% of the total population by 2082. During this time, the old-age dependency ratio (the ratio of individuals aged 65 and over to those aged 20 to 64) will surge from 28% today to 155%. The combination of a shrinking and ageing population poses a formidable challenge to sustaining social insurance systems and maintaining living standards. Labour shortages will intensify as retirees make up an increasing share of the population, and the fiscal cost of health, long-term care and pensions is set to more than double to 17.4% of GDP by 2060

In Korea, every woman had six children on average over her lifetime in 1960. This dropped to just below one child per woman in 2018, and fell further year by year to reach 0.72 in 2023. From the 1960s to the mid-2010s, the decline in fertility came about as Korean women postponed the age at which they get married and reduced the number of children they had once married. During this time period, the vast majority eventually married and had at least one child. The period starting in the late 2010s marks a change, as falling fertility from this time on has increasingly been driven by married women having no children and women foregoing marriage altogether. This trend seems to have continued into the 2020s, even though the numbers remain difficult to interpret due to the Covid-19 pandemic.

To an extent falling fertility reflects that young people around the world have better access to birth control and increased freedom to use it to live the lives they want with the number of children they prefer, which increases welfare for those concerned and reduces environmental pressures. However, in several countries, including Korea, young generations bring very few children to the world despite their preferences for more, and despite society needing more children to dampen the consequences of rapid ageing.

When gender-unequal norms and a large gender wage gap meet long hours and inflexible working practices, many Korean mothers are constrained to choose family over career for an extended period of time, while men have little choice but to become the family breadwinner. This reduces the well-being of both men and women as well as family income. Seniority-based wages and a dual labour market compound the loss of lifetime income for any extended labour market absence. In previous times, when strong social norms dictated women to marry and have children, and women's career opportunities were limited, women more easily chose family over employment. As Korea has grown richer, women have gained more equal opportunities to men in education and working life, and families increasingly rely on two incomes, the sacrifice of family income for each child has grown and pushed fertility to new lows.

Beyond the family budget constraint, it also matters to fertility that mothers bear a heavier individual career burden than fathers, as decisions to have a child normally require agreement between the parents. The importance of this individual cost of parenthood may have increased as an increasing share of marriages end in divorce, and it may have been pushed up by a shift in preferences. When Korean married women were in employment in the past, this tended to be either out of necessity because their husband's incomes were too low to feed the family, or because the financial rewards were substantial. However, since the early 2000s, the elasticity of married women's labour supply in response to their own wages and spouses' income have been decreasing considerably, which indicates that women's preferences may have shifted in favour of career.

Direct costs add to the loss of income associated with parenthood. While expenditures for food, clothing and childcare have declined as a share of average family income, increases in housing expenditure have reduced fertility rates across the OECD, including Korea. In a reflection of Korea's dual labour market, many parents allocate a sizeable portion of their income to private tutoring to help their children get ahead, making education expenditure another major hurdle to have children. In 2023, almost 80% of Korean schoolchildren participated in private tutoring for which their parents spent roughly 10% of their disposable income on average.

Family policies, including early childhood education and care, paid parental leave and family benefits, can make it easier to combine career and parenthood and partially compensate parents for cost from having and raising children. A major policy reform in 2013 made all preschool-aged children eligible for free childcare regardless of parental income, accompanied by the introduction of a parental home-care allowance for parents opting to care for their child at home. Parental leave has also been expanded and strengthened considerably over time in Korea, with the result that both the duration and the level of payment eligible parents are entitled to compare well with the OECD average. Even so, the effects of these policies in terms of female employment and fertility have been underwhelming. Empirical evidence points to a sizeable income effect in which cash transfers and subsidised services provided in-kind increase household disposable income, enabling mothers to stay at home. Individual situations and preferences play an important role, with for example mothers living in areas with quality childcare available being more likely to increase their labour supply as a response to the 2013 reform. The career maintenance effect of family policies will likely be weaker and the income effect stronger in countries like Korea where labour market institutions make it difficult to combine career and children at the outset.

The Covid-19 pandemic led to postponed marriages and childbirths, temporary pushing fertility below its trend. A recent uptick in marriages and births reflects a catch-up effect from the pandemic years. However, it is not possible to untangle the effects of the pandemic from other forces acting, and the possibility of a trend shift in fertility therefore cannot be ruled out. The working hour reduction reform which was phased in from 2018 to 2021 represents a major shift towards work-life balance. Cumulating with the strengthening of family policies the past couple of decades it could potentially have tipped the scales for prospective working parents. However, a fertility revival will at best be slow and gradual until policies, gender norms and working practices taken together support a large majority of women to pursue career and family in tandem.

# 1 Overview: Reversing the demographic meltdown

Jon Pareliussen, Economics Department of the OECD

Birth rates are falling across the world. This is arguably good news for the environment and for the women and men across the world who have gained access to birth control and have the freedom to use it to live the lives they want with the number of children they prefer. Even though this message of sustainability and empowerment is true, there is also another side to the story. In several countries, young generations bring very few children to the world despite their preferences for more, and despite society desperately needing more children to dampen rapid ageing. In Korea, every woman had six children on average over her lifetime in 1960 (Total Fertility Rate, TFR). The TFR dropped to just below one child per woman in 2018, and fell further year by year to reach 0.72 in 2023. This is the lowest in the world, lower than in Japan (1.2), China (1.2), Singapore (1.0) and Chinese Taipei (0.9) (Yang et al., 2024). Most importantly, it is far less than the number of children Korean women say they would like to have.

Ultra-low fertility in Korea is a symptom of structural traits of Korean society constraining people's possibilities to combine career and family. Parents need to reallocate some of the time that would otherwise have been spent on paid work to childcare. For a variety of reasons discussed in this book, mothers tend to reallocate more time away from work and towards childcare than fathers. The value of this time increases with average incomes, and it increases as women gain more equal access to education and careers. These forces, which are largely common across countries, nonetheless yield very different outcomes, as some countries successfully soften the trade-off with a combination of family-friendly labour practices, family policies like subsidised childcare, and more gender-equal norms and more equal sharing of caring responsibilities between mothers and fathers.

Korea's ultra-low birth rates reflect Korea's rapid achievements in raising incomes and empowering women in a society where young people's fertility choices remain constrained by the realities of life, notably gender norms and labour practices which are remnants of a different time when men were breadwinners and women home-makers by default. This constrained choice is the main reason why low fertility is rightfully among the top priorities of the government, who declared it a national emergency and announced new policy initiatives in 2024, including a plan to establish a new ministry (tentatively named the Ministry of Population Strategy Planning) to achieve the target of raising the fertility rate to 1 by 2030.

## Ageing is largely irreversible, but can be slowed

Ageing caused by low fertility is a major societal challenge in several OECD countries, and nowhere more so than in Korea (Figure 1.1). This said, Korea's ageing challenges have just barely begun. The Korean labour force has experienced demographic tailwinds for decades. The share of the population in working age is today close to its peak, as large generations born in the 1960s, 70s, 80s and even 90s are all in working age. Some signs of ageing are nonetheless becoming apparent. The population begun to decline in 2021. Kindergartens are increasingly converted into nursing homes and wedding halls into funeral parlours, while the sales of pet strollers exceeded those of baby strollers on a leading e-commerce platform for the first time in 2023. This anecdotal evidence only foreshadows the profound changes to come as large cohorts of baby-boomers reach retirement and new cohorts reaching working age are continuously shrinking in size.

Once it has taken hold, ageing is largely irreversible. The dynamics of low fertility in the past rapidly diminish the generations of women in childbearing age today (Table 1.1), with the consequence that population decline can only be slowed marginally in the short term. A fertility rate of 0.72 means roughly that for every 100 people in the current parent generation there will be only 36 children and 13 grandchildren. Assuming that fertility remains around the current level and immigration follows past trends, the Korean population is expected to halve over the next six decades and the elderly (aged 65 or older) will account for around 58% of the total population by 2082. During this time, the old-age dependency ratio (the ratio of individuals aged 65 and over to those aged 20 to 64) will surge from 28% today to 155%. The combination of a shrinking and ageing population poses a formidable challenge to sustaining social insurance systems and maintaining living standards. Labour shortages will intensify as retirees make up an increasing share of the population, and the fiscal cost of health, long-term care and pensions is set to more than double to 17.4% of GDP by 2060 (Chapter 2; OECD, 2024a).

Figure 1.1. The population will decline more rapidly in Korea than elsewhere

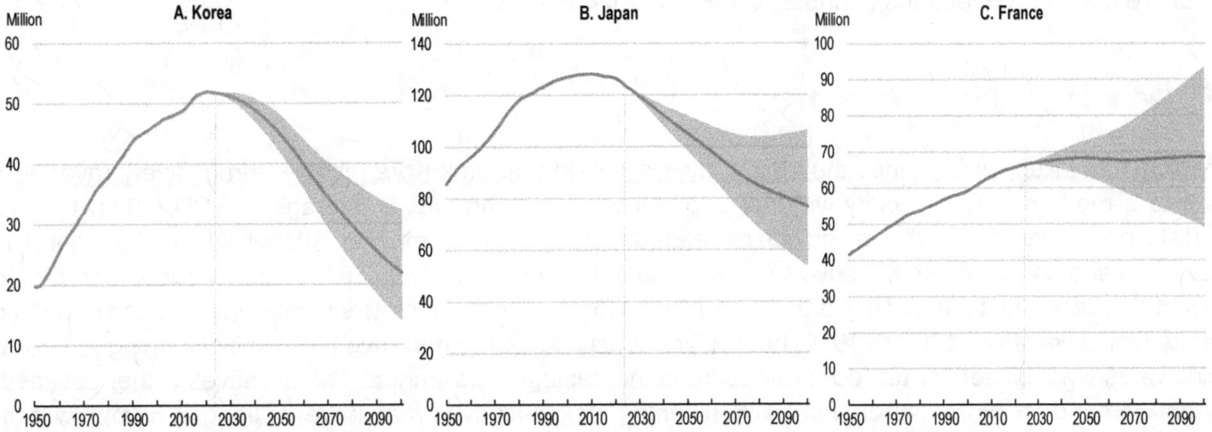


Note: The line represents the UN's medium scenario and the shaded area is bounded by the UN's low and high scenarios.
Source: UN, World Population Prospects 2024.

StatLink https://stat.link/i8cmoq

Table 1.1. The total fertility rate has fallen steadily from generation to generation

Completed and uncompleted cohort-specific total fertility rates[1], number of women and births

| Birth cohort | Cohort-specific fertility rate | Number of women per cohort[2] | Number of births per cohort |
|---|---|---|---|
| 1936-40 | 4.97 | 1151342 | 5720443 |
| 1941-45 | 3.95 | 1169586 | 4623958 |
| 1946-50 | 2.94 | 1287335 | 3786696 |
| 1951-55 | 2.43 | 1617090 | 3931146 |
| 1956-60 | 1.89 | 2207268 | 4170633 |
| 1961-65 | 1.95 | 2269201 | 4429480 |
| 1966-70 | 1.89 | 2185784 | 4128946 |
| 1971-75 | 1.69 | 2167499 | 3661990 |
| 1976-80 | 1.51 | 1946316 | 2947696 |
| 1981-85 | 1.34 | 1850484 | 2474097 |
| 1986-90 | 1.06 | 1516056 | 1605503 |
| 1991-95 | 0.81 | 1651828 | 1343762 |
| 1996-00 | 0.73 | 1543635 | 1133028 |
| 2001-05 | 0.72 | 1209243 | 868841 |
| 2006-10 | 0.72 | 1098975 | 787416 |

Note: 1. Cohort-specific fertility rates are obtained by summarising age-specific birth rates transposed from Table 2.1. Missing numbers are extrapolated by assuming that they are equal to the age-specific birth rates of the preceding cohort (for the 1981-85 and subsequent cohorts) and the subsequent cohort (in the case of the 1936-40 cohort).
2. The sizes of the birth cohorts from 1936-55 are derived from Statistics Korea's 1960 Projected Population Database, and cover South Korea only.
Source: Author's calculations based on Kwon, T. and D. Kim (2002), *Understanding Population (revised edition)*, Seoul National University Press (in Korean), and Statistics Korea.

This rapid ageing is perhaps the most intuitive and well-documented reason why politicians do and should care about low fertility, but measured in GDP per capita and the fiscal balance, increasing fertility will have immediate negative consequences with gains materialising only in the very long term. Children do not pay much taxes, their mothers may reduce their labour supply, while children and their families receive substantial transfers and in-kind services like schooling, childcare and health services from the public sector. As an example, if Korea's fertility rate were to miraculously increase by two and a half times from today to reach 1.85, the dependency ratio would still increase to 117%. This is a sizeable improvement from 155% but would still turn the country from one of the youngest in the OECD to the oldest by a margin over the coming six decades (Chapter 2; OECD, 2024a).

## Korea's era of ultra-low fertility

Fertility has fallen rapidly since the 1950s, over a period that took Korea from a rural society ravaged by war to a modern, urban society with per capita incomes at the OECD average (OECD, 2024a). Falling fertility in the beginning of the period can be related to rising female employment, but also to high population pressure and a wish to escape poverty. The TFR plummeted from 4.5 in 1970 to 2.1 in 1983, a drop of 2.4 in just 13 years. The timing of this dramatic fall inevitably links it to the state's family planning and population control initiatives from 1962 to 1979, but the previously accepted narrative that family planning and falling birth rates was caused by top-down pressure is increasingly challenged. The initiatives rather satisfied a latent demand for birth control and family planning. The initiatives may have influenced norms, with the need for birth control becoming a widely shared social value, and the ideal number of children dropping to stabilise around two, a level at which it remains today. A possible negative long-term effect of the family planning programme is that it may have contributed to the norm that workers are expected to let work take priority over family (Chapter 2; Choi et al., 2024).

After a period of stabilisation and a temporary rebound around 1990, the TFR continued falling to reach a new low of 1.18 in 2002. This was the first time it fell below 1.3, marking the beginning of what is often called in Korea the era of ultra-low fertility (or "lowest-low" in Korean). It temporarily edged up to around 1.3 in the early 2010s before declining again, falling below one for the first time in 2018. Since then, fertility continued falling until it bottomed out at 0.72 in 2023 and started edging up again from the summer of 2024. Postponed marriages during the pandemic and the sequencing of childbirths after marriage means that even fewer babies were born in 2021, 22 and 23 than what would have been the case without by the 2020-21 pandemic. Likewise, the recent uptick reflects a catch-up effect which will at least in part be temporary. The big question, which is further discussed at the end of this chapter, is if there are also other factors pulling up fertility. It cannot be ruled out that 2024 will mark a turning point of Korea's era of ultra-low fertility, but it would be premature to draw this conclusion, and fertility remains extremely low.

Since the start of the millennium, a number of studies have decomposed the fertility trend into various driving forces. They all point to marriage patterns and childbearing behaviour within marriage as key forces behind falling fertility rates. Childbearing outside of marriage has only had a very limited impact, as almost all births occur within marriage in Korea. Some earlier studies looking at the fertility behaviour of cross-sections of women at a given point in time ("synthetic cohorts") observed that people married and had children later in life than before. Fertility in younger age groups (women in their 20s) had fallen as a result, while it had increased in older groups (women in their 30s). These studies inaccurately concluded that couples had approximately the same number of children as before, but only later in life, so birth rates were bound to catch up in the future (Chapter 2; Choi et al., 2024).

With the benefit of hindsight and better methods, it became clear that the number of children each woman has over her lifetime has been falling consistently from one cohort of mothers to the next (Table 1.1). From the 1960s to the 2000s, a reduction in the number of children per married woman and a continuous increase in the age at which women first got married both contributed to the decline in fertility. Already by the end of the 1980s it had become so rare that married couples had three or more children that a continued fall in third and higher-order births had little effect on overall fertility. From the 1990s to the mid-2010s, the falling incidence of second births was the main driving force of the declining birth rate. Up until the mid-

2010s, a vast majority of Korean women ended up marrying and having at least one child, likely partly due to a strong social norm towards the duty to marry and have children. The period starting in the late 2010s marks a change, as falling fertility from this time on has increasingly been driven by married women having no children and women foregoing marriage altogether (Chapter 2; Choi et al., 2024). This trend seems to have continued into the 2020s, but numbers remain difficult to interpret due to the effects of the Covid-19 pandemic, as further discussed below.

## Career-family trade-offs have increased with economic and social progress

Any parent in any country knows that having children comes with costs. There are some direct costs to having children, for example food, clothing, housing, childcare and education. In addition, there is the opportunity cost of lost income, as parents reallocate some time that they could otherwise have spent in paid employment on raising their children. The opportunity cost affects the overall family budget, and it entails an individual career cost to the parent disproportionately shifting efforts from career to childcare.

In Korea, the direct costs of having children are magnified compared to many OECD countries by fierce competition to enter prestigious universities and high private education expenditure (credentialism). The opportunity cost of having children is high due to a dual labour market with unequal pay, working conditions and social insurance coverage, and largely seniority-based career progression combining to create a very high cost for any temporary absence from the labour market. Taken together, credentialism, seniority-based careers and gender discrimination lead to a misallocation of human capital and likely a substantial loss of productivity. Literacy skills and tertiary education, objective measures of skills which are highly correlated with employment and productivity in most OECD countries, do not significantly affect the likelihood of employment in Korea (Figure 1.2). The weak link between objective skills and labour market outcomes also raises normative questions about fairness and the intrinsic value of equal opportunities.

**Figure 1.2. Literacy skills and tertiary education matter little for employment in Korea**

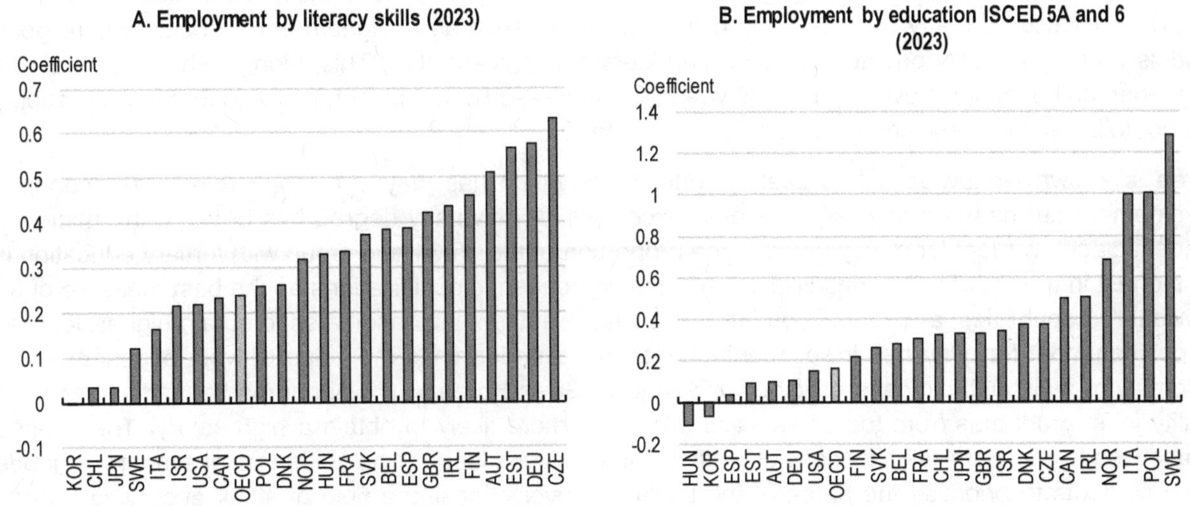


Note: The log likelihood of being employed is estimated in a logistic regression controlling for 10-year age-gender cohort, parental status (by gender), education level, literacy skills and work experience (relative to age). Literacy skills are measured in PIAAC score points on a scale from 0 to 100. Education is measured by the International Standard Classification of Education (ISCED). ISCED 5A and 6 corresponds to tertiary education at Bachelor level or above. For details, see Pareliussen (2022), "How labour market outcomes reflect age, gender and skills in Korea", *OECD Economics Department Working Papers*, No. 1739, OECD Publishing.
Source: Author's calculations based on OECD Survey of Adult Skills (2023).

StatLink https://stat.link/ij2vnb

While the costs of career breaks are high, they are also difficult to avoid for women who choose motherhood. A culture of long work hours and a lack of flexibility where work is expected to take priority over family makes it hard to reduce work efforts for a period while children are young. When choosing parenthood, Korean fathers therefore typically become fully committed breadwinners and mothers typically become fully committed carers for an extended period of time. At the family level this translates into a sizeable loss of family income. At the individual level, most women and men would likely be happier spending reasonable amounts of their time on both career and family. When they are constrained to specialise in one of the two, this is a welfare loss for both (Cavapozzi et al., 2024). The individual cost to Korean mothers is particularly high. They suffer on average a long-term labour income loss of about 66%, mainly due to a decline in their labour force participation after childbirth (Chapter 3). Women therefore increasingly choose not to marry, or to marry but having fewer babies than in the past or not having any at all, a trend which has given rise to the terms "birth strike" and "marriage strike".

### *Parents invest more in their children: The golden ticket syndrome*

The demographic transition is closely connected to economic development, industrialisation, and widespread access to contraception. New technologies are increasingly skill-intensive, while education has a cost. Parents therefore respond to economic development by reducing the number of children while investing more in the human capital of each of them. This is the so-called quantity-quality trade-off. Investments in one's offspring also include items such as food and clothing, which have been continuously falling as a share of total household expenditure in developed countries and are therefore unlikely to be related to falling fertility. The same is the case with childcare, which is increasingly subsidised and affordable across the OECD, and has been provided free of charge since 2013 in Korea. Other items, notably housing and private education expenditures have become more burdensome.

A cross-country empirical study found that increases in household expenditure on housing had a significant negative effect on fertility rates across the OECD (OECD, 2024b). This is also the case in Korea, where the doubling of housing prices between 2013 and 2019 was found to reduce the likelihood of people getting married by between 4 and 5.7% (Kang, 2022). Seoul is one of the most densely populated cities in the OECD. In particular, many parents flock to popular areas such as Gangnam and Seocho, where good schools and high-quality private education providers are concentrated. This, along with the increase in single-person households over the past 20 years, has increased demand for housing in Seoul, while supply has not followed suit, resulting in rising prices (Chapter 3).

Korea is known worldwide for its zeal for education, which has played a major role in its economic development but has in many ways become excessive. A university degree has become the minimum academic achievement for a majority, and the proportion of the 25-34 age group with tertiary education is the highest in the OECD. Credentialism, a reliance on academic qualifications as the best measure of an individual's capabilities, and "education inflation", which requires job candidates to obtain higher degrees for positions that formerly had lower requirements, have undermined the value of work experience and diplomas from all but the most prestigious universities. Given Korea's dual labour market and a scarcity of quality jobs, graduates from top universities are much more likely to obtain a high salary. The intense competition to gain admission to these prestigious universities, dubbed "the golden ticket syndrome", leads many students to prioritise the name of the institution over choosing a field of study according to their interests and skills (OECD, 2022). As a result, the share of working-age Koreans who are over-qualified for their jobs is among the highest in the OECD, and the share of employees with qualifications that are mismatched to the job they actually do is almost 50%, which is the highest in the OECD (Figure 1.3).

Figure 1.3. People's formal qualifications are often mismatched to their jobs in Korea

Incidence of field of study mismatch among adults aged 25-64 (2023)

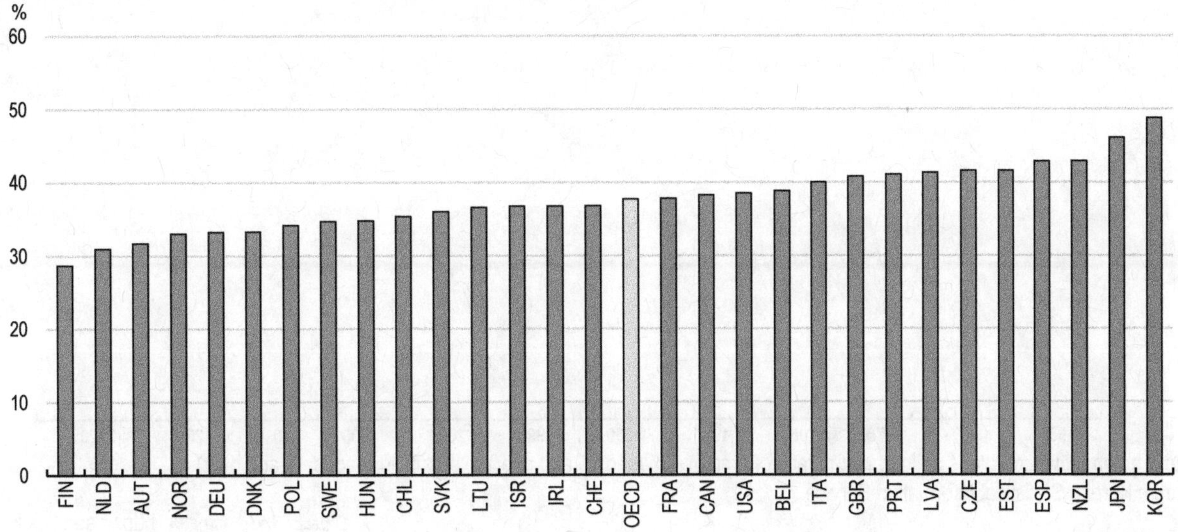


Note: A worker is classified as well-matched by field of study if the area of study of their highest qualification is related to the field that is most relevant to their job. Caution is required when interpreting results for Poland due to the high share of respondents with unusual response patterns. BEL refers to the Flemish region and GBR refers to England.

Source: OECD (2024), Do Adults Have the Skills They Need to Thrive in a Changing World? Survey of Adult Skills 2023, OECD Publishing, Paris.

StatLink https://stat.link/zasdje

In a race to secure their offspring a "golden ticket" to top universities and quality employment, many Korean parents allocate a sizeable portion of their income to private tutoring, making education expenditure another major hurdle to have children. In 2023, almost 80% of Korean schoolchildren participated in private tutoring for which their parents spent roughly 10% of their disposable income on average. Tutoring is positively correlated with academic achievement and likely contributing to Korea's high academic performance as measured by for example the PISA survey (OECD, 2023). These gains in academic achievement are likely outweighed by the cost of provision and negative side-effects, including postponed entry into working life, weaker adolescent mental health and life satisfaction, lower equality of opportunity, and lower fertility.

## *Prosperity and gender equality in education and work accentuate the motherhood cost*

Raising children consumes some of the time that was previously available for paid work, which lowers the household's combined income. In previous times, when women had very limited roles in the labour market, this so-called opportunity cost of having children was also low. In most OECD countries, until around 1930, married women were simply not hired, and almost all births happened within marriage. The labour market participation of married women rose gradually in most OECD countries in the 1930s and 1940s, and much more rapidly after World War II. Korea follows a similar pattern, but with different timing (Figure 1.4). Before the 1980s, Korean employers selectively recruited men and unmarried women. Women's educational attainment made little difference to their likelihood of marriage or career. Since the 1980s, both the government and businesses began to recognise the need to utilise the labour force of married women, but a lack of public support for pregnancy, childbirth and childcare made combining work and motherhood largely impossible. Women therefore tended to participate in the labour force until marriage, after which they exited. Since 2000, women's employment rates have been on a continuous upward trend, only interrupted by the credit card crisis in the early 2000s, the Global Financial Crisis in the late 2000s and Covid-19 in 2020-21. The gender gap in employment has also narrowed over the past two decades, although it remains among the highest in the OECD.

### Figure 1.4. Female employment has risen rapidly since the 1960s

Note: The employment rate is defined as the ratio of employed (aged 15 and over) to population (aged 15 and over).
Source: Korean Statistical Information Service.

StatLink https://stat.link/khve2y

The trend towards more gender-equal access to education (Figure 1.5) and employment increased the opportunity cost of motherhood and gave rise to a negative relationship between women's labour force participation and fertility both between countries and within countries, where women who worked full-time usually had fewer children than those not in employment and women who worked part-time fell in between. Likewise, earnings prospects and the opportunity cost of having children are higher for women with higher education. Before the 1990s, there was therefore a negative cross-country correlation between fertility and female labour force participation (Fluchtmann et al., 2023).

### Figure 1.5. Women are increasingly highly educated

Female to male ratio, students at tertiary level education

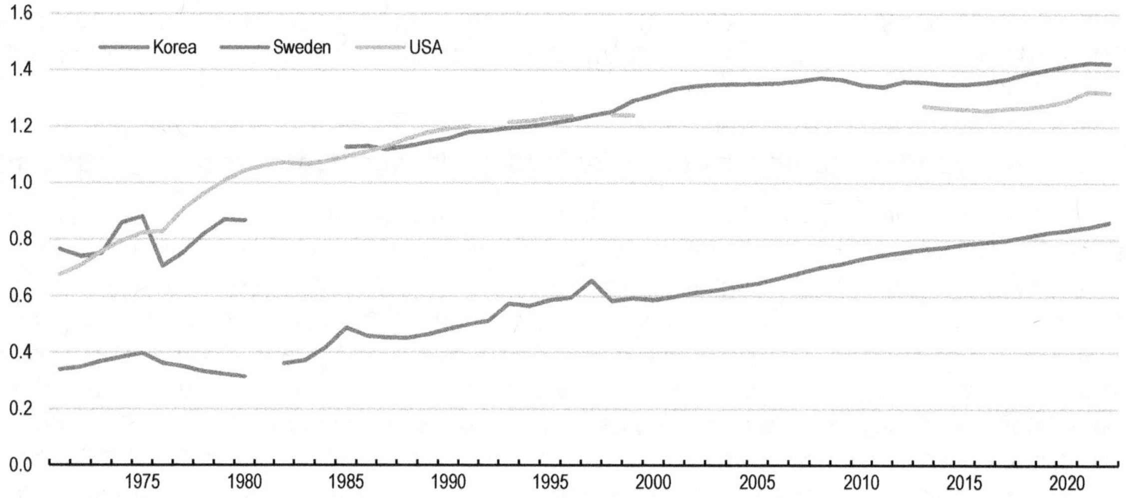


Source: The World Bank.

StatLink https://stat.link/s6aqlc

However, this relationship turned positive by the year 2000, as some countries like Sweden, Norway, Denmark, France and the United States managed to ease the time constraint for mothers by combinations of labour market structures, family policies and more equal sharing of caring responsibilities between mothers and fathers. In contrast, the fertility rate declined sharply in low-participation countries such as

Italy and Spain between the 1970s and 1990s. Korea's experience resembles that of Italy and Spain, but lags in time and the fall in fertility rate has been even more dramatic (Figure 1.6).

**Figure 1.6. Fertility rates have been falling fast in Korea**

Total fertility rate

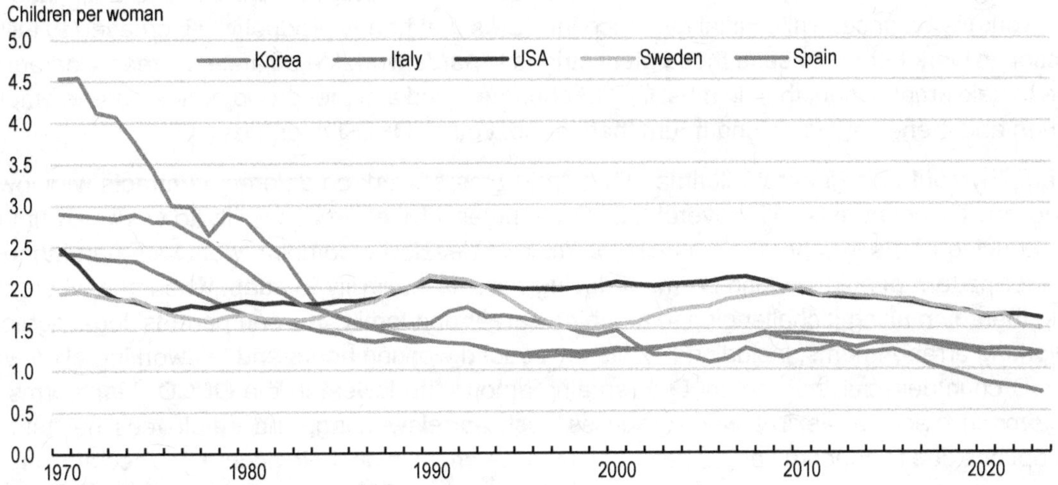


Source: OECD (2024), Fertility rates (indicator). doi: 10.1787/8272fb01-en.

StatLink https://stat.link/8bx54d

Chapter 3 discusses how the career-motherhood trade-off varies between countries and with income levels. Countries with salient trade-offs include middle-income countries like Türkiye, Mexico, Colombia and Costa Rica, who combine fertility rates on par with for example Iceland and France with male employment rates 25-35 percentage points higher than those of women (compared to 5-10 percentage points in France and Iceland). In high-income countries with strong trade-offs like Korea, Italy, Greece and Japan, the gender employment gap is in the range of 15-20 percentage points, while fertility rates are the lowest in the OECD. Rising incomes have sharpened the quantity-quality trade-off and the opportunity cost of motherhood in these countries and turned the balance towards lower fertility and higher female employment.

The sharp opportunity cost of motherhood in Korea comes about because many women leave the labour market for an extended period when they marry or have children, and because these absences have severe long-term consequences for their lifetime earnings. Despite a rapid rise of dual-income families in Korea, driven by a rise in the employment rate of married women with children, a series of studies confirm that the conflict between motherhood and employment remains strong. Kim and Park (2019) found that only 8.7% of women were continuously employed both before and after marriage. A recent survey found that 16% of married women aged 15-54 were currently on a career break due to marriage, family and childcare. Around 41% of them had been away from the labour market for more than 10 years, while 23% had a 5-10-year break (Chapter 3).

Together with the long durations of women's labour market absences, Korea's dual labour market is an important reason for the large income loss. Regular workers enjoy social insurance coverage, good working conditions and high wages, while non-regular workers, including part-time employees, face lower wages, reduced access to social insurance, and precarious job conditions. There is a rigid distinction between regular and non-regular workers, with limited opportunities for transitions. Women often quit their regular contracts as a consequence of motherhood, but find that low-paid non-regular jobs are the only way back in when they seek to re-enter the workforce. As a result, mothers are three times more likely to be in non-regular employment than fathers. Conscient of this, women tend to delay family formation and have fewer children (OECD, 2022; OECD, 2021a).

Long work hours, little flexibility regarding when and where to work and a general expectation that work should take priority over family needs make it difficult to combine two careers with family. This is a main reason why mothers tend to take long career breaks in Korea. Korea's statutory 40-hour regular workweek aligns well with most other OECD countries, and the average usual weekly hours of full-time workers have fallen faster than in any other OECD country over the past two decades. A reform reducing the maximum weekly working hours including overtime from 68 to 52 hours in stages from 2018 to 2021 has greatly improved work-life balance, while initial evidence indicates that hourly productivity increased to fully offset the reduction in work hours. Despite these giant strides towards work-life balance, Korean workers devote more time to paid employment than in most OECD countries, and a higher proportion of Korean employees, both women and men, work very long hours than in most other OECD countries.

Regular employment is in general full-time, while "part-timers" work on different contracts with lower pay and protection. This contrasts with several OECD countries where the possibility to work part-time by for example reducing hours in a person's career job makes it easier to combine work with parenthood. This fits a broader pattern of rigid working norms reducing parents' flexibility to adapt when and where they do their work, thereby making it challenging to combine career and family. Korean parents' legal rights to use flexible working arrangements, including flexible or reduced working hours and teleworking align well with other OECD countries, but their actual use remains among the lowest in the OECD. Many firms do not have systems in place for flexible work practices such as teleworking, and employees hesitate to use available options due to concerns about potential negative impacts on their income, job security, promotion prospects, and career evaluations. Findings by Shin and Lee (2021) indicate that they are right to be worried. They found that even though the use of flexible work arrangements prevented career interruptions for women, increased job satisfaction and improved employees' ability to concentrate on their work, it also increased the risk of scoring low on performance evaluations (Chapter 3; OECD, 2024a).

Since the career-family trade-off is very much alive in Korea, continuously rising female education and employment has come at the expense of fewer childbirths. What has changed is that when facing a conflict between family formation and work, women increasingly prioritise work with the consequence that they postpone marriage and childbirth and have fewer children over their lifetime, or even forgo motherhood altogether. This reflects that with more gender-equal access to education and employment, women's earnings have become an important part of family income and the loss of household income resulting from motherhood has therefore increased.

### *Birth strike: Women may veto parenthood when they have a lot to lose personally*

Some of the ongoing changes are less tangible than those directly related to the household budget constraint. A typical trait of the male breadwinner-female carer model is that prime-aged men's labour supply is not very sensitive to their wage level, while married women's labour supply is largely determined by their spouse's income, and is also very sensitive to the level of their own wages. In other words, men will be fully dedicated to work and providing for their families, while women will only work out of necessity or if the financial reward is substantial. These stylized facts described the situation in Korea very well until the early 2000s, but the elasticities of married women's labour supply in response to their own wages and spouses' income have been decreasing considerably since then (Jung, 2019). This finding indicates that when women today choose to work, they tend to do so less out of necessity and more out of preference than in the past.

A shift towards individualism and away from conformity to traditional norms designating people's duties and their rightful place in the collective, such as the male breadwinner – female carer norm and women's duty to marry and have children, can help explain this potential shift in Korean women's work-family preferences. More practically, as an increasing share of marriages end in divorce, it matters to fertility decisions if one person in a couple bears a disproportionate share of the individual career cost of having children. Children are only likely to be born if both partners desire to have a baby, and the partner carrying the largest individual cost can "veto" the decision. Therefore, countries with more gender-equal sharing of domestic work and lower motherhood penalties in the labour market generally have higher fertility.

Marrying and having children have traditionally been seen as duties in Korea, but young people increasingly reject this idea. Unmarried women are much more likely than unmarried men to cite the loss of freedom from having children and the desire to keep their career as important reasons for not wanting children. Norms towards having children have also changed among those who choose to get married. The duty to have children was an almost universally held norm among married women in 1994, while only approximately 30% agreed to this in 2021 (Chapter 3).

The male breadwinner – female carer norm still stands strong in Korea compared to other OECD countries. The share of the population agreeing that a pre-school child suffers with a working mother and the share of the population agreeing or strongly agreeing that men should have more right to a job than women if jobs are scarce are higher in Korea than in any other OECD country. These attitudes are largely reflected in large gender gaps in time spent per day on paid and unpaid work, although Korea ranks slightly better in these outcomes than it does in norms. If a woman in a childless couple does a disproportional part of the housework this may not prevent her from pursuing a full-time job, but this may become very difficult once a child is born.

The male breadwinner – female carer norm is also perpetuated by a vicious cycle of gender discrimination in the labour market. Korea's gender wage gap is the highest in the OECD, despite narrowing from 37.2% in 2015 to 31.2% in 2022. There is consensus in empirical studies that gender discrimination is a major driver of this gap, with different studies finding evidence of considerable gender discrimination in all age groups, for women with and without children, for employed women, and in hiring (Chapter 3). For example, Kim et al. (2021) decomposed the reduction in the gender wage gap between 2002 and 2020 with changes in observables such as education, industry and occupation. They found that these observables had narrowed the gender wage gap while the practice of paying women less than men under the same conditions had increased the wage gap over this period when seen in isolation. Empirical studies also generally find that this discrimination is limited to the private sector, while public sector jobs such as government officials and teachers, which have strong legal controls in the hiring process, show almost no gender wage gap (Kim and Oh, 2019).

Such a gender wage gap likely contributes to a gendered role separation among couples during childbearing years, as couples will minimise income loss if the lower-paid women work fewer hours or leave the labour force altogether. Employer expectations that women are less likely to work during their childrearing years thereby become a self-fulfilling prophecy, reinforcing a vicious cycle of statistical discrimination and employment discontinuity of mothers which cannot be easily resolved without public intervention. Such discrimination is illegal in Korea, but women who have been discriminated against have faced difficulties in making a case, and many cases have been dismissed due to a lack of supporting evidence or resolved only through corrective measures without imposing penalties. Legal protections, sanctions and enforcement have all been strengthened in Korea in the past few years, but it remains an open question whether or not this is sufficient to make a fundamental difference (OECD 2024a).

## Family policies alone cannot bridge time and money constraints

Family policies, including early childhood education and care, paid parental leave and family benefits, can reduce and compensate for the direct cost from having and raising children, and they can limit the loss of income and future career prospects. Publicly financed childcare and paid parental leave are designed to make it easier to combine work and parenthood, and Korea has made giant strides to implement such family policies. Publicly financed childcare is in particular found to be important across OECD countries. Many studies show that quality childcare boosts female employment and fertility (e.g. OECD, 2017).

Children benefitting from high-quality childcare services also perform better in school than children who do not attend.

Outcomes of other common family policies are more mixed, with their effects on fertility often found to be low compared to their cost, while their effect on female employment is in many contexts insignificant or even negative. Maternity, paternity, and parental leave entitlements provide employment protection for parents absent from work to care for their young children combined with income replacement benefits. While leaves of absence might have a short-term negative impact on career progression, the idea is that they should have a positive effect on women's employment in the long run by maintaining attachment to the labour market and employer-employee matches. However, empirical evidence from various countries does not always show a positive impact on women's labour market participation, nor do such policies always encourage mothers to return to their original jobs. A key mechanism behind this is that any cash transfer or subsidised service provided in-kind will increase a household's disposable income, directly in the case of cash transfers, and indirectly by lowering household expenses in the case of in-kind or subsidised services. As discussed above in the context of spouse's income, this income effect enables parents (usually mothers) to stay at home. For example, a stay-at-home mother who already has her child enrolled in childcare while it is payable will not start working if it becomes free, but the savings on childcare expenses could enable her to stay at home longer than previously planned.

The overall effects of such policies will therefore depend on individual situations and preferences. The career maintenance effect will likely be weaker and the income effect will likely be stronger in countries like Korea where it is difficult to combine career and children at the outset. These insights also create a fairly clear order of priority between the main types of family expenditure if the objectives sought are to boost employment and fertility. Childcare- and parental leave expenditures contribute to both, while the income effect can reduce their aggregate effectiveness in boosting female employment. Child benefits or tax credits, be they recurrent or baby bonuses, will at the outset subsidise fertility, and can improve the livelihoods of families with children, but at the expense of female employment. They will do nothing to bridge the career-family trade-off. In recognition of this, many OECD countries have in recent years shifted their family policy packages towards public support for early childhood education and care and promoting paid leave for both parents.

Korea has introduced a number of family policies in recent years. The enrolment rate in childcare facilities has increased significantly with higher public investment in preschool childcare. Income loss from parental leave gave the right to employment insurance from 2001 and the parental leave benefit for dual-income parents has been increased since 2022 conditional on both parents using parental leave (OECD, 2024a). The eligibility for child allowances has been expanded to children up to the age of eight (previously five), and the allowance amount for infants under two years has been significantly increased. Public spending on family benefits increased from 0.7% of GDP in 2010 to 1.5% in 2020, and is estimated to have increased further by about 0.1-0.2% of GDP since then. It remains lower than the OECD average of 2.3%. This may be an unfair comparison as Korea has a relatively low share of children in the population, but spending per child as a share of GDP per capita is also lower than the OECD average (Chapter 4).

The Korean government has sharply increased public spending on childcare by introducing a series of major reforms aimed at increasing the availability and affordability of early childcare and education services, including extensive subsidies to childcare providers and generous cash benefits for parents (OECD, 2019). A major policy reform in 2013 made all preschool-aged children eligible for free childcare regardless of parental income, accompanied with the introduction of a parental home-care allowance for parents opting to care for their child at home. Public childcare expenditure per child as a share of GDP per capita is approximately 20%, which is third highest in the OECD and on par with the Nordics. Empirical evidence shows that the 2013 reform has had positive effects on fertility, but only limited positive effects on women's employment rates, these being conditional on quality childcare options being available in the vicinity. Childcare support from the extended family, notably on the mother's side, has been found to be a stronger determinant of maternal employment. This appears to be because, even after returning from parental leave, mothers find it difficult to balance work and childcare in practice due to long working hours and an inflexible working culture, as discussed above and in Chapter 3. Against this backdrop, the current childcare system falls short of meeting the needs of working parents, with approximately 30% of mothers citing a lack of suitable childcare options as a reason for career interruption (MOHW, 2022). This reflects quality differences between different categories of suppliers, a scarcity of the high-quality childcare options in high demand, gaps in the service offer after school hours, and a mismatch between parents' long and inflexible working hours and the shorter regular opening hours at childcare centres.

Parental leave has also been expanded and strengthened considerably over time in Korea, with the result that both the duration and the level of payment eligible parents are entitled to compare well with the OECD average. The main problems with parental leave in Korea are that only around half of the total workforce are eligible, and that even those who are eligible are reluctant to take leave in fear of adverse career consequences. The result is that despite increasing rapidly, the share of parents taking parental leave remains among the lowest in the OECD, especially so among men. Research also shows that the income effect of parental leave is dominant, and female leave-takers do not have an increased likelihood of returning to their jobs (Chapter 4).

## Turning the corner of the era of ultra-low fertility?

In the third quarter of 2024, the number of births rose compared to the same period the year before for the first time in 14 years. The marriage rate has also been on the rise after reaching all-time lows during the Covid-19 pandemic. This increase is of course good news, but both marriage rates and birth rates remain very low and below their pre-pandemic levels (Chapter 2). It seems clear that the rebounding marriage rate is largely a catch-up effect after the pandemic, when many marriages were postponed. Childbirth typically follows marriage with a lag, and the rebound in birth rates can therefore also be interpreted as a lagged effect of the pandemic, which is likely to be temporary in nature.

However, it is too early to quantify the effect on fertility of the Covid-19 pandemic in 2020 and 2021, and thereby too early to conclude that this is the full story. A reform was rolled out from 2018 to 2021 to limit the statutory work week including overtime from 68 to 52 hours. This momentous change in favour of family-work balance is not obviously visible in fertility statistics, but positive effects on fertility could have been masked by the subsequent pandemic and cost-of-living crisis. Designating low fertility as a national emergency along with a steady expansion of family policies over time can also have helped to give young couples the needed confidence to bring children to the world. It is not inconceivable that the sum of these changes can have turned the tide on fertility rates, but there is so far no evidence to support such a claim.

In any case, any fertility revival will at best be slow and gradual until policies, gender norms and working practices taken together enable a large majority of women to pursue career and family in tandem. In the meantime, the cohorts of women in childbearing age keep shrinking and the large cohorts born in the 1950s, 60s and 70s keep ageing. Even in a very optimistic scenario, where birth rates more than double, Korea will turn from one of the youngest countries in the OECD to the oldest in a few decades.

Declaring victory on ultra-low fertility would for these reasons be wishful thinking. Rather than stabilisation at a low level, the goal of policy should be that young people in general are given the means and confidence to have and raise the number of children they desire. Policymakers should therefore continue to strengthen family policies, reform labour markets and nudge people's norms towards more gender-equal sharing of paid work and caring responsibilities. Simple patches like increasing baby bonuses will incite some to choose motherhood over career, but may prove to be little more than costly distractions, as they will not solve the underlying problem. Removing constraints to live balanced lives where family and career can be combined should have priority, but will require much more fundamental changes, including reforming labour market duality and winning over people's hearts and minds in support of family-friendly and gender-equal norms and working practices.

## References

Cavapozzi, D., M. Francesconi and C. Nicoletti (2024), Dividing Housework between Partners: Individual Preferences and Social Norms, *IZA Discussion Paper,* No. 17370.

Choi, S., S. Ham, Y. Yang and J. Pareliussen (2024), “Women's employment and fertility in South Korea: A review of recent research”, *OECD Economics Department Working Papers*, No. 1825, OECD Publishing, Paris.

Fluchtmann, J., V. van Veen and W. Adema (2023), "Fertility, employment and family policy: A cross-country panel analysis", *OECD Social, Employment and Migration Working Papers*, No. 299, OECD Publishing, Paris.

Jung, S. (2019), “Part-time work and non-voluntary part-time employment”, *Monthly Labor Review*, March (in Korean).

Kang, D. (2022), Impact of Housing Price Fluctuations on Marriage and Birth Rates and Policy Implications, Korea Institute of Public Finance (in Korean).

Kim, C. and B. Oh (2019), “No gender discrimination before career disruption? Gender earnings gap at the early stage of work career among college graduates in South Korea”, *Korean Journal of Sociology*, Vol. 53/1 (in Korean).

Kim, E. and K. Park (2019), “Life course of Korean women: conflictual gender differentiation and enforced classification”, *Economy and Society*, Vol. 122 (in Korean).

Kim, J., S. Jung and W. Noh (2021), *Changes in the Structure of the Korean Women's Labor Market since 2000*, Korean Women’s Development Institute (in Korean).

Ministry of Education (2024), *Survey on the Private Education Cost for Primary and Secondary Students in 2023*, Ministry of Education of Korea (in Korean).

MOHW (2022), *2021 National Childcare Status Survey - Kindergarten Survey Report*, Ministry of Health and Welfare (in Korean).

OECD (2024a), *OECD Economic Surveys: Korea 2024,* OECD Publishing, Paris.

OECD (2024b), *Society at a Glance 2024: OECD Social Indicators*, OECD Publishing, Paris.

OECD (2023), *PISA 2022 Results (Volume II): Learning During – and From – Disruption*, OECD Publishing, Paris.

OECD (2022), *OECD Economic Surveys: Korea 2022*, OECD Publishing, Paris

OECD (2021a), *Inclusive Growth Review of Korea: Creating Opportunities for All*, OECD Publishing, Paris.

OECD (2019), *Rejuvenating Korea: Policies for a Changing Society*, OECD Publishing, Paris.

OECD (2017), *The Pursuit of Gender Equality: An Uphill Battle,* OECD Publishing, Paris.

Shin, K. and E. Lee (2021), “The necessity and dilemma of flexible working arrangements from the gender perspective”, *Family and Culture*, Vol. 33/4 (in Korean).

Yang, Y., H. Hwang and J. Pareliussen (2024), “Korea’s unborn future: Lessons from OECD experience”, *OECD Economics Department Working Papers*, No. 1824, OECD Publishing, Paris.

# 2 Fewer children, later in life - changing fertility behaviour and its consequences

Hyunjeong Hwang, Economics Department of the OECD
Sunyoung Choi, Korea Institute for Health and Social Affairs
Sunyu Ham, Korea Institute for Health and Social Affairs
Yoonyoung Yang, Economics Department of the OECD
Jon Pareliussen, Economics Department of the OECD

Fertility rates have been steadily declining across the OECD, but the decline has been especially pronounced in Korea. As a consequence, the old-age dependency ratio is projected to increase faster than in any other OECD country, putting considerable strain on labour supply and public finances. Family formation patterns have evolved over time. In the decades up until around 2010 women increasingly delayed marriage and childbirth and reduced the number of children over their lifetimes, but almost all women eventually got married and had at least one child. From the 2010s, more women have chosen to remain unmarried or married and childless. The recent increase in births and marriages represents a catch-up after COVID-19. It is too soon to say if it also marks the start of a more durable increase in birth rates.

The average number of children women have over their lifetimes (Total fertility rate, TFR) has been steadily declining across the OECD, but the decline has been especially pronounced in Korea (Figure 1.2, Panel A). Korea's TFR, which was six children per woman on average in 1960, dropped to just below one child per woman in 2018, and fell further year by year to reach 0.72 in 2023. This is the lowest in the world, well below the rate of 2.1 which is necessary to stabilise the population over the long term (abstracting from migration), and lower than Japan (1.2), China (1.2), Singapore (1.0) and Chinese Taipei (0.9) (Panel B; Yang et al., 2024). A fertility rate of 0.7 means roughly that for every 100 people in the current parent generation there will be only 35 children and 10 grandchildren (OECD, 2024).

Figure 2.1. Fertility rates in Korea have declined reaching, the lowest in the world

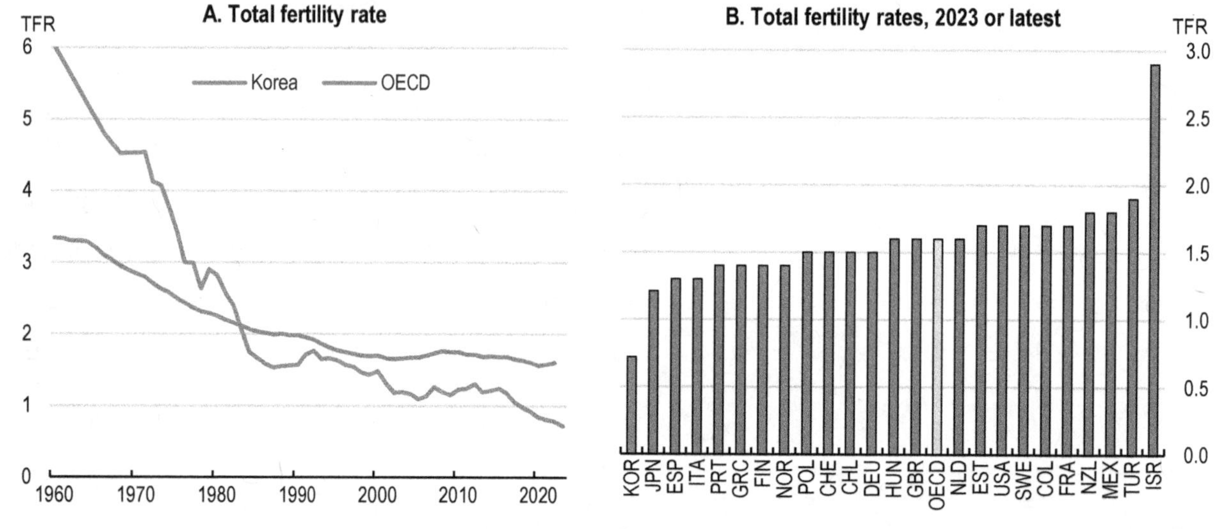


Source: OECD Economic Surveys: Korea 2024.

Fertility only affects society with considerable lags. A large share of the Korean population is today in working age, so from a labour force, macroeconomic and fiscal point of view the challenges associated with low fertility and ageing have barely started. Some changes are nonetheless becoming apparent. The population already began to decline in 2021. Kindergartens are increasingly converted into nursing homes and wedding halls into funeral parlours (JoongAng, 2024) and the sales of pet strollers exceeded those of baby strollers on a leading e-commerce platform for the first time in 2023 (The Korea Times, 2023). This anecdotal evidence foreshadows the profound changes to come as large cohorts of baby-boomers reach retirement and working-age cohorts are continuously shrinking in size (Figure 2.2, Panel A).

Assuming that fertility remains around the current level and immigration follows past trends, the population is expected to halve over the next six decades with the elderly (aged 65 or older) then accounting for around 58% of the total population (Panel B). During this time, the old-age dependency ratio (the ratio of individuals aged 65 and over to those aged 20 to 64) will surge from 28% today to 155%. In the second and the third quarter of 2024, the number of births rose compared to the same period the year before for the first time in 14 years. This increase is at least in part a temporary rebound after the sharp drop in marriages and childbirths during the COVID-19 pandemic, but it cannot be ruled out that birth rates are now stabilising or even edging up on a more long-term basis (Statistics Korea, 2024a). However, even in a very optimistic scenario, where the fertility rate bounces back to 1.85, the dependency ratio would surge to 117%, still turning the country from one of the youngest in the OECD to the oldest (Panel C). The combination of a shrinking and ageing population poses a formidable challenge to sustaining social insurance systems and maintaining living standards. Labour shortages will intensify as retirees make up an increasing share of the population, and the fiscal cost of health, long-term care and pensions is set to more than double to 17.4% of GDP by 2060 (OECD, 2024).

**Figure 2.2. The labour force will shrink and the old-age dependency ratio surge at an unprecedented pace**

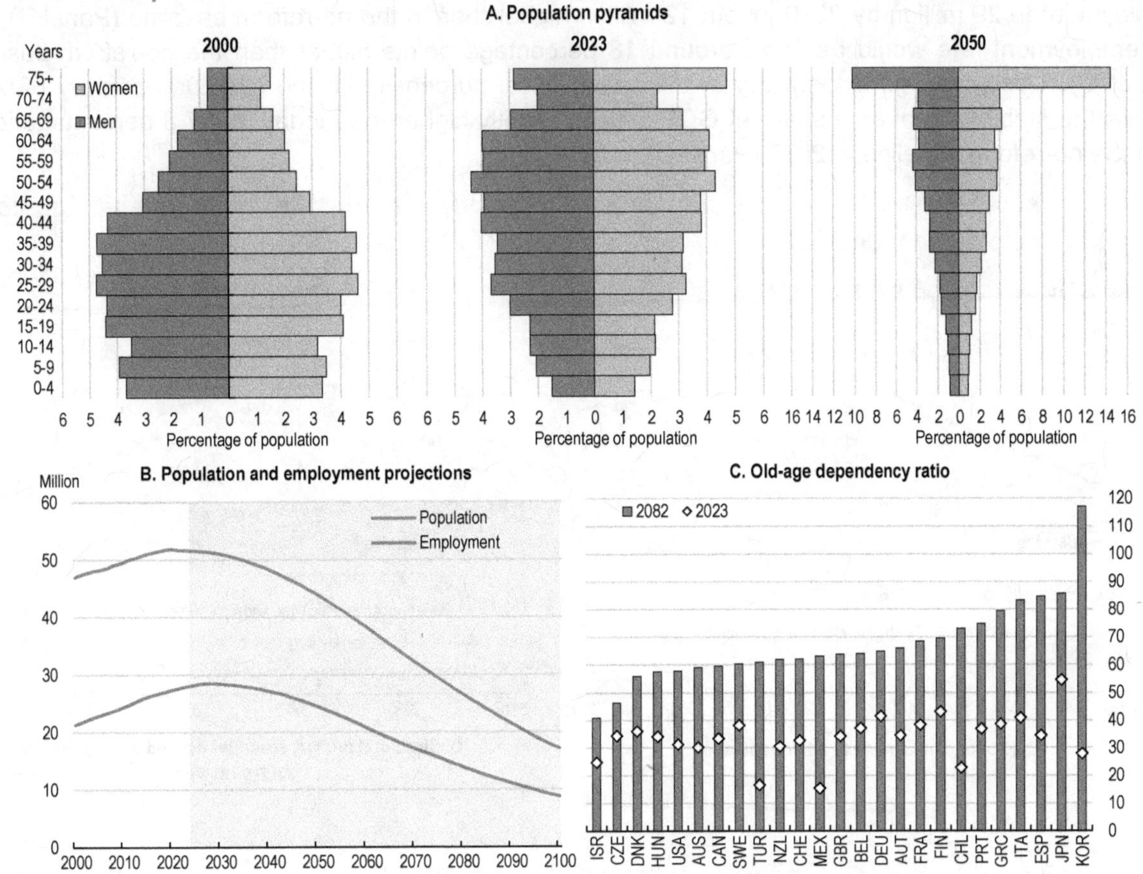


Note: Panels A and B assume that employment rates by age group, the total fertility rate (0.7), net immigration inflows (30,000 per year), and employment rates by gender and five-year age cohorts all remain constant at current levels. Panel C assumes that the total fertility rate in all countries eventually converges to 1.85 children per woman, a medium-variant forecast from the United Nations' World Population Prospects 2022. The old-age dependency ratio is defined as the ratio of individuals aged 65 and over to those aged 20 to 64.
Source: OECD Economic Surveys: Korea 2024.

Boosting fertility alone will not suffice to offset the rapid decline in the workforce. Even if a successful reform programme would almost miraculously succeed in tripling fertility to 2.1 children per woman by 2040, the level associated with a stable population in the long term, this would not prevent the workforce from declining. Lengthening working lives and increasing elderly employment are essential strategies to counteract the adverse consequences of ageing. Many workers in Korea express a desire to remain employed longer. According to a 2023 government survey of individuals aged 55-79, approximately 70% expressed a preference to continue working (Statistics Korea, 2024b). However, the average retirement age from their main career was only 52.7. Careers are often shortened by the seniority-based wage system, which makes older workers less appealing to firms when wages exceed productivity levels. Additionally, company-specific mandatory retirement ages below the legal pension age, along with practices encouraging older employees to retire early, contribute to premature retirement from primary careers. Reforming these systems, raising the statutory retirement age, and offering upskilling opportunities for older workers could help retain them in the workforce longer (OECD, 2024).

Increasing the supply of foreign labour is another vital strategy to remedy labour shortages going forward. Although immigration has increased and Korea has significant further potential to boost immigration, various visa hurdles for skilled immigration as well as poor working conditions for low-skilled immigrants hold back immigration and integration (OECD, 2024).

Lengthening working lives and boosting immigration, alongside a modest rise in the total fertility rate to 1.1, would result in a 12% higher level of GDP by 2070 (Figure 2.3, Panel A). These reforms could increase employment to 29 million by 2070, about 12 million higher than in the no-reform baseline (Panel B), and the employment rate would be 75%, around 18 percentage points higher than the no-reform baseline (Panel C). This would go a long way in alleviating fiscal burdens, with the structural primary revenue required to stabilise debt as a share of GDP settling slightly higher than today, but 7.8 percentage lower than the no-reform baseline in 2070 (Panel D).

Figure 2.3. Increasing fertility, harnessing underutilised labour resources and higher immigration would limit employment decline

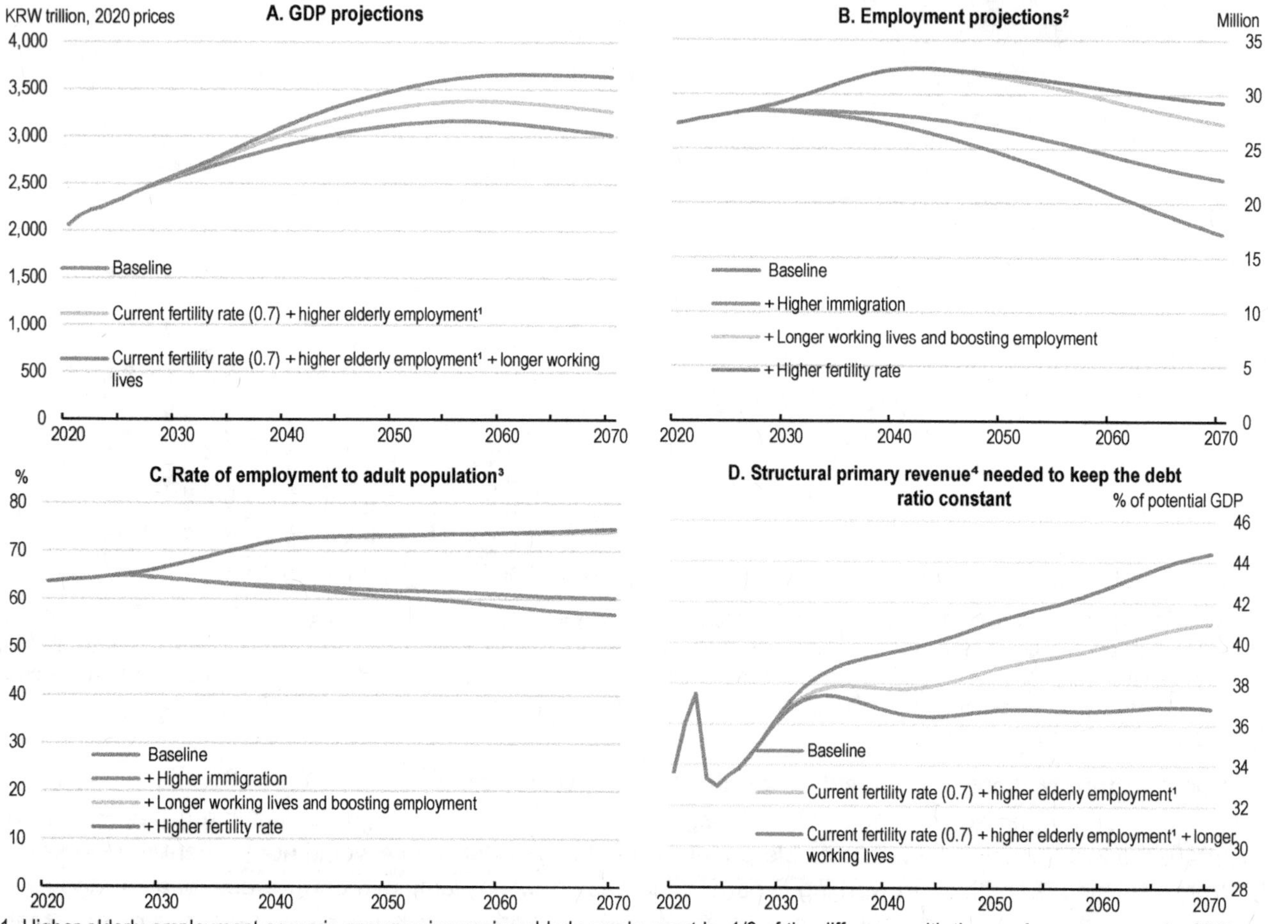


1. Higher elderly employment scenario assumes increasing elderly employment by 1/3 of the difference with the previous age group by 2040 (e.g., the rate for the 60-64 group would rise to 1/3 of the 2022 rate for the 55-59 age group).
2. The baseline scenario is constructed by maintaining the current fertility rate of 0.7 throughout the projection period. In the higher immigration scenario, the net annual immigration inflow increases from the current 30 thousand to 250 thousand by 2040. In the longer working lives and boosting employment scenario, the following reforms are assumed: a) bringing up female employment rates to male employment rates by 2040; b) bringing up the youth employment rate to the current OECD average level by 2040; c) increasing elderly employment by one third of the difference with the previous age group by 2040 (e.g., the rate for the 60-64 group would close one third of the gap to the 55-59 age group in 2022); and d) increasing the legal retirement age to 68 by 2035, and raising it by two thirds of life expectancy gains thereafter. In the higher fertility rate scenario, the fertility rate is increased to 1.1 by 2040 which was the rate recorded in 2023 in Sejong city, the highest among cities in Korea. The scenarios are cumulative, so that, for example, the 'higher fertility rate' scenario also incorporates the effects from the 'higher immigration' and 'longer working lives and boosting employment' scenarios.
3. The rate of employment to adult population is defined as the ratio of total employment to population aged 20 and over.
4. The revenue that must be raised to keep the government debt ratio stable over time.
Source: OECD Economic Surveys: Korea 2024.

A low fertility rate does not mean that young people do not want children anymore. It rather reflects that obstacles are preventing would-be parents from having more children even though they want it and Korea as a nation needs it (OECD, 2024). Over the past two decades, the average number of children per married couple has decreased from around 1.5 to less than 1, while the ideal number of children married women desire has remained much higher (Figure 2.4, Panels A and B). This partly reflects a rapidly rising mean age of marriage, which has in turn increased the age when women have their first child to the highest in the OECD (Panel C). Foregone and delayed marriage have also led to a significant rise in childlessness. The share of women who have not experienced any live births by the age of 50 almost doubled from 7% in 2000 to 13% in 2020 (Panel D).

This chapter describes the declining fertility trend, while its causes are discussed in more detail in Chapter 3. A main takeaway is that Korean women have over time postponed childbearing and reduced the number of children they had over their lifetime at least partially as a response to the conflict between employment and childbirth. Until at least around 2010, Korean women would generally marry and have at least one child, reflecting the societal norm towards the duty to marry and have children. They would typically give up employment for childbirth when faced with a choice between the two, reflecting traditional male breadwinner – female carer norms. However, since around the mid-2010s married women's employment and fertility choices seem to have become increasingly based on their individual work-family preferences, while obstacles to combine the two remain. As a result, fewer people are getting married, and a larger share of married couples remain childless.

Figure 2.4. The disparity between the actual and desired number of children is widening

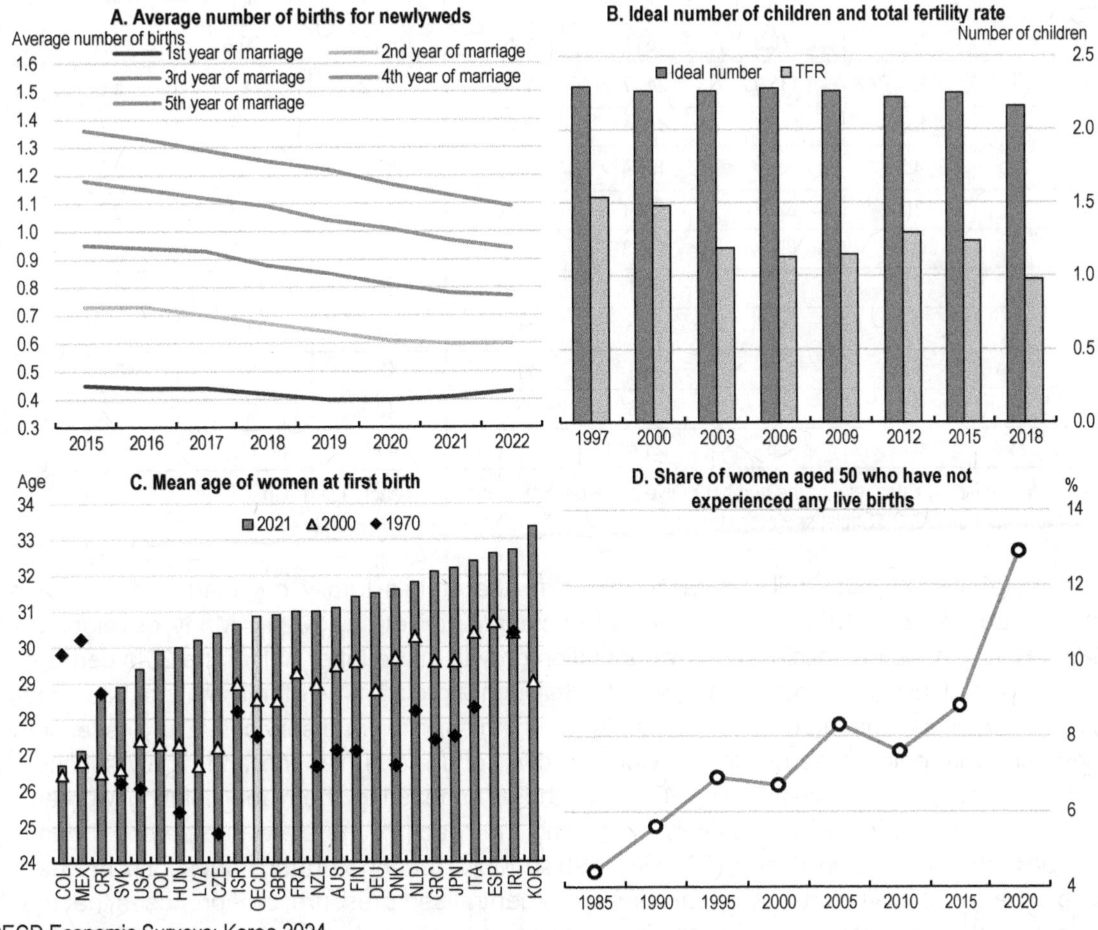


Source: OECD Economic Surveys: Korea 2024.

## Describing and understanding falling fertility in Korea

Fertility has fallen rapidly since the 1950s, over a period that took Korea from a rural society ravaged by war to a modern, urban society with per capita incomes at the OECD average (OECD, 2024). Falling fertility in the beginning of the period can be related to rising female employment, but also to high population pressure and a wish to escape poverty, and active family planning initiatives from the state.

Dramatic changes occurred in the 1970s and the early 1980s, with the TFR plummeting from 4.5 in 1970 to 2.1 in 1983, a drop of 2.4 over just 13 years (Figure 1.2, Panel A; Kwon 1997; Kwon and Kim 2002). Between 1965-70 and 1985, the fertility rate decreased in all age groups (Table 1.1). The fall in fertility rates for ages 15 to 24 can be attributed to the rising age at first marriage, while the decline for ages 25 to 34 can be interpreted as the result of fewer births within marriage.

### Table 2.1. Age-specific fertility rates

| Period | 15-19 | 20-24 | 25-29 | 30-34 | 35-39 | 40-44 | 45-49 | Total fertility rate |
|---|---|---|---|---|---|---|---|---|
| 1955-1960 | 38 | 308 | 335 | 270 | 194 | 96 | 18 | 6.3 |
| 1960-1965 | 20 | 255 | 351 | 274 | 189 | 92 | 17 | 6.0 |
| 1965-1970 | 12 | 180 | 309 | 223 | 134 | 59 | 10 | 4.6 |
| 1975 | 14.3 | 178.3 | 263.8 | 146.1 | 58.1 | 20.8 | 5.0 | 3.47 |
| 1980 | 12.4 | 135.9 | 242.7 | 114.0 | 40.2 | 15.1 | 5.6 | 2.83 |
| 1985 | 10.1 | 118.7 | 159.1 | 41.1 | 8.8 | 2.2 | 0.5 | 1.67 |
| 1990 | 4.2 | 83.2 | 169.4 | 50.5 | 9.6 | 1.5 | 0.2 | 1.59 |
| 1995 | 3.6 | 62.9 | 177.1 | 69.6 | 15.2 | 2.3 | 0.2 | 1.65 |
| 2000 | 2.6 | 39.2 | 150.3 | 84.1 | 17.6 | 2.7 | 0.2 | 1.48 |
| 2005 | 2.2 | 18.0 | 92.1 | 82.1 | 19.0 | 2.5 | 0.2 | 1.09 |
| 2010 | 1.8 | 16.5 | 79.7 | 112.4 | 32.6 | 4.1 | 0.2 | 1.23 |
| 2015 | 1.4 | 12.5 | 63.1 | 116.7 | 48.3 | 5.6 | 0.2 | 1.24 |
| 2020 | 0.7 | 6.2 | 30.6 | 78.9 | 42.3 | 7.1 | 0.2 | 0.84 |
| 2023 | 0.3 | 3.8 | 21.4 | 66.7 | 43.0 | 7.9 | 0.2 | 0.72 |

Note: Age-specific fertility rates refer to the number of live births per 1,000 females in each age group.
Source: Kwon and Kim (2002), Statistics Korea.

The timing of this dramatic fall inevitably links it to the state's family planning and population control initiatives from 1962 to 1979, but causality is unclear (Choi et al., 2024). Many developing countries, including Korea, adopted policies to slow population growth in the latter half of the 20th century. In Korea, these aimed to reduce women's unwanted births through a programme of information, basic maternal and child health services, and the provision of family planning supplies and services. Early assessments of the policies vary from being essential for economic growth and modernization and highly successful (Korea Institute for Health and Social Affairs, 1991) to those lambasting them for violating women's privacy, eroding their autonomy, and excessively expanding the reach of the state into personal domains, all in pursuit of birth suppression (Lee,1989; Kim, 1993). More recent literature questions the narrative that family planning and falling birth rates was caused by centralised pressure, and proposes that the initiatives rather satisfied a latent demand for birth control and family planning (Kwon and Kim 2002; Bae 2012). In contrast to the 1960s, the need for birth control became a widely shared social value, and the ideal number of children dropped to about two. A possible negative long-term effect of the family planning programme is that it may have contributed to the norm that workers are expected to let work take priority over family.

The developmentalist population policy pitted economic growth against childbirth and failed to recognise the value and contributions of parenthood (Hwang, 2005). This historical legacy hindered public discourses about these issues even during the 1980s and 1990s, when economic growth and democratisation had been achieved and fertility had dropped well below two children per woman.

After a period of stabilisation and a temporary rebound around 1990, the TFR continued falling to reach a new low of 1.18 in 2002. This was the first time it fell below 1.3, marking the beginning of what is often called in Korea the era of 'ultra-low fertility'. It temporarily edged up to around 1.3 in the early 2010s before declining again, falling below one for the first time in 2018. In 2021, Korea already had the lowest TFR in the world at 0.81, followed by Spain at 1.19, Italy at 1.25, and Japan at 1.30 (OECD, 2023). By 2023, the TFR had fallen to 0.72, which is remarkably low, both in historical and cross-country comparison (Statistics Korea, 2023a). The annual number of births, which had stayed above 600,000 before 2000, has also declined considerably since. While it fluctuated between 400,000 and 500,000 during the first 15 years or so of the millennium, it was down to 230,000 by 2023.

### *1980s-2000s: The number of children within marriage falls towards one*

Since the start of the millennium, a number of studies have decomposed the fertility trend into various driving forces. They all point to marriage patterns and childbearing behaviour within marriage as key forces behind falling fertility rates. Childbearing outside of marriage has only had a very limited impact, as almost all births occur within marriage in Korea. From the 1960s to the 2000s, a reduction in the number of children per married woman and a continuous increase in the age at which women first got married both contributed to the decline in fertility. Before the 2000s the decline in the number of married couples having three or more children lowered the birth rate, while in the 2000s a decline in the number of married couples having two or more children was the driving factor. From the 2010s, however, falling fertility was increasingly driven by married women having no children and women foregoing marriage altogether.

Earlier decomposition exercises pooled age-specific marriage- and fertility rates at a given point in time (synthetic cohorts), thereby masking behavioural changes within age cohorts. These studies tended to conclude that delayed marriage was the main cause of falling fertility, while falling fertility within marriage had a relatively small effect (Jun, 2002) or even that the birth rate within marriage increased during this period (Lee, 2012; 2018; Table 2.2). In other words, these studies concluded that couples had approximately the same number of children as before, but only later in life, so the TFR was bound to catch up in the future.

**Table 2.2. Decomposition of changes to the total fertility rate into changes in marriage rate and marital fertility rate using synthetic cohorts, 2000-2016**

| | 2000-2005 | 2005-2012 | 2012-2016 |
|---|---|---|---|
| | Contribution to △TFR | Contribution to △TFR | Contribution to △TFR |
| Marriage rate | -0.337 | -0.334 | -0.179 |
| Marital fertility | -0.050 | 0.438 | 0.042 |
| Non-marital fertility | -0.003 | 0.006 | -0.009 |

Source: Lee (2018).

In general, analysing age-specific TFR based on synthetic cohorts has limitations for capturing rapidly changing fertility behaviours. Breaking down changes in the TFR into components such as delayed childbearing and changes in fertility levels using synthetic cohorts underestimates the actual decline in the

TFR, since delayed childbirth in older cohorts can wrongly be interpreted as a temporary delay also for younger cohorts, while childbirth does not necessarily recover over time within cohorts. This is especially important to understand the decline in fertility rates in Korea and other East Asian regions (Frejka et al., 2010, as cited in Shin, 2020).

Figure 2.5 shows that the fertility of women aged below 30 was higher in 2002 than in 2012, while fertility for women above this age was considerably higher in 2012 than in 2022. This illustrates why confounding the two trends of women delaying childbirth and having fewer children over their lifetime could lead researchers to interpret falling fertility as a mere delay when relying on synthetic cohort data in the past. In contrast, by 2022, fertility was either considerably lower or approximately the same as a decade earlier for all age groups, removing with the benefit of hindsight any earlier misconceptions that women would "catch up" by having more children later in life.

**Figure 2.5. The evolution of age-specific fertility rates**

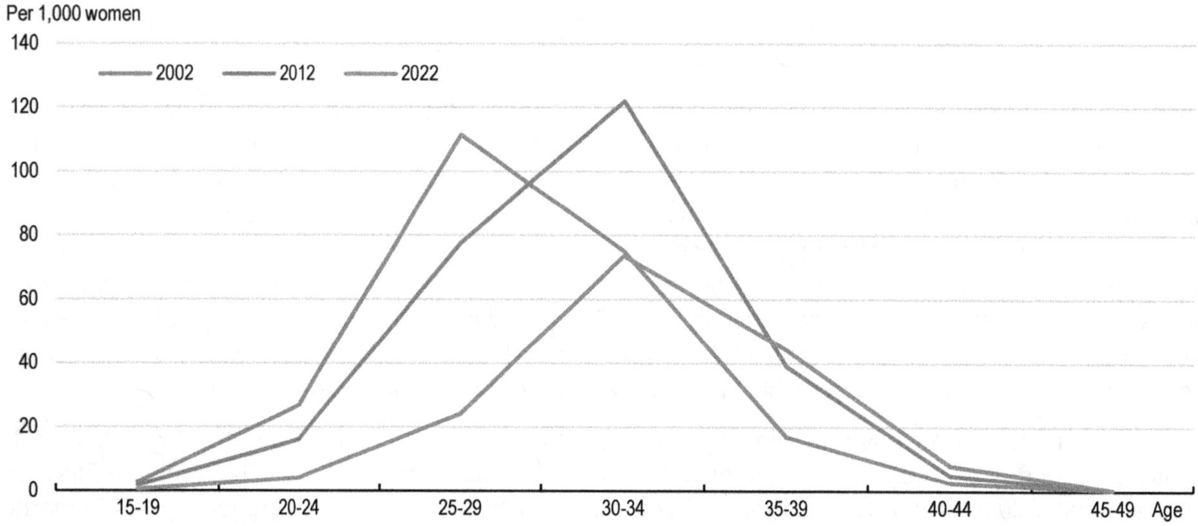


Source: Statistics Korea, Vital Statistics of Korea.

StatLink https://stat.link/jm4h0u

To overcome the methodological issues of synthetic cohorts, Yoo and Sobotka (2018) focus on a tempo-adjusted TFR, namely the counterfactual TFR that would have been achieved if there had been no significant changes in the mother's age of childbirth by birth order (first child, second child, third child and so on). In line with previous findings, they showed that mechanically, without the shift to later childbearing, the TFR would have stayed higher. For example, the TFR was just below 1.2 in 2002. Adjusting for the tempo-effect, the TFR would have been around 1.7. In contrast to previous conclusions, they highlighted that a trend towards fewer children per woman had contributed decisively to lowering the TFR. They showed for example that having more than two children had become rare already by the late 1980s, and that the further falling incidence of having three or more children therefore had little impact on the subsequent decline in the overall TFR. The tempo-adjusted TFR for second births, which was around 0.9 (approximately 90% of women would have had at least two children, adjusting for the tempo-effect) in the 1980s and early 1990s, decreased steadily from the late 1990s to below 0.6 in 2015. The adjusted TFR for first births sat slightly below 1.0 in the early 1980s, and started to decline from the early 2000s. It dropped further to levels approaching 0.8 in the early 2010s.

Woo and Jang (2018) support these findings by studying the parity progression ratio, the share of married women with a certain number of children who later have an additional child (zero children to one, one to two and so on), with data from the Korean Longitudinal Survey of Women and Families. They show that the share of women (age 15-49) having at least one child fell only modestly from 97% during the 1965-1983 period to 92% during the 1984-1997 period to 87% during the 1998-2014 period. The likelihood of having a second child has fallen steadily from one time period to the next, while the likelihood of having three or more children was severely diminished already in the 1984-1997 period (Table 2.3).

Table 2.3. Changes in parity progression ratios over time

| year / PPR | 1965-1983 | 1984-1997 | 1998-2014 |
|---|---|---|---|
| Childless→First | 0.966 | 0.920 | 0.866 |
| First→Second | 0.932 | 0.711 | 0.543 |
| Second→Third | 0.614 | 0.128 | 0.111 |
| Third→Fourth | 0.493 | 0.095 | 0.081 |
| Fourth→Fifth | 0.412 | 0.080 | 0.065 |
| Fifth→Sixth | 0.356 | 0.071 | 0.056 |
| Sixth→Seventh | 0.314 | 0.065 | 0.049 |

Note: Parity progression ratios are defined as the proportion of women with a certain number of children that later have an additional child, measured for the total population of women aged 15-49 in any given year.
Source: Woo and Jang (2018).

To overcome the shortcomings of previous studies and give a more accurate and complete picture of fertility behaviour, a number of studies are now focusing on estimating and analysing cohort fertility rates (both completed and uncompleted) (Shin et al., 2019; Yoo, 2020, 2022; Oh, 2018; 2019; Kye et al., 2022). These studies have all found that since the 1969 birth cohort, the age of women's first childbirth has steadily increased and fertility levels have decreased (Figure 2.6). For instance, Yoo (2020) showed that while the most frequent childbearing age has shifted from the mid to late twenties to the early to mid-thirties, the fertility levels of women in their early to mid-thirties today do not compensate for the past fertility levels of women in their mid to late twenties.

Figure 2.6. Cohort total fertility rate and average age of childbearing: 1946 to 1977 cohorts

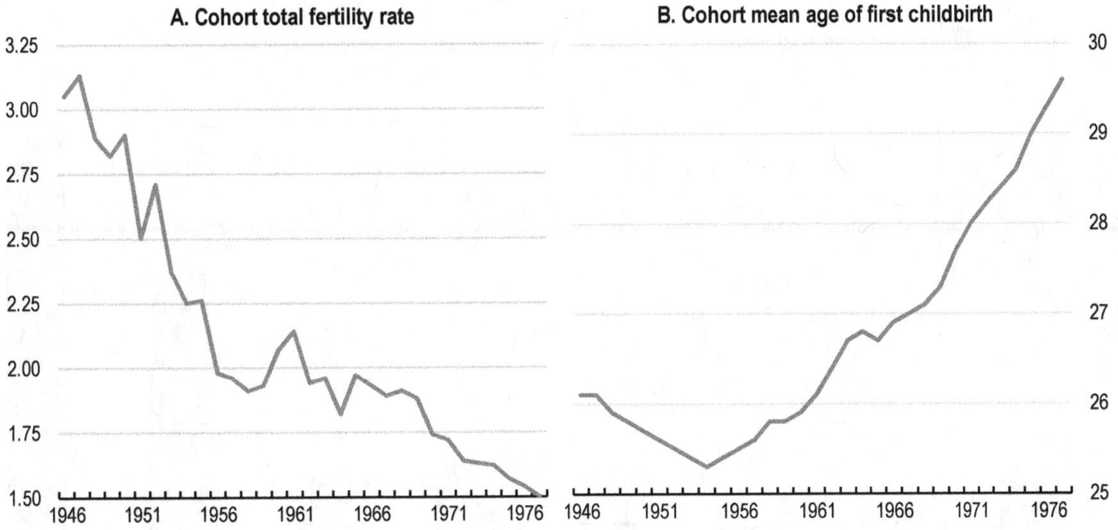


Source: Shin et al. (2019).

### *2010s and onwards: people increasingly forego marriage and children*

In the 2000s, fertility was mainly related to the childbirth behaviour of women born from the late 1960s to the late 1970s, while childbirth behaviour in the 2010s was associated with women born between the late 1970s and the early 1990s. There are important differences between these two generations, with rising education levels among the most obvious. It is still too early to study the fertility decline from the mid-2010s until today based on completed cohort fertility rates, as women in childbearing age at any given time span decades of birth cohorts.

However, past patterns and the composition of current childbearing cohorts point to a continued downward trend in fertility. First, childlessness among married women is increasing in every relevant age group (Figure 2.7). This trend is also evident from the perspective of birth cohorts. According to the analysis by Cho et al. (2024), the rate of childlessness among married women born before 1970 was very low at around 3%. However, women in more recent birth cohorts are far more likely not to have children. For instance, 9.6% of married women born in 1980 did not have children until they became 40 years old (Figure 2.8).

Figure 2.7. Proportions of childless married women by age group

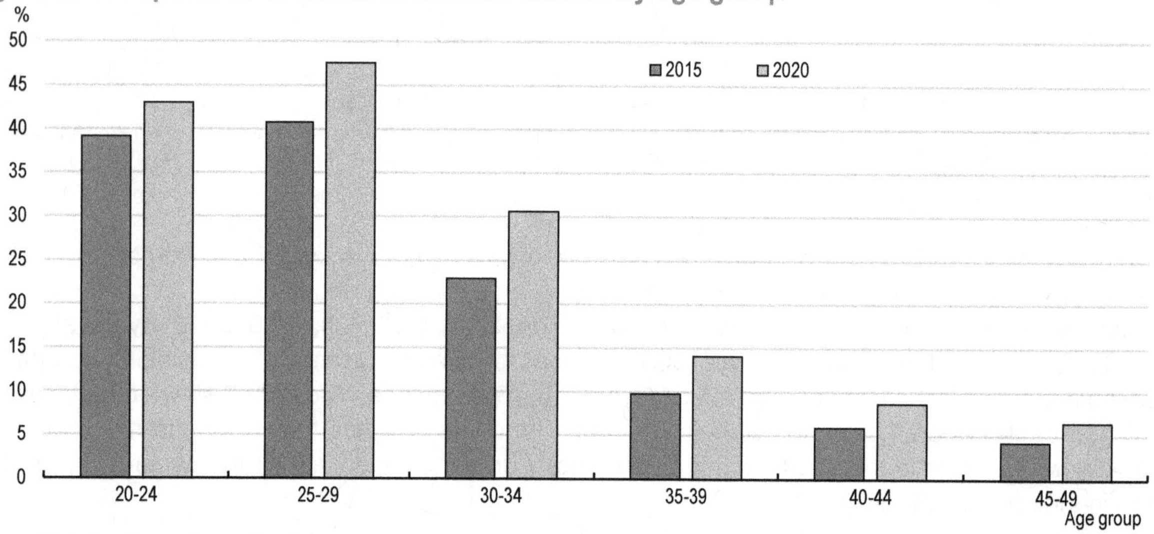


Source: Statistics Korea, Population Census.

StatLink https://stat.link/5mtar2

Figure 2.8. Childlessness rate among married women by birth cohort up to age 40

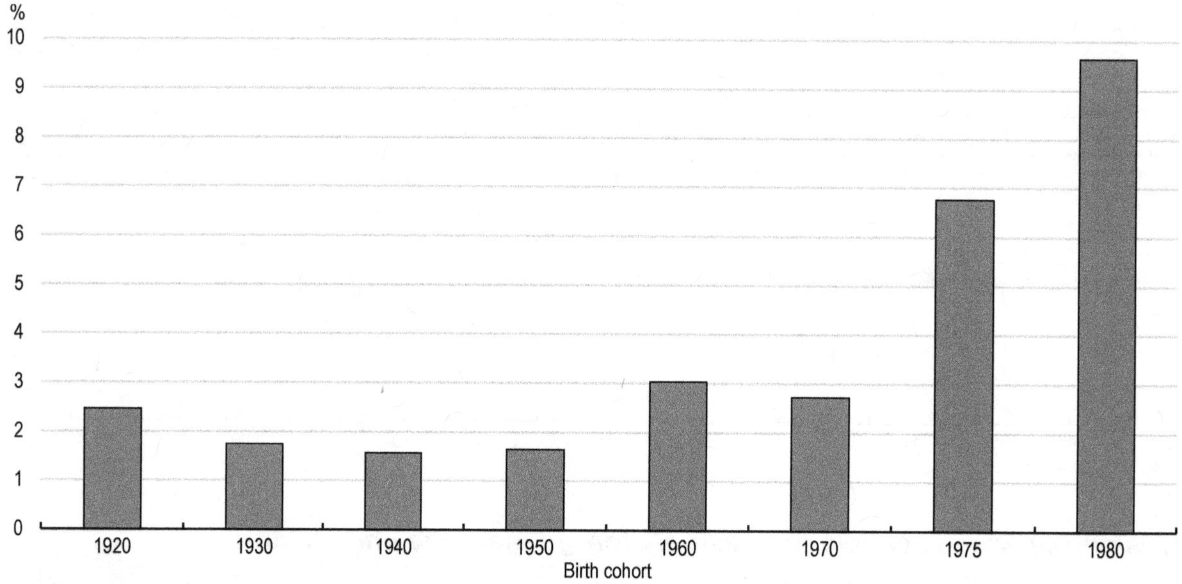


Source: Cho et al. (2024).

Second, childbirth outside of marriage remains highly uncommon, and the share of the population which is married has kept falling across age groups and gender. In 2000, over 90% of men in their early forties and women in their late thirties were married (Figure 2.9). For most of the 20th century, marriage was common in Korean society. However, the portion of married individuals has declined significantly across nearly all age groups from the early 2000s. By 2020, the marriage rate did not surpass 80% even in the age groups most likely to have tied the knot. Even taking into account that marriages in 2020 were delayed due to the pandemic would likely not affect these numbers much, since this is the stock of married people, which will not change drastically based on one single year for most age groups. The reduction was particularly dramatic in age groups where first marriages were most common, namely people in their late twenties and early thirties. For instance, in 2000, 59.6% of women aged 25-29 were married, but by 2020 this had dropped to 18.9%. Over the same period the marriage rate for women in their early thirties fell from 87.2% to 53.1%. The rate for women in their late thirties dropped from 90.9% in 2000 to 72.9% in 2020. For men of the same age, it fell even more sharply from 86.9% to 60.1%.

Figure 2.9. Proportion of married individuals by age group in 2000 and 2020

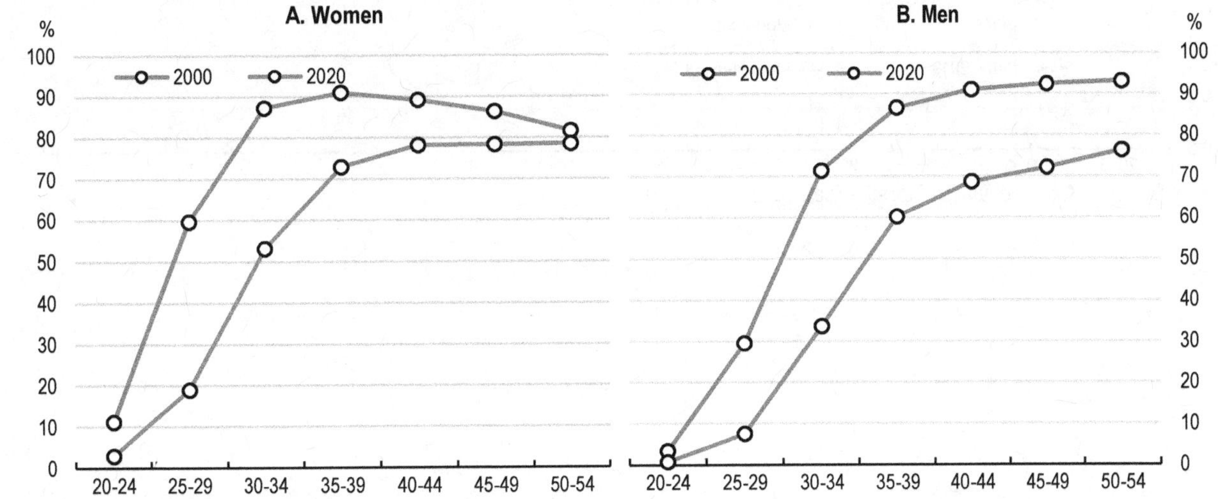


Source: Statistics Korea , Population Census.

StatLink https://stat.link/decuf3

Some question marks remain, which could potentially change this assessment as more data becomes available in the future. In the third quarter of 2024, the birth rate rose compared to the same period the year before for the first time in 14 years. The marriage rate has also been on the rise after reaching all-time lows during the Covid-19 pandemic. This increase is of course good news, but both marriage rates and birth rates remain well below their pre-pandemic levels (Figure 2.10). It seems clear that the rebounding marriage rate is largely a catch-up effect after the pandemic, when many marriages were postponed. Childbirth typically follows marriage with a lag, and the rebound in birth rates can therefore also be interpreted as a lagged effect of the pandemic, which is likely to be temporary in nature. However, it is too early to quantify the effect on fertility of the COVID-19 pandemic in 2020 and 2021, and thereby too early to conclude that this is the full story. In 2018, the statutory work week was limited to 52 hours. This momentous change in favour of family-work balance is not obviously visible in fertility statistics, but positive effects on fertility could have been masked by the subsequent pandemic. Designating low fertility as a national emergency along with a steady expansion of family policies can also have helped to give young couples the needed confidence to bring children to the world.

However, as discussed in subsequent chapters, any fertility revival will at best be slow and gradual until policies, gender norms and working practices taken together enable a large majority of women to pursue career and family in tandem. In the meantime, the cohorts of women in childbearing age keep shrinking and the large cohorts born in the 1950s, 60s and 70s keep ageing. Even in a very optimistic scenario, where birth rates more than double, Korea will turn from one of the youngest countries in the OECD to the oldest in a few decades.

**Figure 2.10. Rates of births and marriages have picked up, but remain below pre-pandemic levels**

Rates of birth and marriage (12-month moving average) per 1000 women aged 20-45

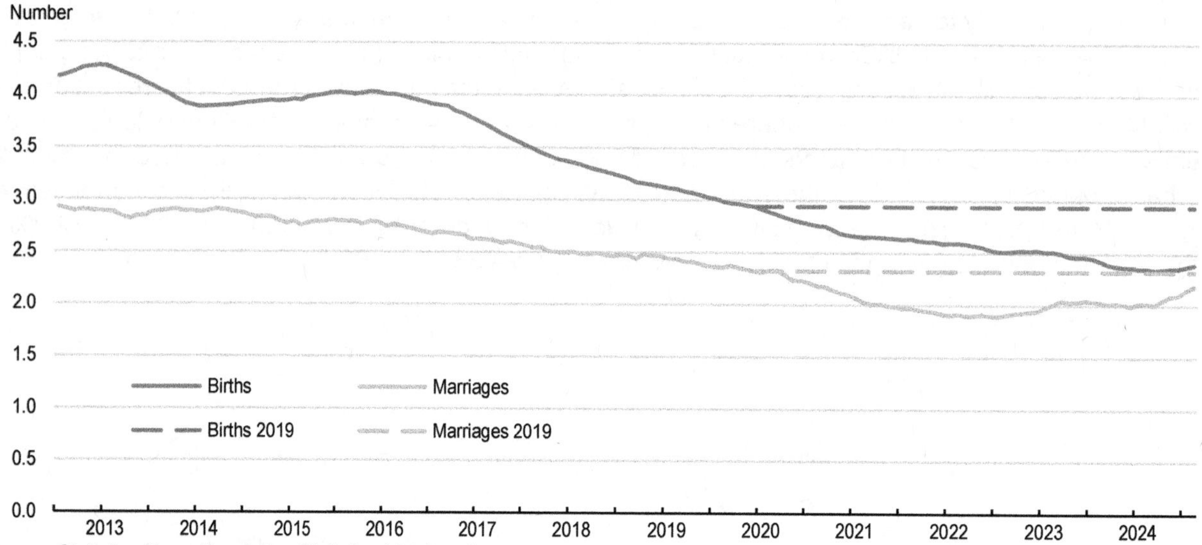


Source: Statistics Korea Population Statistics (database).

## References


Bae, Y. (2012), Human Reproduction in the Korean Modernity, Sigan Yeohaeng (in Korean).

Choi, S., S. Ham, Y. Yang and J. Pareliussen (2024), "Women's employment and fertility in South Korea: a review of recent research", *OECD Economics Department Working Papers*, No. 1825, OECD Publishing, Paris.

Cho, S., Y. Shin, K. Kim, D. Hyun, J. Choi (2024). *A Comparative Study of Life Course Transitions Across Birth Cohorts: Focusing on Young Adulthood*. Korea Institute for Health and Social Affairs, Statistics Research Institute (in Korean) (forthcoming).

JoongAng Daily (2024), "As birthrates plummet, kindergartens become nursing homes", *Korea JoongAng Daily,* 17 January.

Jun, K. (2002), "Fertility", *Population of Korea*, Statistics Korea (in Korean).

Kim, E. S. (1993), The Making of the Modern Female Gender: *The Politics of Gender in Reproductive Practices in Korea*, PhD Thesis, University of California, Berkeley.

Korea Institute for Health and Social Affairs (1991), Thirty Years of Population Policies, Korea Institute for Health and Social Affairs (in Korean).

Kwon, T. et al. (1997), "The process and meaning of fertility transition in Korea", *Understanding Fertility Transition in Korea*, Ilsinsa (in Korean).

Kwon, T. and D. Kim (2002), *Understanding Population* (revised edition), Seoul National University Press (in Korean).

Kye, B., S. Yoo and S. Choi (2022), "Trends in marital fertility, 2005~2020: duration-based approach", *Korea Journal of Population Studies*, Vol. 45/4 (in Korean).

Lee, C. (2018), "Did pro-natal policy in Korea fail?: a decomposition of fertility change from 2000 to 2016", *The Korean Journal of Economic Studies*, Vol. 66/3 (in Korean).

Lee, C. (2012), "A decomposition of the decline in the total fertility rate in Korea: effects of changes in marriage and marital fertility", *Korea Journal of Population Studies*, Vol. 35/3 (in Korean).

Lee, M. (1989), "A feminist analysis of the state policy in birth control", *Women's Studies Review*, Vol. 6 (in Korean).

OECD (2024), *OECD Economic Surveys: Korea 2024*, OECD Publishing, Paris.

Oh, J. (2019), "Forecast of and factors driving a double-dip in Korea's fertility rate", *The Korean Journal of Applied Statistics*, Vol. 32/4 (in Korean).

Oh, J. (2018), "A Study on forecasting cohort incomplete fertility for Korea", *Korea Journal of Population Studies*, Vol.41/1 (in Korean).

Shin, Y., M. Lee and S. Park (2019), *Analysis and Outlook of Korea's Long-term Trends in Lowest-low Fertility*, Korea Institute for Health and Social Affairs (in Korean).

Statistics Korea (2024a), *Population Trends for September and the Third Quarter of 2024.*

Statistics Korea (2024b), *Statistics Korea Supplementary Surveys on the Economically Active Elderly Population*, Statistics Korea.

The Korea Times (2023), *Sales of Pet Strollers Surpass Baby Strollers for 1st time*, The Korea Times, 27 December.

Woo, H. and I. Jang (2018) "Fertility transition in South Korea: application of survival analysis", *Journal of the Korean Official Statistics*, Vol. 23/2 (in Korean).

Yang, Y., H. Hwang and J. Pareliussen (2024), "Korea's unborn future: lessons from OECD experience", *OECD Economics Department Working Papers*, No. 1824, OECD Publishing, Paris.

Yoo, S. (2022), "Postponement and recuperation of fertility in South Korea: estimating and projecting completed fertility", *Journal of the Korean Official Statistics*, Vol. 27/1 (in Korean).

Yoo, S. (2020), *Analysis of Total Live Birth Changes*, The Population Association of Korea (in Korean).

Yoo, S. and T. Sobotka (2018), "Ultra-low fertility in South Korea: the Role of the tempo effect", *Demographic Research*, Vol. 38/1.

# 3 When family aspirations clash with realities of life - underlying causes of low fertility

Jon Pareliussen, Economics Department of the OECD

Yoonyoung Yang, Economics Department of the OECD

Hyunjeong Hwang, Economics Department of the OECD

Sunyoung Choi, Korea Institute for Health and Social Affairs

Sunyu Ham, Korea Institute for Health and Social Affairs

Falling fertility is a global phenomenon related to the increasing opportunity cost of motherhood as incomes rise and women gain more equal opportunities in education and the labour market. Rising direct costs of having children, such as housing and education also matter. Effective family policies, a family-friendly working life and more gender-equal sharing of parenting responsibilities making it easier to combine career and family can counteract these trends and increase fertility. In Korea, the direct costs of having children are magnified by fierce competition to enter prestigious universities and high private education expenditures. Most importantly, the opportunity cost of having children is high, as a large gender wage gap compounds norms of mothers as the main carers, while working and caring are difficult to combine in an uncompromising work culture. A dual labour market and largely seniority-based career progression combine to create a very high cost for any temporary absence from the labour market.

Low fertility is a global phenomenon as countries go through their demographic transitions from high birth rates and high mortality rates to low fertility and low mortality. While this was originally seen as the final "steady-state" stage of the demographic transition where the population would stabilise, it has become clear that there is nothing steady and universally predictable about it. Fertility rates differ widely between countries, reflecting economic forces, social norms and intervening policies (Zaidi and Morgan, 2017).

The demographic transition is closely connected to economic development, industrialisation, and widespread access to contraception. New technologies are increasingly skill-intensive, while education has a cost both directly and historically in terms of lost income from child labour. Parents therefore respond to economic development by reducing the number of children while investing more in the human capital of each of them. This is the so-called quantity-quality trade-off. Other factors could reinforce this trend, including the decline in child labour (by law) and a rise in life expectancy, increasing the value of investments in human capital (Delventhal et al., 2021; Galor, 2005; Doepke et al., 2022).

The quantity-quality trade-off literature focuses on household income and treats the married couple as a single decision-making unit. This is also the point of departure for a second major strand of the literature focussing on the trade-offs between fertility and women's labour force participation and thereby family income. Labour market participation of married women (very few births happened outside of marriage at the time) was low since the onset of the industrial revolution until the beginning of the twentieth century, but then started to rise gradually in most OECD countries in the 1930s and 1940s, and much more rapidly after World War II. This increased the opportunity cost of childrearing in terms of lost family income from women's employment. It gave rise to a negative relationship between women's labour force participation and fertility both between countries and within countries, where women who worked full-time usually had fewer children than those not in employment and women who worked part-time fell in between. Likewise, earnings prospects and the opportunity cost of having children are higher for women with higher human capital. Before the 1990s, there was therefore an inverse relationship between female education and fertility both within and between countries (Doepke et al., 2022).

However, the negative cross-country correlation between fertility and female labour force participation observed in most industrialised countries until the 1980s had turned positive by the year 2000 (Doepke et al., 2022; Fluchtmann et al., 2023). The average total fertility rate increased after 1980 in countries with high female labour force participation such as Sweden, Norway, Denmark and the United States, while it declined sharply in low-participation countries such as Italy and Spain between the 1970s and 1990s. From 1990 onward, the average fertility rate in high-participation countries has remained higher than that of low-participation high-income countries. Korea's experience resembles that of Italy and Spain, but lags in time and the fall in fertility rate has been even more dramatic.

This new pattern does not mean that the quantity-quality trade-off and the opportunity cost of motherhood no longer matter, but rather that other factors intervene to make these trade-offs more or less salient in different high-income societies. This point can be illustrated in a scatterplot of the employment gap between men and women and the total fertility rate (Figure 3.1). Considerable differences exist between countries. Middle-income OECD countries including Turkiÿe, Mexico, Colombia and Costa Rica have relatively high fertility, while a high gender employment gap indicates a trade-off between female employment and fertility in these countries. Some countries, best exemplified by Italy, Greece, Poland and Japan exhibit a somewhat lower, but still high gender employment gap combined with low fertility rates. This implies that there is a trade-off between fertility and female employment, but as incomes are higher in these countries than in Turkiÿe, Mexico, Colombia and Costa Rica, the quantity-quality trade-off and the opportunity cost of motherhood are more salient. A balance is therefore found at higher female employment and lower fertility. Korea shares the qualitative characteristics of this group but is an outlier in terms of its large gender employment gap and very low fertility rate, indicating stark trade-offs between career and motherhood. A cluster of countries exhibit higher fertility rates, combined with a considerably lower gender employment gap. The lowest trade-offs are found in the Nordics and France. Israel, owing to Haredi's large families and low male employment rate, is an outlier, with very high fertility combined with a low gender employment gap.

### Figure 3.1. Total fertility rate and gender employment gap

2020

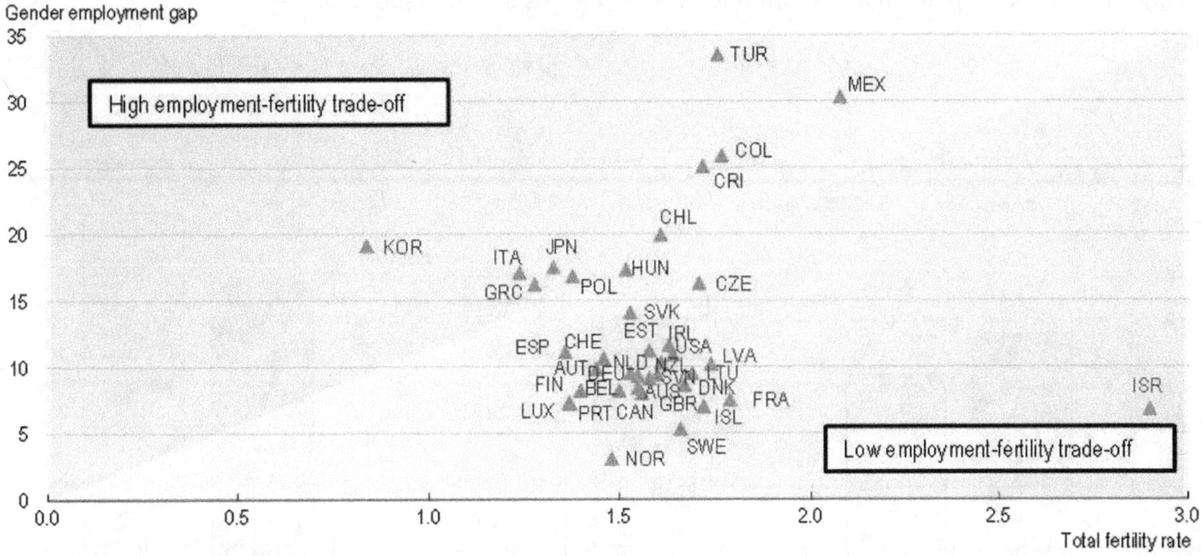


Note: This figure is meant for illustration purposes only. Countries towards the bottom and the right experience the least salient trade-offs, while countries towards the top and left experience higher trade-offs.
Source: OECD, Social Protection and Well-being (database).

StatLink https://stat.link/jtik39

Factors mitigating the earlier established trade-offs include the expansion of public education, which has reduced the cost to parents of investing in their children's human capital. Marketisation of childcare (and other home-produced goods and services) has partially converted the time cost of having children into a monetary cost, facilitating female labour force participation especially for high-income families, while public funding of childcare and parental leave can further ease the opportunity cost of parenthood across the earnings distribution (Doepke et al., 2022).

Frictions in the labour market can on the other hand accentuate trade-offs. When unemployment is high, temporary jobs common, and permanent jobs hard to obtain, even a temporary leave to start a family can have long-term repercussions for labour market prospects. Fertility rates may consequently be lower than in a setting where secure, long-term jobs are easier to find (Doepke et al., 2022).

The negative relationship between female education and fertility within countries has also shifted since the 1990s in advanced countries (Hazan and Zoabi, 2015; Bar et al., 2018). For instance, in high-income countries such as the United States, Germany and France, the relationship between education and fertility was negative along the entire education distribution in the 1980s, while fertility has increased at the highest education levels (such as an MA or PhD) since the 2000s. Korea has also moved in this direction in recent years with the fertility rate falling faster among the less educated (KIHASA, 2019). An average 83% of women with a university degree or higher are employed in OECD countries, while only 69% are in Korea (Figure 3.2), where many highly educated women also exit employment upon motherhood.

Analysing households as a single decision-making unit may overlook some important aspects of fertility behaviour. Individuals in high-income countries increasingly value individual self-expression and self-realisation (Inglehart and Welzel, 2005). Individual careers and income prospects also increase in importance as divorces (and break-ups in the case of cohabitation) become more common. In this new reality, it matters to fertility decisions if one person in a couple bears a disproportionate share of the individual career cost of having children. Indeed, Doepke and Kindermann (2019) show that in high-income countries, the mapping from partners' fertility preferences to outcomes is well described by a veto model: children are likely to be born only if both partners desire to have a baby, implying that a "veto" from one of the potential parents is sufficient to block the decision. Therefore, countries with more gender-equal sharing of domestic work and lower motherhood penalties in the labour market generally have higher fertility. Social norms play an important role in how parents share responsibilities.

Figure 3.2. Female employment rate of tertiary graduates is lower than the OECD average

2022

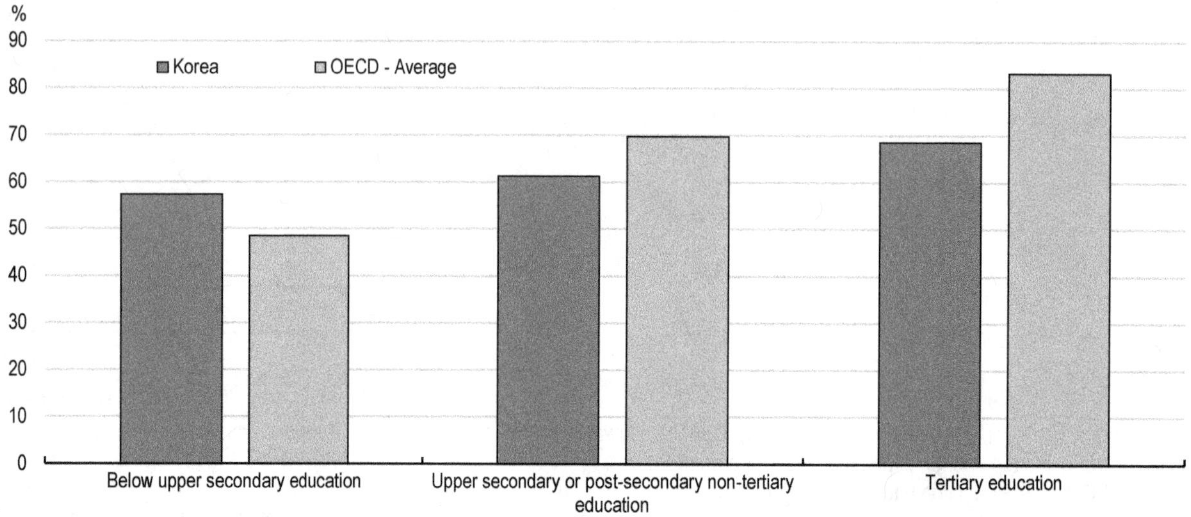


Source: OECD (2023a), Education at a Glance 2023.

StatLink https://stat.link/xlesou

These various insights help understand why fertility has fallen in Korea despite a considerable strengthening of family policies. The country combines relatively poor performance compared to other OECD countries on several features relevant to fertility. The direct costs of having children (in line with the quantity-quality trade-off hypothesis) are magnified compared to many OECD countries by fierce competition to enter prestigious universities and high private education expenditure. Norms dictating that children should be born within marriage, and that buying a home is a necessary condition to marry may also raise the bar to family formation. The opportunity cost of having children is high due to a dual labour market with unequal pay, working conditions and social insurance coverage, and largely seniority-based career progression combining to create a very high cost for any temporary absence from the labour market (OECD, 2022). A culture of long work hours and a lack of flexibility where work is expected to take priority over family makes it hard to reduce work efforts for a period while children are young, and even the rapid expansion of publicly funded childcare is not sufficient to bridge the demands of a full-time career with having a family (see below). The options available are therefore for many to either remain fully committed to work at the expense of family formation or to temporarily halt working altogether and commit fully to taking care of children and household, with severe long-term career repercussions. This is a choice mostly faced by women, since gender and family norms place the responsibility for childrearing mostly on mothers, and a large gender wage gap makes it rational to forgo the mother's income instead of the father's. Women therefore increasingly choose not to marry, not to have babies, or to have fewer babies than in the past, a trend which has given rise to the terms "birth strike" and "marriage strike". Some men may also object to the expectations to become a breadwinner dedicated to his career that traditionally comes with family formation (Cho et al., 2020).

## Direct costs of family formation are high in many countries, including Korea

Having children is a costly affair, as all parents know. Items such as food and clothing make up an ever-decreasing share of outlays in the typical household in OECD countries, while most countries including Korea are increasingly subsidising childcare, lowering the out-of-pocket cost to parents. Housing prices and education costs have on the other hand been on the rise for decades in a number of countries including Korea. In Korea, 41% of unmarried men aged 19 to 34 and 26% of women identify financial constraints as their primary deterrent to getting married. Housing, education and tutoring are expensive. More than half of young people (51.2%) think that they have to own a house to get married, especially in big cities (KRIHS, 2023). The housing price-to-income ratio in metropolitan areas increased from 6.7 in 2012 to 10.1 in 2021 (KOSIS, 2023), making home ownership challenging to achieve for young people. High private education costs is another factor reducing fertility rates. Korea's private tutoring participation rates are very high, largely reflecting fierce competition to enter prestigious universities. Many parents therefore allocate a significant portion of their income to private tutoring. Meanwhile, the income of young adults has decreased compared to other age groups over the past 10 years, while their debt has increased (Figure 3.3).

Figure 3.3. Financial insecurity among young people has increased

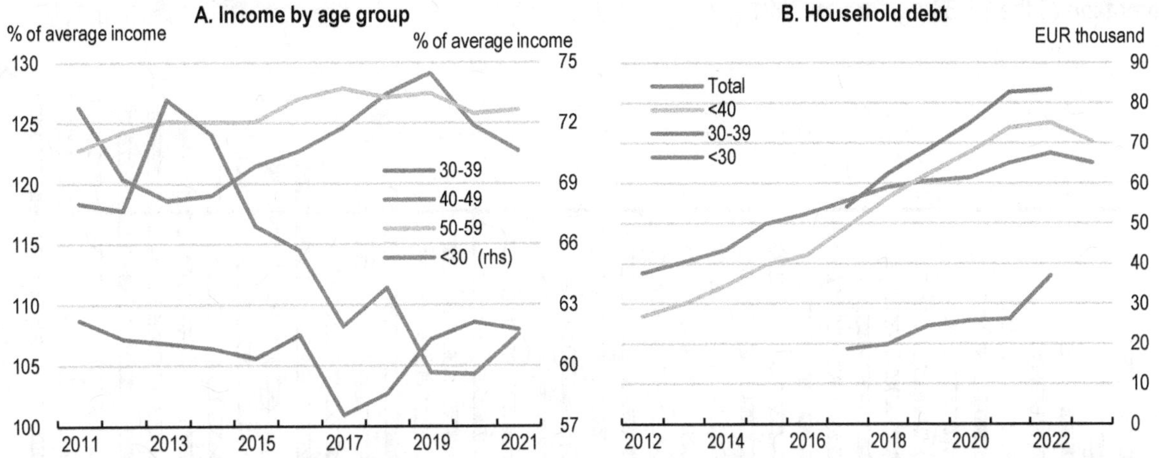


Note: Panel A represents a four-quarter moving average for three age groups. Panel B shows debt for individuals under age 40 and for the total population.
Source: OECD Economic Surveys: Korea 2024.

### *Korea stands out internationally with high private outlays on education*

Korea is known worldwide for its emphasis on education, which has played a major role in its economic development. In recent decades, a university degree has become the minimum academic achievement for a majority. More than 80% of teenagers plan to obtain at least a four-year university degree and 90% of parents share that ambition (Jones, 2013). Indeed, nearly three-quarters of high school graduates advanced to college or university in 2021, and the proportion of the 25-34 age group with tertiary education is the highest in the OECD (Figure 3.4). Korea's extraordinary zeal for education has strengthened credentialism – a reliance on academic qualifications as the best measure of an individual's intelligence or ability to perform a particular job (OECD, 2022).

Credentialism has led to "education inflation", which requires job candidates to obtain higher degrees for positions that formerly had lower requirements. This trend is in part reflected in the declining share of students in two-year colleges, traditionally significant providers of vocational education, and a larger share in four-year universities. For example, a two-year college degree in cosmetology faces competition from a four-year university (bachelor) degree in cosmetology (OECD, 2019b).

Education inflation has undermined the value of work experience and diplomas from all but the most prestigious universities (Choi, 2021). Given the dual labour market and a scarcity of quality jobs, graduates from top universities are much more likely to obtain a high salary. Lee and Koh (2023) found that graduates from top-tier universities earn 24.6% more than graduates from bottom-tier universities at the time of labour market entry in Korea, and the wage gap peaks at 50.5% between the ages of 40 and 44. The intense competition to gain admission to these prestigious universities, dubbed "the golden ticket syndrome", leads many students to prioritise the name of the institution over choosing a field of study according to their interests and skills (OECD, 2022). According to a government survey on factors influencing university choice, 24% of respondents considered university prestige most important, while 32% prioritised aptitude and interest. The survey further suggests that over the past three years, more youth have prioritised prestige, while fewer have prioritised aptitude and interest (MOE and KRIVET, 2023). There is also significant competition to enter medical schools. Doctor pay is high compared to other OECD countries, especially for specialists (OECD, 2023b), and doctors can remain in their career until they reach old age, unlike many other professionals who are typically forced out around the age of 50 due to seniority-based wages and the practice of honorary retirements.

**Figure 3.4. The share of tertiary graduates among young Koreans is the highest in the OECD**

Percentage of the 25-34 age group, 2021

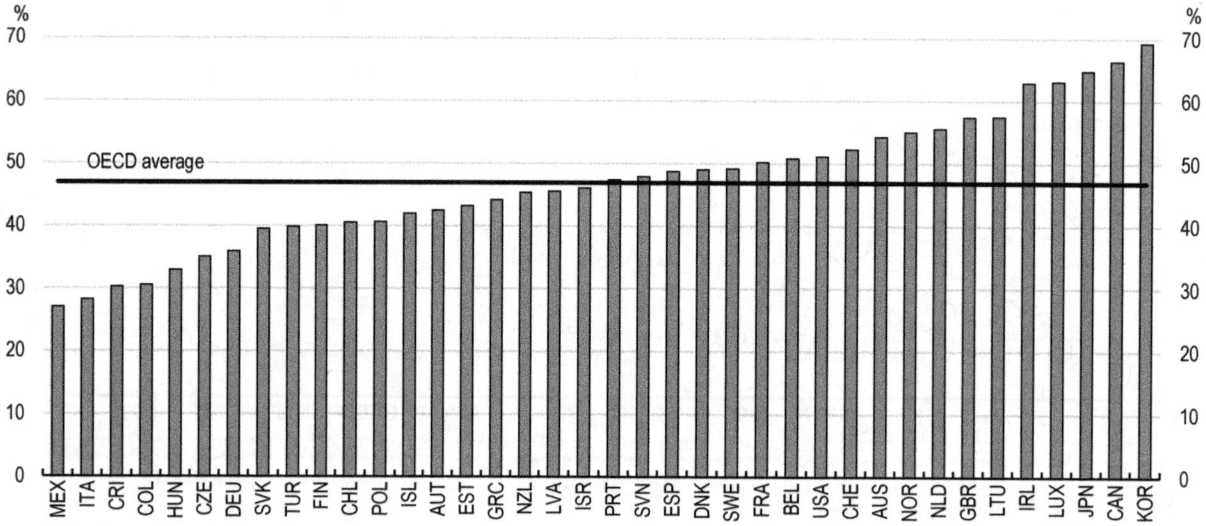


Source: OECD (2021a), Education at a Glance.

StatLink https://stat.link/4vo8ei

Against this backdrop, many Korean parents allocate a sizeable portion of their income to private tutoring, making education expenditure another major hurdle to have children. In 2023, 78.5% of Korean primary and secondary school students participated in private tutoring (Ministry of Education, 2024). The monthly average expenditure for private tutoring per student has increased since 2015, reaching KRW 434 thousand, roughly 10% of average household disposable income in 2023 (Figure 3.5). Empirical analysis suggests that prevalence of private tutoring is negatively associated with a country's total fertility rate (Anderson, 2018). Indeed, 49.2% of Korean parents think the cost of private tutoring is very burdensome (KEDI, 2022), and 27% point to the burden of their children's education and childcare as one of the main reasons for the falling fertility rate (PCASPP, 2023).

Figure 3.5. Private education expenditure has increased in recent years

Monthly private education expenditure per student, at constant prices

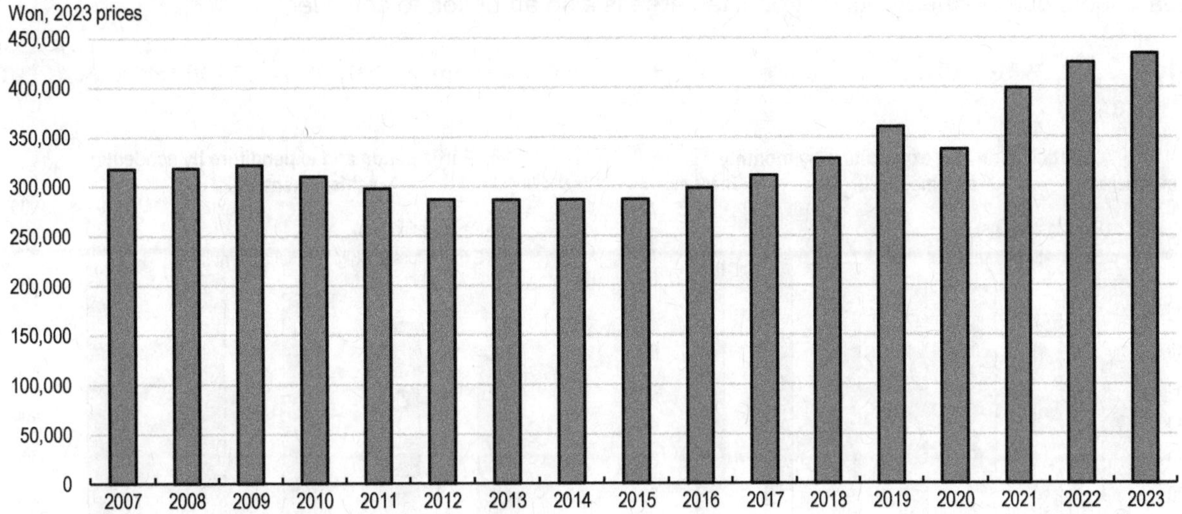


Note: Private education expenditure has been deflated using CPI.
Source: OECD Economic Surveys: Korea 2024.

This "Golden ticket syndrome", a situation where almost all students participate in inefficient competition from which only a few emerge as winners is a huge waste for the country. The situation tends to hold back intergenerational social mobility because parents with higher incomes can spend more on private tutoring Figure 3.6, Panel A), and tutoring works in the sense that it is positively correlated with academic achievement (Panel B). However, in terms of net benefits to society, gains in academic achievement are likely outweighed by the cost of provision and negative side-effects, including postponed entry into working life (OECD, 2022). Intensive tutoring has a detrimental effect on adolescent mental health (Xu and Lee, 2023), and Korean youth report low life satisfaction relative to other OECD countries (OECD, 2023f). More than 80% of Korean college students perceive high school as a "life-or-death battlefield", a significantly higher proportion than in the United States (40%), China (42%) and Japan (14%), countries with relatively comparable entrance exam systems (Kim, 2017).

Efforts to reduce the use of private tutoring have ranged from enhancing the quality of public education to directly regulating private tutoring institutions. Investment in public education has increased to the OECD average, and the number of students per teacher is relatively low (Minea-Pic, 2023). The university entrance exam, the College Scholastic Ability Test (CSAT), has also been reformed to reduce the burden on students, including by removing off-curriculum "killer questions" as of 2023. The government has also directly regulated tutoring centres (hagwons) by recommending them not to offer tutoring ahead of the curriculum from 2014, and banning classes after 10 PM from 2008. Such reforms have so far been unsuccessful, as they did not address the core issues of elite universities and labour market dualism.

Many OECD countries have university entrance systems with low levels of competition and hence little private tutoring. More than half of OECD countries adopt open admissions systems for tertiary education, meaning that there are no restrictions on the number of students accepted into Bachelor's or Master's programmes at universities in general. In Germany, for instance, where public universities are free and unranked, all upper secondary graduates who passed the university entrance exam are secured a seat in the university and the major of their choice except for some popular majors. Introducing a credit transfer system which allows credits taken at one university to be counted towards a qualification studied for at another and facilitating joint degrees as in most European universities (EC, 2024) could also help students pursue their academic interests at various institutions, reducing the emphasis on a few prestigious universities. Investment in higher education is low compared to the OECD and additional investments targeted to selected universities outside of the Seoul metropolitan area, for example in the Regional Innovation System and Education (RISE) programme and Glocal College 30 Project, could help reduce the preference for Seoul-based universities. Relocating some prestigious universities or certain popular departments outside the Seoul metropolitan area is also an option to consider.

#### Figure 3.6. Private education spending is positively correlated with parents' income and academic achievement

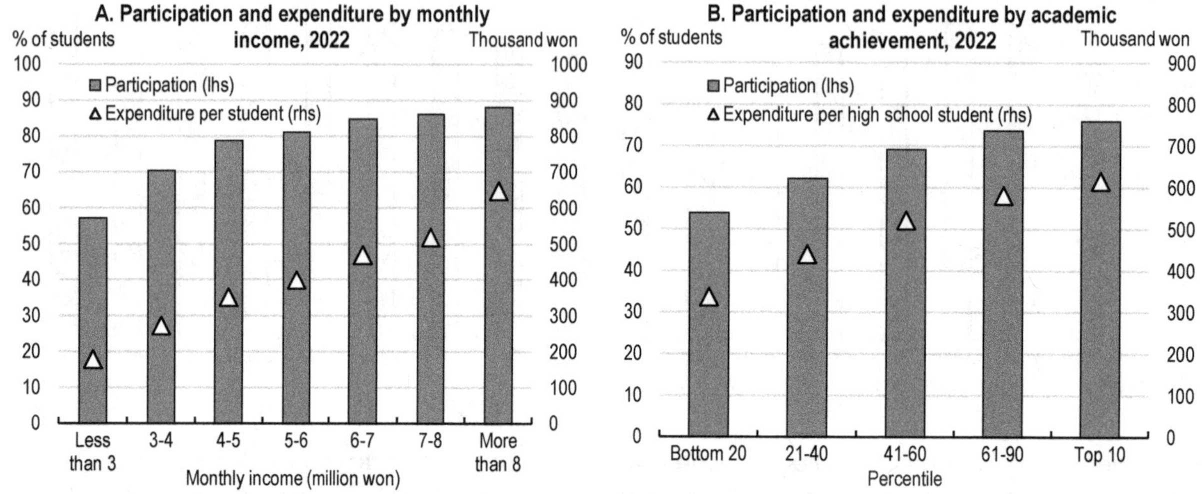


Source: OECD Economic Surveys: Korea 2024.

Another way to dampen competition is by lifting some restrictions to supply more of the study places that are in high demand. In the mid-1990s, study places at universities located in non-Seoul metropolitan areas increased due to deregulation, while enrolment caps on universities in the Seoul metropolitan area were maintained. Since then, competition for admission to universities in the Seoul metropolitan area has grown. Han (2022) found that regulated universities within the Seoul metropolitan area tend to be less responsive to student demand. Moreover, the deregulation of student enrolment in non-Seoul metropolitan areas led to a 9 to 10% decrease in participation in private tutoring in those regions (Park et al., 2018). In line with the recommendation of the 2022 *Economic Survey of Korea*, the Korean government allowed universities to adjust student enrolment across majors from the 2024 school year (Ministry of Education, 2022). The Yoon administration has also taken the initiative to increase the medical school enrolment quota to address doctor shortages and reduce the intensity of competition to enter medical schools. The increase seems to be going ahead despite fierce resistance from the medical profession.

Another way to reduce the money and time spent on private tutoring is to improve the public supply of education services. One issue is opening hours. School ends before 2 PM in the lower primary grades. Until 2024, extracurricular classes were open until 5 PM for first and second-grade students in primary school, shorter than full-time normal working hours for parents. The lack of quality daycare services for young school-age children pushed one in five parents with a primary school child to use private tutoring (Ministry of Education, 2024), and it compelled mothers to exit employment or take parental leave (Choi et al., 2022). The government is rolling out a reform extending extracurricular class hours further to 8 PM ("Neulbom School" programmes) for first-grade primary school students in 2024, second-graders in 2025 and all primary school students in 2026. To ensure its success in competition with private tutoring providers, the reform needs to be implemented with a keen eye on quality.

Strengthening the quality of regular school lessons would also help reduce private education costs. In a recent survey, 50% of parents answered that their children take private tutoring to supplement regular school classes (Ministry of Education, 2024). According to an analysis in Germany, students who received quality individualised and personalised learning during regular classes were less likely to engage in private education (Guill et al., 2020). Similarly, in Scandinavian countries, which seem to have been least affected by the rise of private tutoring, both slow learners and high achievers are entitled to receive education tailored to their needs within the framework of public education (Bray, 2021). Increasing the time teachers spend on preparation and teaching could help teachers to better cater for students' individual learning needs, as Korean teachers spend a higher-than-average proportion of their working time on administrative tasks (OECD, 2024a).

High-quality tutoring lessons delivered digitally for free to students would help ease the inequality of opportunity and financial strain on parents that private tutoring creates. For example, Seoul Metropolitan City runs the "Seoul-Learn" platform, which provides online learning contents from private tutoring institutions to students in vulnerable households. More broadly, digital technologies, including artificial intelligence (AI), could improve the quality of education, increase cost-effectiveness and make education more inclusive by for example personalising education in low-cost ways, and thereby making it accessible to pupils of different means and backgrounds.

### *Rising housing costs hold back family formation*

A cross-country empirical study found that increases in household expenditure on housing had a significant and negative effect on fertility rates across the OECD (Fluchtmann et al., 2023; OECD, 2024c). In another study, the doubling of housing prices in Korea between 2013 and 2019 was found to reduce the likelihood of people getting married by between 4 and 5.7% (Kang, 2022). The Yoon administration has a target of providing 2.7 million homes nationwide and 1.58 million homes in the Seoul metropolitan area from 2023 to 2027, a 32% increase compared to the addition to housing supply from 2018 to 2022. The strategy involves invigorating private housing supply by simplifying regulations and procedures and direct supply of social housing. However, due to the recent real estate downturn and escalating construction costs, housing starts decreased by 37% nationwide and 56% in Seoul in 2023 compared to the previous year. Given the two- to three-year construction timeline, this implies a considerable reduction in new units available for occupancy in 2025, potentially exerting upward pressure on market prices going forward.

Seoul is one of the most densely populated cities in the OECD (OECD, 2021c). In particular, many parents flock to popular areas such as Gangnam and Seocho, where good schools and high-quality private education providers are concentrated (Jones, 2020). This, along with the increase in single-person households over the past 20 years, has increased demand for housing in Seoul, while supply has not followed suit, resulting in rising prices (BOK, 2021). The housing supply rate in Seoul (the ratio of the total number of housing units to the total number of households) has decreased since 2018, and stood at 93.7% in 2022 (MOLIT, 2024). According to Statistics Korea, the total number of households nationwide is expected to increase until 2039 despite the population decline, due to increasing numbers of single-person households. This means that the supply of housing must steadily increase at least for the next 15 years to improve the balance between supply and demand.

Some regulations hinder private sector involvement, particularly in reconstruction (e.g., rebuilding or repurposing), which is crucial for addressing housing shortages in densely populated Seoul (OECD, 2019d). Since 2006, the Korean government has been collecting 'excess' profits expected from apartment reconstructions. Under the current law, if the average profit per apartment cooperative member of a reconstruction exceeds a certain limit (currently KRW 80 million), the government collects up to 50% of the profit in advance. While the original intent was to promote housing price stability and social equity by reclaiming excess profits, this practice causes financial strain among cooperative members, reducing incentives for residential construction. It could also lead to double taxation, as homeowners are already subject to capital gains tax when selling property.

Presale price caps is another longstanding practice in Korea aimed at stabilising housing prices for privately built new apartments. The Yoon administration lifted presale caps in most areas of Seoul, but they remain in some districts, including popular districts like Gangnam and Seocho which have been at the centre of supply shortages and escalating housing prices. These price caps diminish housing project profitability and keep down both the quantity and quality of housing supply, with the likely long-run effect of housing prices rising even further (Jones, 2020; Yun and Kim, 2014; KDI, 2009).

Social housing is an important source of affordable housing for young people. With increases over the past few years, social housing represents around 8% of the total housing stock, slightly higher than the OECD average (Cournède et al., 2022). However, a significant share of the social housing stock is vacant. From 2009 to 2019, on average, 17 000 public housing units were supplied to newlyweds annually, but only 51% were occupied because the quality, location, and size did not match the needs of newlywed couples (Board of Audit and Inspection, 2021). Despite efforts to enhance the quality and aesthetics of public housing in Korea over the years, these units still generally lag behind private housing, resulting in a persistent stigma attached to public rental housing residents (Woo et al., 2021). This potentially deters some newlyweds from considering these housing options. Additionally, public housing units targeted at newlyweds have predominantly been smaller than 50m², potentially falling short of the desired size. Indeed, smaller-sized public housing has shown a higher non-occupancy rate compared to larger units.

## Childbirth leads to substantial income losses in Korea for a number of reasons

While Korean women in the past may have chosen to leave their jobs when they married and had their first child, many women today are making different choices. The share of dual-income households is on the rise, but the conflict between motherhood and employment remains. What has changed is that when facing a conflict between family formation and work, women increasingly prioritise work. This reflects that women's earnings have become an important part of family income and likely a shift in women's labour supply preferences. In this regard, labour market conditions and policies such as work hours, workplace flexibility and job quality and stability affect fertility and female employment by making career and family more or less compatible. Rigid work patterns and long working hours, as in Japan and Korea, may also make family policies less effective than in other countries with shorter work hours and more flexibility as to where and when to work (Sobotka et al., 2019). This is because when individuals are expected to be fully committed to working long and rigid hours, even well-designed and generous family policies may for many not be enough to make it possible to combine career and children. Moreover, the quality and stability of jobs influence fertility decisions as they determine families' and individuals' financial security, work-life balance, and overall confidence in their ability to provide for and support a family.

### *Female employment has increased, but the work-family conflict remains*

Research shows that among high-income countries, those countries with norms and policies facilitating a combination of career and motherhood achieve both high female employment rates and high birth rates compared to their peers. The female employment rate in Korea has increased over time, but remains, at 61.4% (of the population aged 16-64, in 2023), lower than the 63.2% OECD average (Figure 3.7, Panel A). The employment gap to men is among the highest in the OECD in 2022 (Panel B). The gender wage gap is the largest in the OECD, and the proportion of non-regular workers among women is higher than that among men (Pareliussen, 2022).

Figure 3.7. Female employment has increased over time in most OECD countries

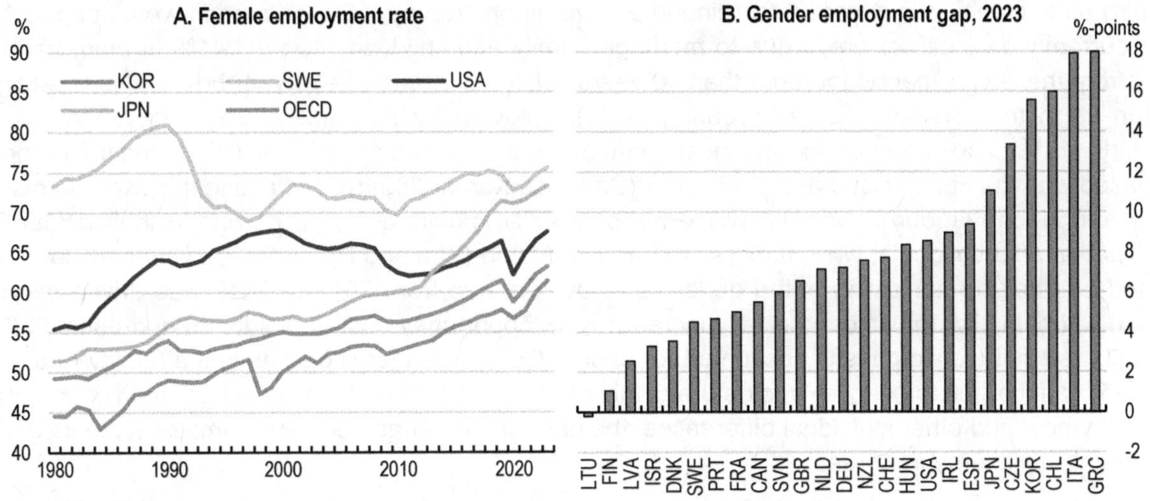


Note: Employment rates for 15-64-year-olds.
Source: OECD, Labour Force Statistics (database).

StatLink https://stat.link/3jmeqr

Since the 1980s, the employment of married women increased in urban manufacturing and service industries in Korea (Kang, 2007). Between 1985 and 1990, the labour force participation rate of married women rose from 41.0% to 46.8%, whereas during the same period, the participation rate of unmarried women increased only marginally from 44.7% to 45.6% (Lee, 2012), marking a shift away from the previous practice of selectively employing unmarried women. Both the government and businesses began to recognise the need to utilise the labour force of married women, but public legal and institutional support for pregnancy, childbirth, and childcare was limited. In this situation, where responsibility for childrearing lay with the family, and specifically with women, combining work and childcare was structurally almost impossible. Women therefore tended to participate in the labour force until marriage, after which they exited the labour market. With improved income levels and the spread of middle-class family norms, this reinforced gender-divided roles and responsibilities dictating that women should take care of the home in late 20th-century Korea (Choi and Chang, 2004).

Since 2000, women's employment rates have been on a continuous upward trend, only interrupted by the credit card crisis in the early 2000s, the Global Financial Crisis in the late 2000s and COVID-19 in 2020-21. The employment rates of women aged 15-64 rose by close to 10 percentage points from 50.1% in 2000 to 61.4% in 2023, while the employment rate of women aged 25-49 rose from 56.3% to 68.3%. Men generally have a higher level of employment than women, and the employment rate of men aged 15-64 has been modestly increasing to reach 76.9% in 2023. The employment rate of men aged 50 and older has increased, while employment of men aged 25-49 has trended down slightly. In 2000, the overall employment rate for women aged 15 and over was 23.8 percentage points lower than that of men. As of 2023, this gap had narrowed to 17.2 percentage points (15.5 percentage points for 15-64 year-olds). (Statistics Korea, 2024a).

### *Marriage and childbirth reduce women's employment*

A series of studies analysing women's employment in relation to marriage and childbirth from a life-course perspective emphasise that in contrast to the OECD average, women's employment over their lifetime has not significantly deviated from the traditional "M-shaped" pattern (Figure 3.8; Min, 2012; Kim and Park, 2019; Choi and Lee, 2022). It is slightly higher for young women than young men before dropping sharply as a share of women drop out of the labour force to marry and raise children in their 30s. Women's employment gradually picks up after childrearing age, when they are in their 40s, and drops again in their late 50s as they start to retire. This sequencing of career and family illustrates that career and motherhood are difficult to combine in Korea. According to a government survey, 16% of married women aged 15-54 were currently on a career break due to marriage, family and childcare. Around 41% of them had been away from the labour market for more than 10 years, while 23% had a 5–10-year break. The most typical reason for career breaks was child-rearing (41%), followed by marriage (25%) and pregnancy and childbirth (24%). The career break was most frequent among women aged 35-39 (25%) and the proportion increased with the number and age of children (Statistics Korea, 2024b). Reflecting this, Korean mothers suffer a long-term labour income decrease of about 66%, mainly due to a decline in their labour force participation after childbirth, while fathers are hardly affected (Kim and Hahn, 2022). Cho and Han (2024) pointed out that the narrowing of the gender employment gap from 2013 to 2019 was driven by young women without children, which ironically increased the opportunity cost of childbirth, and estimated that this increase in the child penalty accounted for about 40% of the overall decline in the fertility rate. While there are variations in the degree and nature of this trend depending on the time period, birth cohort quality of employment and other individual differences, the phenomenon has been and remains a steady feature of women's life course in Korea.

Figure 3.8. The gender employment gap opens up as Korean women enter their 30s

2023

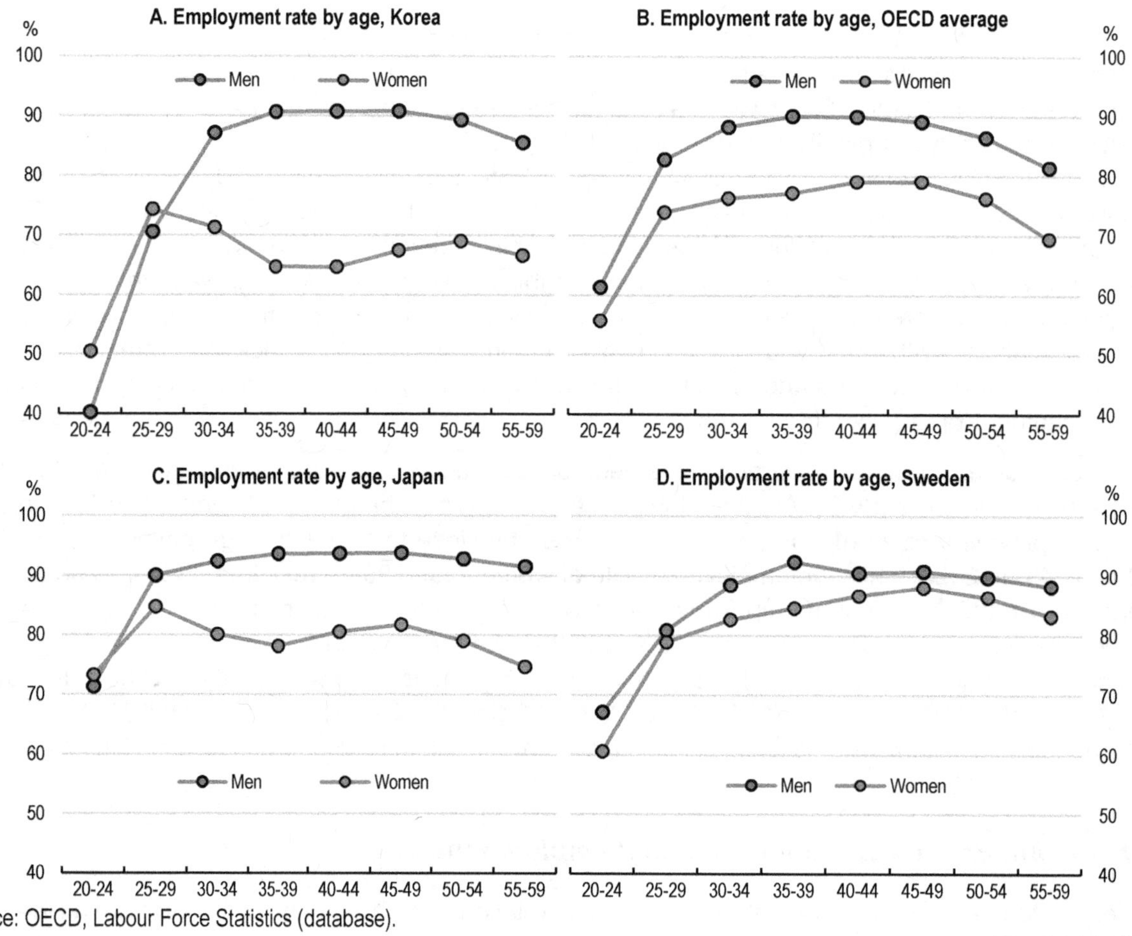


Source: OECD, Labour Force Statistics (database).

StatLink https://stat.link/5gw0a1

Yoo and Lee (2020) found that the employment rate of women who married between 2002 and 2012 dropped by about 12 percentage points in the year of marriage from 82% to 70%, dropped further to 57% after one year and to 45% after six years, a cumulative 37 percentage points drop. Since most women who married in the 2000s had at least one child, the decline in employment after marriage estimated in this study can be understood to include both the effects of marriage and childbirth. Kwak (2020) found that having a first child reduced the probability of a woman being employed by 45% compared to the year before, with the probability of being employed dropping by 17.7 percentage points between two years and one year prior to childbirth.

Kim and Park (2019) created seven categories of life courses and populated them using individual and occupational history data from the Korean Labor and Income Panel Study (2016). According to them, 48.0% of the women could be categorized into either the "M-shaped life" category or the "potentially M-shaped life" category, which means they left their jobs after marriage. This finding indicates that the most typical employment pattern for women across all generations in Korean society is one where they work until marriage (or first childbirth), leave employment thereafter, and then re-enter the labour market after a certain period. Only 8.7% of women were continuously employed both before and after marriage. A significant portion of 17.1% remained in employment while staying unmarried. This study shows that while the share of married women experiencing career interruptions has been decreasing in recent times, life courses that exhibit a balance of work and family remain rare.

Studies measuring changes between birth cohorts reach similar conclusions (Min, 2012; Kim and Park, 2019; Choi and Lee, 2022). Women from the 1970-79 cohort did not show a significant difference compared to women born in the late 1960s in terms of how likely they were to leave employment during periods of childbirth and childrearing (Min, 2012). Women born in the 1970s participated in the labour market more before childbirth compared to women born in the 1960s. However, a greater number of married women in the 1970s cohort withdrew from the labour market immediately after childbirth (Chang and Cheon 2014; Kim 2015; Kim, Park and Shin, 2015). This should be seen in the context of a gradual increase in the age of marriage and childbirth. Women with a higher age at first childbirth were likely to be employed until they had their first child, but were not more likely to stay in employment after childbirth (Min, 2012).

### *Labour market dualism makes work-family balance more challenging*

Job quality and stability promote fertility and female labour participation. Alderotti et al. (2021) suggest that employment instability has a non-negligible negative effect on fertility and the effect has become stronger over time. In countries with a dual labour market where jobs are either temporary or for a lifetime such as has long been the case in Spain (see below) and Korea, women tend to postpone childbearing in the hope of landing a stable job first. The quality of part-time employment is particularly important. The possibility of working part-time when children are young, for example by reducing hours in a person's career job, makes it easier to combine work with parenthood. However, part-time employment will not stimulate fertility if it is of worse quality than full-time employment in terms of job protection, social benefits or hourly earnings (Mcdonald and Belanger, 2016).

Research indicates that a well-calibrated flexicurity approach reduces labour market dualism, making temporary workers feel secure while achieving positive productivity outcomes (Noja and Cristea, 2018; Noja, 2018; Muffels and Wilthagen, 2013). Flexicurity relies on three pillars: freedom to hire and fire (subject to due process), a robust social insurance system ensuring income security in unemployment, and active labour market policies offering workers the opportunity to obtain new skills and look for new jobs in the event that they do lose their job. Several European countries, including the Netherlands and Nordic countries, have adopted variants of this model. For instance, in the early 1980s, the Netherlands adopted flexicurity to reduce unemployment and to enable workers to balance work and life (Becker and Schwartz, 2005). As a result, the Netherlands experienced reduced gender economic disparities, and a drastic decline of unemployment rates, accompanied by a rise of part-time employment (Levy, 1999; Song, 2014). Similar experiences have been observed in other countries, including Denmark and Spain.

Spain's social partners agreed to a labour market reform in 2021 as a condition to access European funds. The reform aimed at reducing labour market duality and improving the ability of firms to adjust to shocks. The reform reduced the number of contract types to three, restricted the conditions for companies to use temporary contracts, given their extraordinary prevalence, and introduced changes to collective bargaining. Social security contributions were increased for contracts of less than 30 days, and fines on companies abusing fixed-term contracts increased. The reform seems to have been successful in improving working conditions, especially for the young and for women. Following the reform, the number of registered temporary contracts fell sharply, while permanent contracts surged. However, it is too early to conclude that the reform was the cause of these improvements. The 2021 reform comes on top of a number of measures to reduce labour market dualism since the early 1990s, including making employers pay severance to non-regular workers from 2010 (Eichhorst and Marx, 2019; OECD, 2023d) and streamlining dismissal procedures in 2012 (OECD, 2013). These reforms were complemented by strengthening the social safety net, such as expanding coverage of unemployment insurance (e.g., making enrolment of the self-employed compulsory).

Dualism is deeply entrenched in Korea's labour market, with regular workers in large companies (often referred to as "the primary labour market") enjoying social insurance coverage, good working conditions and high wages, while non-regular workers ("the secondary labour market"), including part-time employees, face lower wages, reduced access to social insurance, and precarious job conditions. There is a rigid distinction between regular and non-regular workers, with limited opportunities for transitions. Women often quit their regular contracts as a consequence of motherhood, but find that low-paid non-regular jobs are the only options available when they seek to re-enter the workforce. As a result, mothers are three times more likely to be in non-regular employment than fathers. This leads to delayed family formation and fewer children being born (OECD, 2022; OECD, 2021b).

Despite efforts to break down labour market dualism, the share of non-regular workers increased from 32% in 2014 to 37% in 2023 according to Statistics Korea. According to an OECD survey, 61% of 25-54-year-olds reported that the risk of losing their job or income was among their top three worries, as against a 51% OECD average (OECD, 2024c). Chang (2020) analysed how duality in Korea, measured as the risk of job change, has changed across gender and the starting time of first employment for cohorts born in the 1960s, 1970s and 1980s. The results showed that job stability for the 1980s birth cohort improved compared to previous cohorts and that the security of women's jobs notably improved for those in their late twenties and early thirties. However, job stability for those in their early twenties had deteriorated. The gender gap for job stability was greater in the primary labour market than in the secondary labour market and job stability in areas predominantly occupied by women has shown no significant improvement over the past 30 years.

Choi et al. (2020) found that for women in the secondary labour market, the probability of leaving the labour market increased as their children grew older. It began to fall somewhat when the child reached the age of nine or older. The authors observed that the likelihood of women exiting the labour market increases by 15.6% when children are between four and nine years old compared to women without children. For primary labour market workers, no statistically significant difference in employment withdrawal was found compared to childless women for children under nine years of age. However, a 14.3% withdrawal probability was observed when children were over nine years old. In the primary labour market, outside the public sector, even employees with regular contracts (Jeong-gyu-jig) may not have high job security. Additionally, as job responsibilities and workload often increase with higher positions, the time pressure can be higher for older age groups. Furthermore, if the spouses of women are regular workers in senior positions in the primary labour market, this can further strengthen the pressure on women to exit the labour market. In practice, while the long working hours for women in managerial positions did not affect their husbands' career breaks, having a husband who worked long hours was found to increase the likelihood of women in managerial positions leaving their jobs, a finding supported in other research (Cha, 2010). For public sector and large corporation workers, Choi et al.'s (2020) only statistically significant finding was a

10.6% increase in the probability of leaving the labour market for those with children under 3 years old, compared to childless workers.

Other recent studies have corroborated these findings. Oh and Kim (2021) found that the risk of career interruption after marriage is lower for highly educated women and those with higher employment stability. Contrary to Min (2012), Oh and Kim suggested that the risk of career interruption after the first childbirth decreases with age. Jung (2023) conducted a cluster-centred trend analysis of the employment trajectories of women who experienced their first childbirth between 2005 and 2012. The study categorized these trajectories and examined factors affecting employment continuity, finding that women in lower income brackets were more likely to leave employment after having their first child. Maintaining regular employment requires access to various types of caregiving resources, and both caregiving support from family and the use of public childcare were associated with maintaining regular employment.

A root cause of labour market duality is the large productivity gaps among Korean companies, with SME productivity lagging well behind that of large companies and services sector productivity lagging well behind that of manufacturing compared to what is the case in most other OECD countries. A number of policies in place tend to support the survival of low-productivity firms, including subsidy schemes and a scheme for time-limited immigration to low-skilled jobs. Previous OECD Economic Surveys of Korea have recommended a number of reforms to reduce these productivity gaps, focussing on level playing-field competition in the domestic market and increasing openness to in-bound foreign trade and investment (OECD, 2018; OECD 2024b).

However, the most direct and impactful step that could be taken to address this issue would be to relax employment protection for regular workers to reduce the cost and uncertainty of dismissal, while strengthening the social safety net, notably income replacement for the unemployed (OECD, 2022; OECD, 2024b). A survey of 70 employers reports that they hire non-regular workers to ensure labour market flexibility to respond to market fluctuations, thereby avoiding the expenses associated with laying off regular workers (Saram-in, 2021). Employment protection for regular workers is relatively rigid compared to other OECD countries, ranking as the 13th strictest in 2019. Regular workers are strongly protected from dismissal by laws and labour unions, and delays before final court rulings are excessive. Dismissals for economic reasons are strongly regulated, with many procedural hurdles for firms. There must be "an urgent managerial necessity", a criterion that is ill-defined and difficult to prove in court. Consequently, unpredictable layoff costs compounded by lengthy legal processes, drive up incentives for hiring non-regular workers (OECD, 2022). Simplifying and accelerating the remedial procedure for unfair dismissals, clarifying criteria such as providing more explicit guidance on what constitutes "urgent managerial necessity", together with increasing the representativeness of unions as discussed below, could improve the situation.

Korean labour unions are relatively strong but unrepresentative of the majority of workers. Only 3% of non-regular workers are labour union members, compared to 20% of regular workers (Statistics Korea, 2024c). The labour unions' predominant focus on the interests of regular employees, especially those in large companies and the public sector, has contributed to the gap in employment protection compared to non-regular workers. The low unionisation rate is also an issue in general, as fragmented and poorly representative social partners are likely to be less inclusive and increase the level of strife (OECD, 2017). Korean unions received grant funding from the central government until 2023, after which union funding was abolished partly due to the lack of transparency in the use of public funds. Before this time, union fees could also be deducted from income taxes, but were pooled with other deductions and subject to a cap on total deductions. In order to increase the representativeness of unions, public funding could increasingly incentivise membership, for example by applying a separate ceiling for tax deductions of union fees, but could also incentivise the membership of non-regular workers more directly.

Another reason for hiring non-regular workers is their low labour costs, stemming partly from their low enrolment rate in social insurance, reflecting both non-compliance with mandatory enrolment and that not all categories of workers are required to enrol. Hiring workers who are not enrolled in social insurance schemes (i.e., national pension, health and employment insurance) lowers employers' labour costs by about 8-9%. This issue could be mitigated through a stronger monitoring system and labour inspectorate, and integrating social contributions and tax collection. In 2020, Korea outlined a roadmap to achieve full employment insurance coverage by 2025. The original plan was to increase enrolment to 17 million in 2022 and 21 million in 2025. However, as of December 2023, enrolment stood at only around 15.83 million despite some efforts such as expanding employment insurance to platform workers and several occupations such as agency drivers in 2021-22, and easing requirements for employment insurance enrolment in small agriculture and fisheries businesses in 2023. The government plans to integrate social contributions and tax collection as recommended in the 2022 *Economic Survey of Korea*, which would help increase compliance.

### *Long work hours and a rigid working culture are difficult to combine with childrearing*

Shorter work hours and flexibility regarding when and where to work make it easier to combine work and family. Weekly work hours differ across the OECD, with the average being around 42 for men, and only Norway and Denmark displaying average weekly work hours below 40. Working hours in Costa Rica, Türkyie, Colombia and Mexico stand out as the longest in the OECD, at just below 50 hours per week. Men work more hours than women in all countries, but the gaps vary considerably in size, with notably small gaps in the Baltics, Hungary, Slovenia and Chile. Korean workers devote more time to paid employment than their peers in most OECD countries, averaging 44.1 hours per week for men and 41.8 hours for women (Figure 3.9, Panel A).

Working very long hours is generally incompatible with participating actively in parenting and family life. The share of workers working very long hours differs considerably between countries, with the ranking of countries very similar to that of average hours. More men than women work long hours in all countries, but the gender gap varies considerably. Gender gaps are also large in countries like the Nordics, the Netherlands and France, generally seen as relatively gender-equal. The Baltics and Hungary stand out with a very low share of both men and women working long hours. A higher proportion of Korean employees, both women and men, work more than 50 hours per week than in most other OECD countries (Figure 3.9, Panel B).

There has been considerable progress in Korea over the past decade, with the average usual weekly hours of full-time workers decreasing by 8.2 hours, reaching 43.2 in 2022. This marks the fastest reduction in work hours among OECD countries, where the average decline over the same period stands at 1.5 hours, but typically from a lower starting point. Korea rolled out a reform reducing the maximum weekly working hours including overtime from 68 to 52 hours in stages from 2018 to 2021. This has improved work-life balance, while initial evidence indicate that hourly productivity increased to fully offset the reduction in work hours (Shim and Kim, 2020). Korea's statutory 40-hour regular workweek aligns well with most other OECD countries, while the 52-hour cap including 12 hours overtime remains above 48 hours, the statutory limit most commonly observed in OECD countries.

Since the introduction of the 52-hour cap, discussions have been ongoing to increase flexibility in its application by allowing workers to accumulate overtime for extended breaks. Such flexibility could in principle help parents combine work and family if it was balanced between the needs of employers and employees, but in the Korean context there are valid concerns that it would be unbalanced in favour of employers. For example, many Korean workers do not fully utilise their legal annual leave (15 days), with an average annual leave utilisation rate of 76%, due to a number of reasons such as the preference for monetary compensation in exchange for unused annual leave, lack of replacement workers and worries about burdening colleagues (MCST, 2023).

The most direct way policy can influence working hours is by setting minimum labour standards in legislation. The European Union has enforced a regulation capping the workweek at an average of 48 hours over four months since the 1990s. These measures aimed to promote a healthier work-life balance and greater gender equality in terms of working hours and employment prospects, given that men tended to work longer hours than women (Eurofound, 2017). European countries now show relatively minor gender disparities in working hours and wages, with a strong work-life balance as supported by OECD indicators (OECD, 2023c). France reduced the standard weekly working hours from 39 to 35 in the late 1990s (OECD, 2009). Moreover, some OECD countries, including France, Belgium, and Italy, have introduced "right to disconnect" laws, giving employees the right to disconnect from work-related communication outside regular working hours (EU-OSHA, 2023). In France, for instance, the 2013 law requires companies with 50 employees or more to establish a dialogue between employer and employees in order to regulate the use of digital tools beyond working hours, to specify employees' rights to switch off, and to ensure these rights are enforced (EPRS, 2020). The law is complemented by penalties for non-compliance and provides legal recourse for employees if they believe their rights have been violated. Beyond its legal implications, this legislation has served to heighten public awareness of the right to disconnect.

**Figure 3.9. Long working hours are prevalent in Korea**

2023

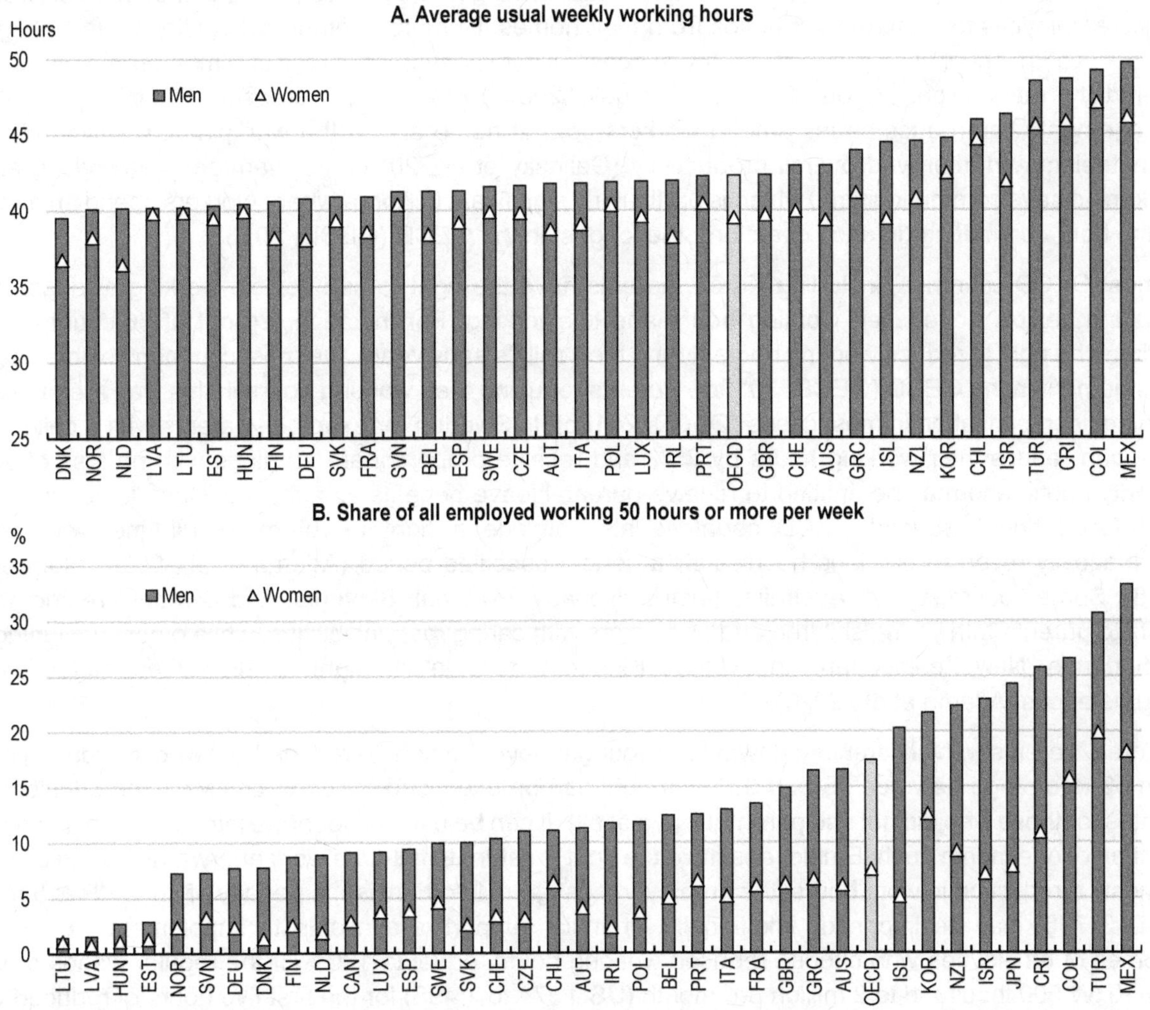


Note: For Panel B, the dataset contains data on employment by long hour bands (50 and over, 60 and over) for usual weekly hours worked in the main job. Actual hours of work instead of usual hours of work are only available in some countries (Japan and Korea). Data are broken down by professional status – employees, total employment – by sex and age groups.

Source: OECD Labour Force Statistics database.

StatLink https://stat.link/ntg4mc

The United Kingdom provides an example of how legal maximum working hours can influence actual working hours. While the European Union, prior to Brexit, set a 48-hour limit on weekly working hours for employees, only the United Kingdom allowed workers to "opt out", permitting them to work up to 60 hours per week. This flexibility, designed to accommodate individual preferences, contributed to a prevailing culture of long working hours in the United Kingdom (Barnard et al., 2003). Compared to Western and Northern European countries like France, the Netherlands, Germany, and Denmark, the United Kingdom stands out with long working hours and a high share of workers working long hours (Figure 3.9). This culture, particularly prevalent among white-collar professionals, managers, and full-time regular employees, normalises long hours and may deter employees from choosing reduced working hours or flexible arrangements for fear of career repercussions (Kwon, 2016; Fagan, 2009).

Flexible working arrangements can allow parents to allocate their time use in ways that reduce conflicting demands from work and family. This, in turn, provides greater possibilities for parents to enter or remain in the labour market. Workplace flexibility options span from reduced working hours, flexitime (starting and finishing work at different times without affecting total daily working hours or earnings), and compressed workweek (where the normal workweek is reduced to fewer than five days, but the total number of hours normally worked per week remains the same, typically through extended daily working hours) to more advanced options, such as "time accounts" to spread working hours across weeks or months. Teleworking allows employees to perform their duties from their homes. Numerous empirical studies have highlighted the positive impact of such practices on the successful combination of career and motherhood, as well as on fertility rates (Tonkikh et al., 2019; Rajgelj, 2007). Moreover, increased availability of these arrangements can reduce stress among workers both at home and in the workplace, resulting in lower absenteeism and improved overall productivity (Galinsky et al., 2011). Furthermore, teleworking allows workers to save commuting time, which is particularly significant in Korea where workers spend an average of one hour commuting (in each direction), the longest in the OECD (OECD, 2016).

In most OECD countries, including Korea, parents have the right to use flexible working arrangements, including flexible or reduced working hours and teleworking. For instance, 24 out of 36 countries give workers the right to reduce working hours during their child's early years, the most common flexible working arrangement in the OECD (OECD, 2019c). Parents reducing their working hours in this way are entitled to earnings compensation in most cases (OECD, 2019c). In Sweden for example, parents with a child under eight can reduce their working hours by 25% and receive proportionate earnings with no loss of social security rights, and may be entitled to receive parental leave benefits as a top-up. Complementing rights to reduced hours, several OECD countries also provide a right to return to full-time work and/or automatically revert to previous hours after a certain specified period (Adema et al., 2020; Blum et al., 2018). Some countries (e.g. Australia, Austria, Norway, Portugal, Slovenia, and Sweden) restrict these rights to parents with young children and/or workers with caring responsibilities, while others, including the Netherlands, New Zealand and the United Kingdom, provide the right to all workers regardless of circumstances (Adema et al., 2020).

In Korea, parents with children aged twelve or younger have the right to reduce their weekly working hours from 52 to a range between 15 and 35. This right can be exercised for up to one year (an additional 24 months for those who did not use parental leave at all). It can be used in separate intervals, with a minimum duration of one month each. Employees have the right to return to full-time work afterwards. When a worker requests a reduction in work hours, the employer must grant it; otherwise, a penalty of up to KRW 5 million (USD 3 735) may be imposed. Additionally, financial support is available to supplement the reduced incomes of employees who choose reduced working hours, equal to 100% of the regular wages ranging from KRW 500 thousand to 2 million per month (USD 374 to 1 495) for the first five hours of reduced work and 80% of the regular wages between KRW 500 thousand and 1.5 million (USD 374 and 1 120) for the remaining hours. To be eligible, two conditions must be met: the worker must be on reduced work hours for a minimum of one month, and must have been enrolled in employment insurance for at least 180 days.

Despite these legal rights, which align well with other OECD countries, the adoption of flexible working arrangements in Korea remains among the lowest in the OECD. In 2015, fewer than 10% of employees used these arrangements, far below the OECD average (Figure 3.10). Although adoption increased to around 16% in 2022, influenced by COVID-19 and government efforts, a survey reveals that over 7.48 million workers, more than double the current users, wish to utilise such arrangements but cannot (Federation of Korean Industries, 2023). Notably, workers in their 30s (58.2%), a key demographic for family formation and fertility, expressed the highest desire to utilise the system. There is also notable mismatch between the preferred types of flexible work arrangements and those actually used in Korea (Statistics Korea, 2022). Presently, among workers utilising flexible work options, the most prevalent are telecommuting and remote work (5.4%), while the least commonly used are compressed workweek (4.6%), flexitime (3.9%), and reduced working hours (1.7%). Conversely, workers who do not currently employ flexible work arrangements express a stronger preference for flexitime (14.6%), compressed workweek (13.6%), and reduced working hours (10.2%).

## Figure 3.10. Few workers utilise flexible working time arrangements in Korea

The share of employees using flexible working time arrangements, aged 15-64, 2015

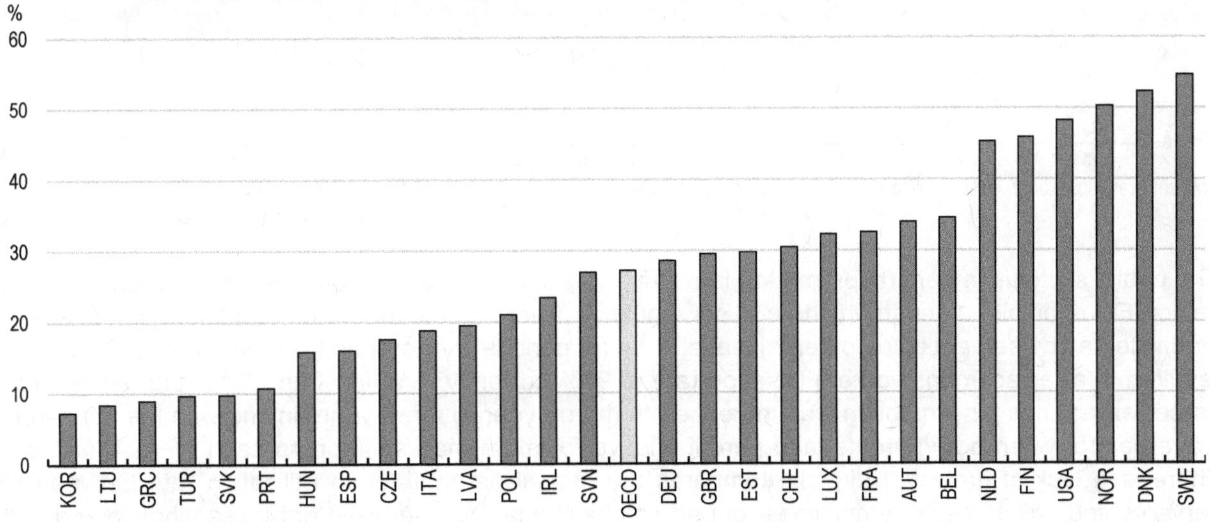


Note: Flexible working hours refer to the situation of employees who can either fully determine or at least adapt within certain limits their working hours (e.g. flexitime). OECD is the unweighted average of the 28 OECD countries shown in this chart.
Source: OECD Employment Outlook 2021.

StatLink https://stat.link/eyaf6z

Opportunities to access flexible working arrangements vary with firm size. For instance, teleworking is taking place in 51% of Korea's large companies, compared to only 27% in companies with 5-30 workers (KIHASA, 2022). This matters, as Korean workers spend an average of one hour commuting (in each direction), the longest in the OECD. Flexible work arrangements are more common among men than women (Figure 3.11). This could be because more men work in large corporations or have secure long-term contracts, contexts where flexible work arrangements are used more and more frequently.

Contributing factors to the limited adoption of flexible work arrangements in Korea despite having a similar legal framework to other OECD countries include the lack of a teleworking system and the career disadvantages for those who utilise teleworking options (KIHASA, 2022). This issue is particularly pronounced among non-regular workers, who, despite having equal rights to flexible working arrangements in principle, face additional barriers in practice (OECD, 2024b). If workplace culture and implicit norms continue to endorse extended work hours and presenteeism as the standard, employees may hesitate to use these arrangements due to concerns about potential negative impacts on their income, job security, promotion prospects, and career evaluations. Shin and Lee (2021) interviewed human resource managers at 30 companies where flexible work arrangements were common and found that flexible work arrangements prevent career interruptions for women, increase job satisfaction and improve employees' ability to concentrate on their work. However, using flexible work arrangements also increased the risk of scoring low on performance evaluation, or made workers anxious about this possibility and made them feel the need to prove themselves.

Figure 3.11. Use of flexible work arrangements by gender

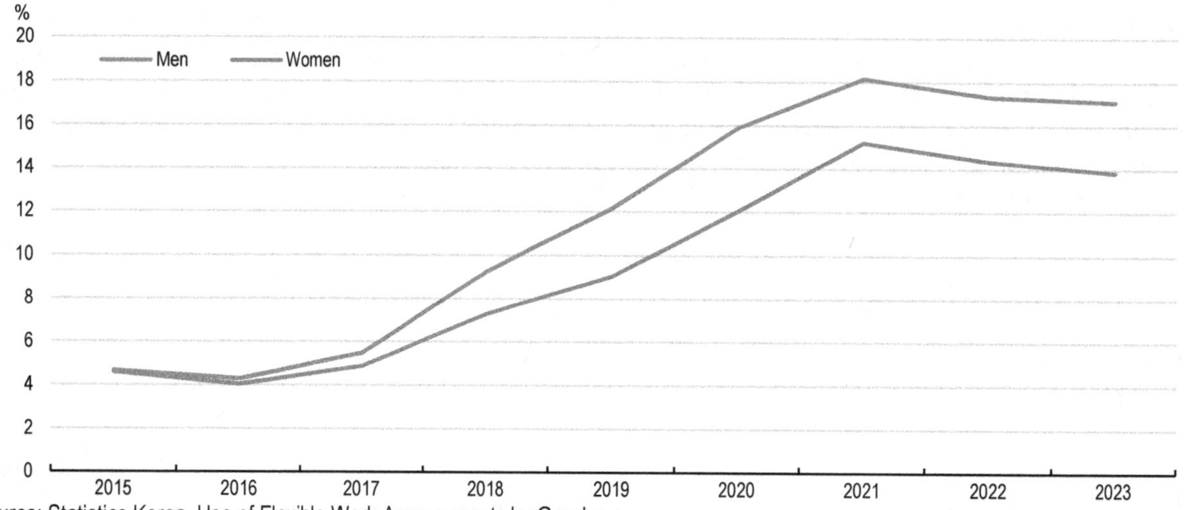


Source: Statistics Korea. Use of Flexible Work Arrangements by Gender.

StatLink https://stat.link/6raiub

The public sector is in general promoting family-friendly and flexible work practices more than the private sector. For example, amendments to civil servant laws now mandate the swift recruitment of replacement staff when a civil servant takes parental leave, even for periods shorter than six months. This initiative has resulted in a replacement worker utilisation rate of 94% currently. Starting from 2018, the recognition of career experience for promotion was increased from one year to three years in line with the full parental leave period, when both parents take parental leave for more than six months each for their first child. There is a lack of data that directly compares the overall parental leave utilisation rate between civil servants and private sector employees, but an empirical analysis suggests that those who worked in the public sector are around four times more likely to perceive parental leave as being accessible (Kim et al., 2021). Furthermore, in 2021, the share of male government officials who used parental leave reached 41.5%, more than doubling from 19% in 2016, and considerably higher than the overall average of 24.1% (average for men and women).

Some private companies have implemented proactive work-family balance policies beyond government requirements, leading to increased productivity and market valuation. A prime example is POSCO, one of the world's largest steel manufacturers. For example, POSCO introduced a "working-from-home for parenting" system, allowing employees with young children to work remotely for either full or half days. In addition to facilitating flexible work arrangements, POSCO provides generous maternity benefits, offering a one-time payment of KRW 2 million (approximately EUR 1 400) for the firstborn and KRW 5 million (approximately EUR 3 500) for the second child on top of the mandatory benefit. After maternity leave, parental leave automatically begins for up to three years without the need for a separate application process or approval from a supervisor. According to POSCO's own surveys and analysis, these policies have increased employee satisfaction levels and the company's market valuation.

Another example is THEVOO Engineering, an SME engineering company. THEVOO Engineering actively promotes flexible work hours and telecommuting for all employees, and currently over half of the workforce is making use thereof. It introduced a 'Selective Time Work System' which allows employees to freely choose working hours. Employees are required to work a minimum of six hours and 30 minutes per day, with the standard workday being eight hours. If they do not fulfil the full eight-hour workday, they have up to three months to make up for the remaining hours. THEVOO put in place software that records all data generated within the company, including PC usage status and activity, as a performance management programme. Since the introduction of the system, the company's revenue has nearly doubled despite a decrease in the number of staff. The company goes to great lengths to facilitate work for parents, for example by allowing parents to bring their children to work when needed and providing a space where they can study or watch videos. The CEO has ambitions to establish workplace childcare, but the company does not have the necessary scale to realise this ambition on its own.

## Changing social norms increase women's opportunities outside of traditional family structures

A norm is defined as something that is usual, typical or a shared standard of acceptable behaviour. These common ideas are products of a country's historical, religious and cultural heritage, but also shaped by its level of economic development. Norms play a key role in economic development, democracy, governance institutions and gender equality. They are important to fertility, as they affect how society organises working life and caring responsibilities in ways that make work and family formation more or less compatible. They may also steer individual choice in fertility decisions through for example norms towards marrying and having children as a duty, and norms towards the desired number of children.

As outlined in Yang et al. (2024), the demographic and industrial transitions are intricately connected and consequential to understand how fertility, economic growth, values and norms have evolved over time and thereby the policy measures needed to address low fertility (Table 3.1). Industrialisation sharpens the quality-quantity trade-off and the opportunity cost of having children in terms of career sacrifices, while access to education and contraceptives make it drastically easier to limit fertility. Persisting gender-unequal norms may still affect how families and workplaces are organised and may make it difficult to combine motherhood with working and other forms of self-realisation. Throughout the industrial transition and subsequent expansion of the services sector, women's opportunities in education and employment increase, while norms generally become more gender-equal and focussed on individual self-expression. Together with intervening policies, these factors contribute to shape fertility rates in a low-fertility, low-mortality setting in societies that have completed the demographic transition (Zaidi and Morgan, 2017; Lesthaeghe, 2014).

### Table 3.1. Societal transitions: stylised features

| Demographic transition | Industrial transition | Economic growth | Values and gender norms | Forces driving fertility and female employment |
|---|---|---|---|---|
| Malthusian stagnation, high fertility and high mortality | Subsistence, primary occupations dominant | Stable low GDP growth, negligible per capita growth | Traditional values, family dominant economic entity with less defined gender roles | Quantity-quality trade-off, with a considerable share of family income from children's labour |
| Mortality decreases, fertility remains high | Industrialisation, early stage | Very high GDP growth driven by population growth and productivity, high per capita growth | Industrialisation and urbanisation move values from traditional towards secular with a defined male breadwinner model | Quantity-quality trade-off sharpened by the increasing value of investments in human capital |
| Low mortality, fertility decreases | Industrialisation, advanced stage | High growth, very high per capita growth driven by productivity increases and slowing population growth | Values move further from traditional towards secular, increasing educational and professional opportunities for women | Quantity-quality trade-off further sharpened by increasing value of investments in human capital. The opportunity cost of lost income following motherhood increases |
| Low fertility, low mortality | Post-industrial with service sector expansion | GDP and per capita growth converging towards levels around the rate of productivity growth | Secular values increasingly dominant, with increasingly individualistic self-expression values and increasingly gender equal norms | Prospective mothers and fathers seek to achieve their aspirations, individually and as a family unit, for fertility and career, within economic and social constraints |

Note: This table is a rough conceptual representation with no claims to causality.
Source: Author compilation.

Countries with stronger individualistic self-expression values tend to have more gender-equal sharing of childcare responsibilities and to have institutions and working lives better adapted to combining parenthood and work for women and men, although there are considerable differences from country to country (Inglehart and Welzel, 2005). A move towards individualistic values is also associated with increasing divorce rates, re-marriage rates, an increasing share of cohabiting couples, and an increasing plurality of family arrangements in general. The Nordics, Netherlands and New Zealand are the countries most aligned with such values, followed by a number of European and English-speaking non-European countries including Austria, France, Belgium, Germany, Australia, Canada and the United States (World Values Survey, 2023).

If considerable gender inequalities in the career cost following childbirth persist while younger generations increasingly value their individual self-expression and self-realisation, couples will have fewer children, as children are likely to be born only if both partners agree to have a baby (Doepke and Kindermann, 2019). Korea is the country with the weakest self-expression values in the OECD, indicating that priority is given to economic and physical security over self-expression and quality of life. Koreans also typically conform to traditional norms regarding issues such as gender equality, divorce, immigration, homosexuality, cohabitation and sex before marriage (Figure 3.12). Korea's very rapid economic development along with its Confucian background are likely partial explanations why this is the case. Norms change more between than within generations, and old generations formed their norms in a very different context than today's modern Korea. Institutions were formed based on older generations' values and younger generations are subject to expectations from their elders, to an extent forming their actions if not always their beliefs. In terms of fertility, Korea's position with high economic development and individual freedom coupled with more traditional gender roles implies that women to a large extent have the means to choose alternative paths from the traditional role as mother and carer, while patriarchal norms in family and work life do not necessarily facilitate combining the two.

Figure 3.12. Norms tie childrearing and marriage closely together

Sex before marriage justifiable never (1) to always (10)

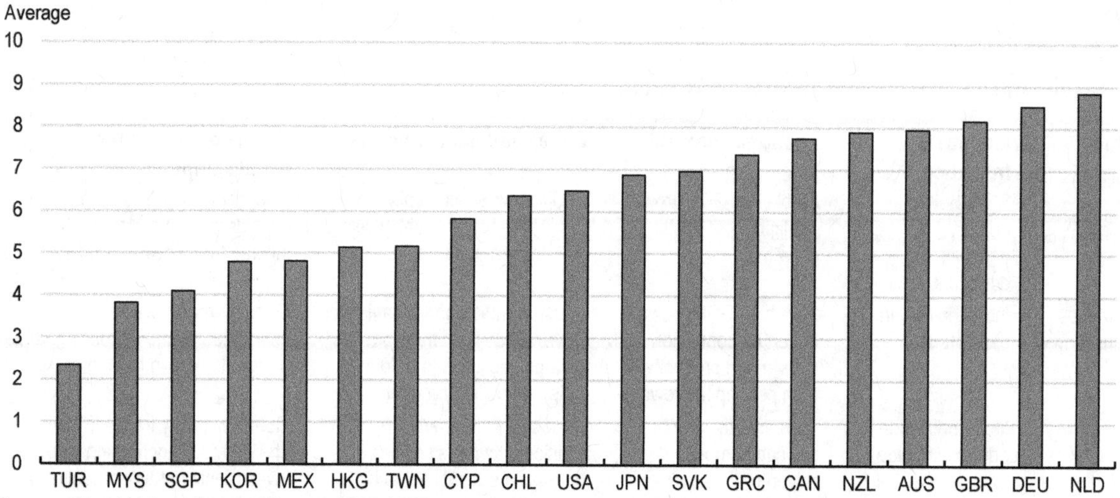


Source: World Values Survey Wave 7: 2017-2022, www.worldvaluessurvey.org.

StatLink https://stat.link/5kfmo1

## *Gender discrimination reinforces traditional gender roles*

Social norms about women's roles in the home and the workplace affect the sharing of paid work and unpaid caregiving work between men and women and thereby the opportunity cost of motherhood. For example, working mothers are often perceived as bad mothers and mothers face expectations to be children's primary caregivers in many countries. The share of the population agreeing that a pre-school child suffers with a working mother is higher in Korea than in any other OECD country, slightly above that in China, and notably higher than in the Nordics, New Zealand, the Netherlands, the United States, Japan and Indonesia (Figure 3.13). Younger generations of Koreans have less negative perceptions of the negative effects on children of working mothers than older ones, but more than 50% of 16-24 year-olds agree or strongly agree that a pre-school child suffers with a working mother.

### Figure 3.13. Korean norms are against working mothers

Share of respondents who agree or strongly agree that a pre-school child suffers with a working mother

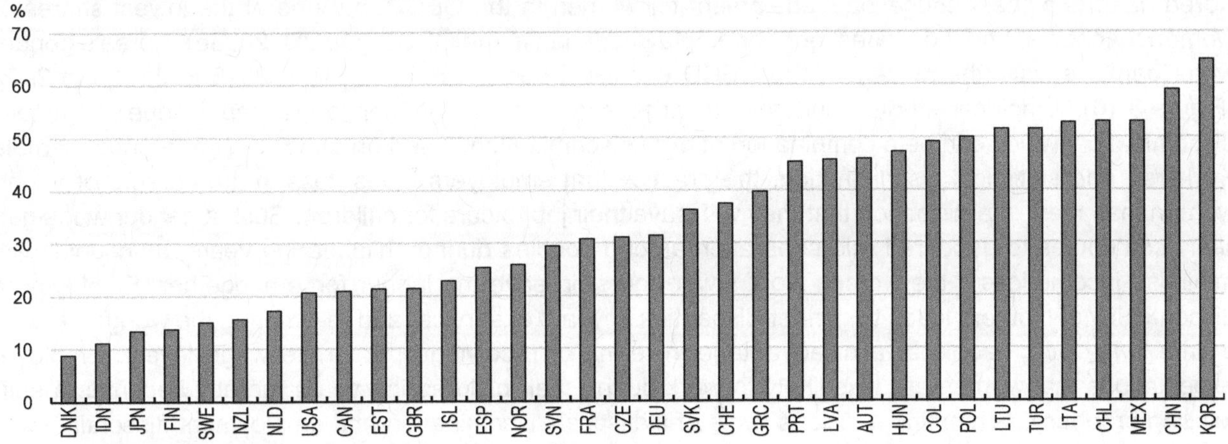


Note: OECD countries, China and Indonesia.
Source: World Values Survey Wave 7: 2017-2022.

StatLink https://stat.link/7ubed6

Similar traditional gender norms are reflected in the share of the population agreeing or strongly agreeing that men should have more right to a job than women if jobs are scarce, where more than half of Koreans agree. This is a higher share than in Türkiye, while the share agreeing in Japan is less than half. 5% or less agree in the Nordics, Netherlands, United States, New Zealand and the United Kingdom (Figure 3.14).

### Figure 3.14. Korean men are seen as the main bread-winners

Men should have more right to a job than women if jobs are scarce: agree or strongly agree

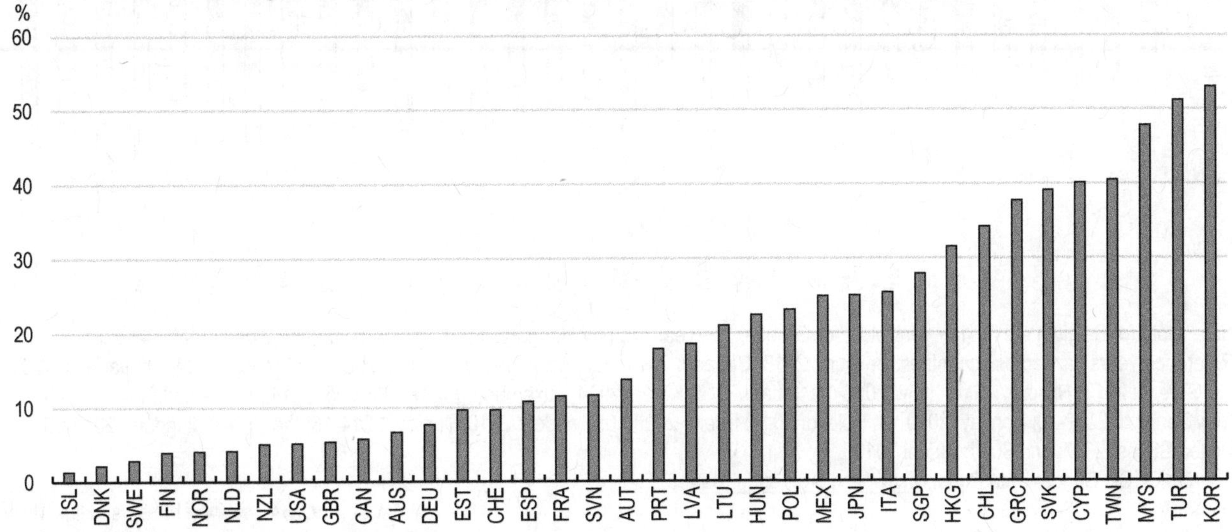


Source: World Values Survey Wave 7: 2017-2022.

StatLink https://stat.link/hs5v10

These attitudes are largely reflected in large gender gaps in time spent per day on paid and unpaid work, even though there are some notable differences in country rankings between norms and outcomes. Countries relying heavily on private provision of childcare to a varying degree compensated by transfers and tax credits, such as the United States and the United Kingdom, rank lower on this indicator than what would have been expected solely based on the above-mentioned attitudes. Despite sizeable gaps between genders, Korea ranks better than Japan on this measure. For most countries, the gaps in time spent on paid work are reflected in fairly similar-sized gaps in unpaid work, but there are some notable exceptions including Estonia, Finland, Italy and Lithuania, where the extra time women spend doing unpaid work is far from matched by the extra time men spend on paid work (Figure 3.15).

Korea has the highest educational attainment for women in the OECD, but one of the lowest shares of women managers, and the highest gender employment gap in the OECD (OECD, 2023e). Korea's gender wage gap is equally the highest in the OECD despite a decline from 37.2% in 2015 to 31.2% in 2022 (Figure 3.16). Empirical studies find that a large share of the gender wage gap is due to gender discrimination, which can be a combination of pure discrimination based on gender (a preference for male workers), and statistical discrimination, the practice that employers invest less in the careers of young women than men, in anticipation that they will leave their job to care for children. Such a gender wage gap likely contributes to gendered role separation among couples during childbearing years, as couples will minimise income loss if the women work fewer hours or leave the labour force altogether. Employment discontinuity of mothers leads to gender disparities in years of service, and re-entering the workforce after a time away puts people at a disadvantage in terms of receiving appropriate wage levels. Employer expectations that women are less likely to work during their childrearing years thereby becomes a self-fulfilling prophecy, reinforcing a vicious cycle of statistical discrimination and employment discontinuity of mothers.

### Figure 3.15. Gender gaps in time spent on paid and unpaid work are relatively large in Korea

Gender gap, women minus men, 15-64 year-olds

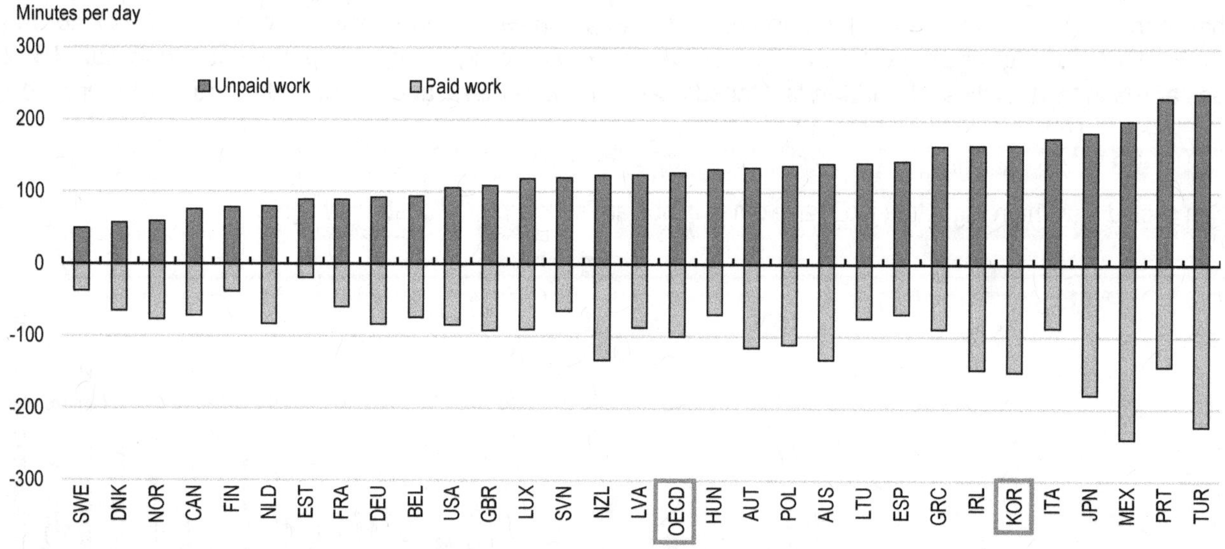


Note: Data for Belgium are for 12+ year-olds; for Greece, 10+ year-olds; for Hungary, 15-74 year olds; and for Sweden, 25-64 year olds. Reference years vary across countries: Belgium: 2013; Canada: 2015; Estonia: 2009-10; Finland: 2009-10; France: 2009-10; Germany: 2012-13; Greece: 2013; Hungary: 2010; Italy: 2013-14; Japan: 2016; Korea: 2014; Luxembourg: 2013; Mexico: 2014; the Netherlands: 2015-16; New Zealand: 2009-10; Norway: 2010-11; Poland: 2013; Spain: 2009-10; Sweden: 2010; Turkey: 2014-15; the United Kingdom: 2014-15; the United States: 2017; and South Africa: 2010.
Source: OECD Gender Data Portal, www.oecd.org/gender/data.

StatLink https://stat.link/1lujw3

**Figure 3.16. Korea's gender wage gap is the highest in the OECD**

2023 or latest

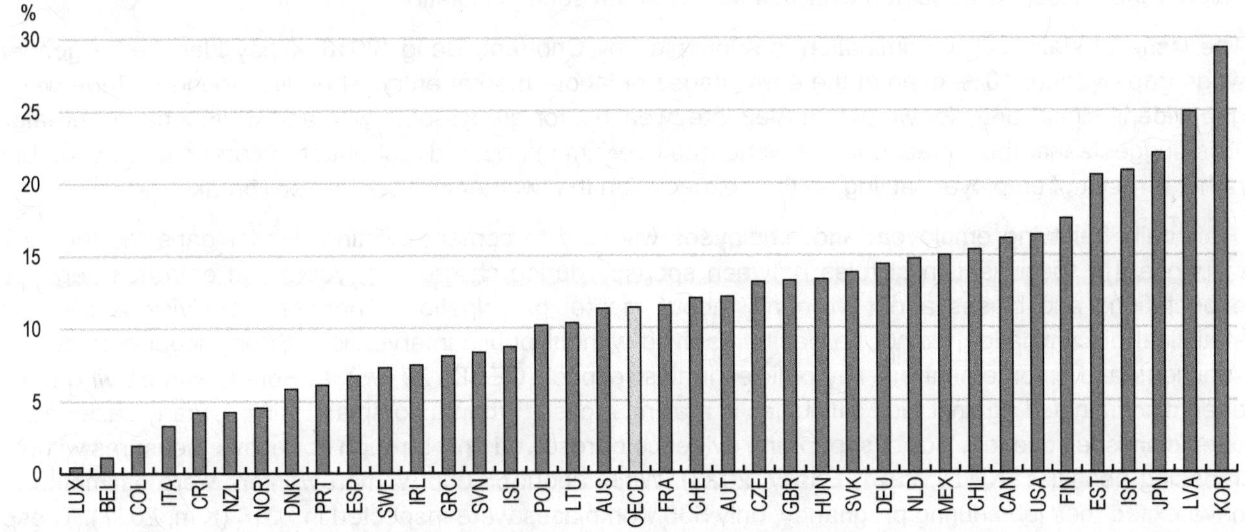


Note: The gender wage gap is defined as the difference between median earnings of men and women relative to median earnings of men. Data refer to full-time employees on the one hand and to self-employed on the other. Data refer to 2021 for Ireland and to 2022 for Austria, Belgium, Chile, Denmark, Estonia, Finland, France, Germany, Greece, Hungary, Iceland, Israel, Italy, Latvia, Lithuania, Luxembourg, the Netherlands, Poland, Portugal, the Slovak Republic, Slovenia, Spain and Switzerland.
Source: OECD, Gender wage gap (indicator). Doi: 10.1787/7cee77aa-en

StatLink https://stat.link/69q0j3

Despite legal prohibitions against discrimination related to pregnancy, childbirth, and parental leave, one in four women reported feeling discriminated against during job recruitment (24.4%) and in terms of pay (25.1%) (KLI, 2023a). In contrast, only 7.6% of men reported similar experiences of discrimination in these areas. In a survey carried out in 2018, 70% of individuals who utilised parental leave reported facing various disadvantages on their return, notably concerning promotions, exclusion from significant tasks, and discrimination in bonus allocation (KWDI, 2018).

Empirical studies confirm that gender discrimination is a key driver of the Korean gender wage gap, even though observable factors like work hours, sector, firm characteristics and tenure also matter (Choi et al., 2024). This discrimination is generally found in the private sector, while public sector jobs such as government officials and teachers, which have strong legal controls in the hiring process, show almost no gender wage gap (Kim and Oh, 2019).

Yoo (2017) found a large unexplained gender wage gap among two- and four-year college graduates at the time of labour market entry. According to this study, female college graduates earned only 78% of what their male counterparts received upon labour market entry. The contribution of observable human capital to this wage gap was relatively small (7.1%), direct wage discrimination accounted for 32.1%, and 62.1% was attributed to differences in labour market positions such as occupation, industry and company size. Kim and Oh (2019) found that women earn 17.4% less than men in entry-level jobs, despite having identical resumes. Kim (2017) analysed the gender disparities by age and found the gender wage gap in the 15-29 age group was smallest, but the proportion of the gap attributed to unexplained discrimination factors was the largest, at 185.6%. For the over-55s, however, factors including education level, job type, and company size accounted for 55% of the total wage gap. In the 30-54 age group, these factors only explained 30% of the wage gap, with the remaining 70% attributed to unexplained discrimination.

Kim et al. (2021) decomposed the reduction in the gender wage gap between 2002 and 2020 into changes in the composition of explanatory variables, such as the increase in the proportion of women in higher education, high-wage industries, and occupations and changes in the price structure. They found that changes in the composition of explanatory variables accounted for 65% of the reduction in the gender wage gap. On the other hand, the practice of paying women less than men under the same conditions actually increased the wage gap over this period, when seen in isolation.

The issue of statistical discrimination is addressed by Choi and Bang (2018). They identified a gender wage gap of about 10%, even at the early stages of labour market entry. They also found that the wage gap widens significantly for women in their late twenties, for groups both with and without career breaks. This suggests that the increase in the wage gap over time is not a direct effect of career interruption but rather a result of employers acting on their expectation that women will take career breaks.

Rationally behaving employers and employees will tend to cement existing gender gaps, as they will influence the specialisation of roles between spouses during childrearing years and entrench negative expectations and biases about women's labour market participation. Therefore, the vicious cycle of statistical discrimination cannot be easily resolved without public intervention. Strong legal protections, sanctions and enforcement are key policies in this respect (OECD, 2019c). In Korea, women who have been discriminated against face difficulties in making a case. When a complaint is filed, many cases have been dismissed due to a lack of supporting evidence or resolved only through corrective measures without imposing penalties (KWDI, 2021; Edaily, 2023). While about 55 000 women workers were estimated to have exited their jobs during pregnancy, only 535 workplaces were inspected in 2016 (Kim, 2017). These gaps can result in a climate where workers feel compelled to endure disadvantages, believing that raising concerns may not yield tangible resolutions or protection. Indeed, according to a survey, three out of four workers tolerate gender discrimination mainly due to perceived ineffectiveness in addressing concerns (Human Rights Commission, 2018).

To improve the situation, since 2016, Korea has conducted "Smart Labour Inspections" in workplaces with staff who are pregnant or have given birth, using relevant information from the National Health Insurance Service and Employment Insurance. The number of labour inspectors nearly doubled from 1 538 in 2016 to 3 058 in 2023. The number of inspected workplaces also increased to 1 028 in 2023. The number of reported discrimination cases related to maternity leave increased from 49 in 2016 to 91 in 2023. In 2022, Korea permitted the existing National Labour Relations Commission, comprised of members representing workers, employers, and public interests, to issue corrective orders to employers. These orders include ceasing discriminatory acts or paying appropriate compensation after investigation and interrogation when affected workers apply for remedy. Failure to comply with a corrective order without justifiable grounds may lead to an administrative fine of up to KRW 100 million (EUR 74 000).

Despite increases, labour inspectors are struggling with chronic manpower shortages (KLI, 2023b), resulting in inadequate supervision of many workplaces (KLI, 2024). Employers face fines up to KRW 5 million (EUR 3 470) when found guilty of gender discrimination in hiring, and up to KRW 30 million (EUR 20 800) with up to five years in prison for gender discrimination in promotions. The fine is lower than in some other OECD countries. For instance, the fine is up to EUR 450 000 in the Netherlands or EUR 300 000 in Germany for gender discrimination cases (OECD, 2019c). In Ireland, in cases of discrimination, employees can seek reinstatement to their previous position and claim financial compensation for the preceding six years without any ceiling for any damages suffered due to the discrimination under the Employment Equality Act (IHREC, 2024). Gender discrimination in the workplace may lead to imprisonment in Belgium, for one month to one year (OHRH, 2018). In France, the fine can be up to EUR 225 000, along with imprisonment for up to three years. The Finnish Penal Code prohibits discrimination at work based on sex and several other grounds with penalties varying from a fine to a maximum of two years imprisonment (ILO, 2023).

Pay transparency can also help close the gender wage gap. This not only holds firms accountable for gender disparities but also empowers workers to challenge inequities and generates public pressure for change, prompting employers to take corrective action. Since 2020, businesses have been required to disclose gender wage data through online systems such as Alio and Clean Eye. Korea mandates gender pay reporting, but firms are not requested to provide the detailed information necessary for meaningful analysis and action. Among the 21 OECD countries that mandate gender pay reporting in the private sector, Korea and the United Kingdom are the only ones that request only an aggregate, company-level estimate of the wage gap (OECD, 2023g). In all other countries, more granular information, such as by job category, parental status or seniority, is required for reporting. Furthermore, Korea mandates reporting only for large firms (with a minimum of 500 employees, or 300 or more full-time employees for companies obligated to provide disclosure under Article 14 of the Monopoly Regulation and Fair Trade Act). Moreover, the absence of mandatory equal pay auditing processes, as practiced in many other OECD countries, including Canada, Finland, France and Sweden (OECD, 2023g; Cowper-Coles et al., 2021), further hinders progress in addressing inequalities (OECD, 2023g).

### *Norms towards marriage, having children and female employment are changing*

Norms towards cohabitation and divorce are among those that can create hurdles to family formation in Korea. The share of children born to unmarried (usually cohabiting) women has increased across the OECD, and has in recent decades been driven by the higher-educated. More than half of births happen outside of marriage in a number of countries including most Nordics, Chile, France, Mexico and the Netherlands (Figure 3.17). Some countries in notably Latin America have relatively high rates of cohabitation for slightly different reasons, as cohabitation was historically socially accepted as a "poor man's marriage". Even so, cohabitation rates have risen considerably also for the higher-educated in many of these countries. There is no clear correlation between the share of children born outside of marriage and total fertility, even though most of the countries with low trade-offs between fertility and female employment also have a higher than average share of children born outside of marriage.

Figure 3.17. Births outside marriage remain extremely uncommon in Korea

2020 or latest

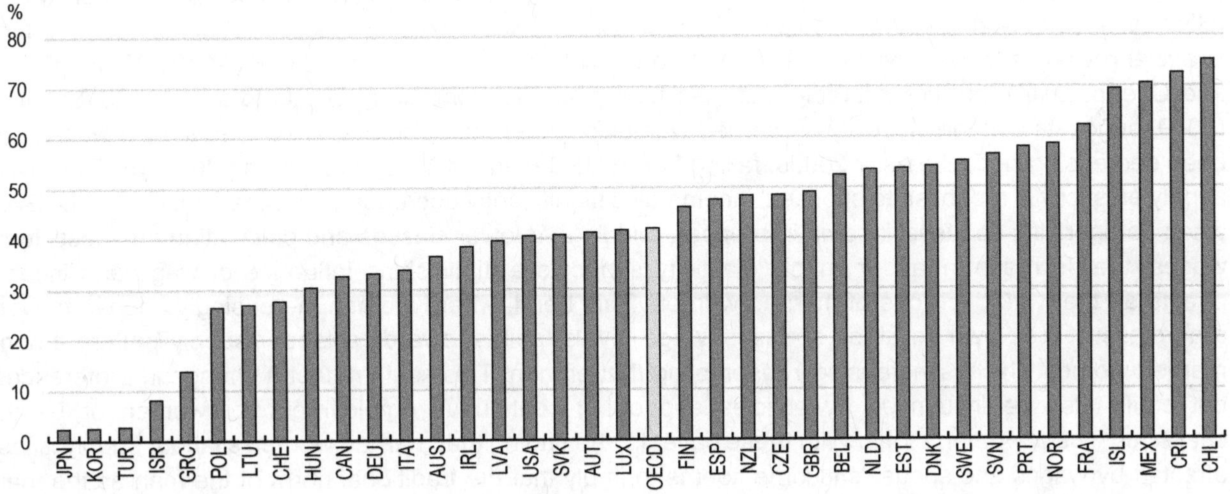


Note: Data for Australia, Japan, Korea and New Zealand refer to ex-nuptial/out-of-wedlock births, that is, where the child's parents are not registered as married to each other (or, for New Zealand only, in a civil union with each other) at the time of the birth. For all other countries, data refer to births to mothers where the mother's marital status at the time of birth was other than married. For Canada, births to mothers whose marital status is other than married as a proportion of births where the mother's marital status is recorded. In 2018, the mother's marital status was not recorded on 8% of births. For Mexico, births to mothers whose civil status is other than married as a proportion of births where the mother's civil status is recorded. In 2018, the mother's civil status was not recorded on 8% of births. Data refers to 2018 for Belgium, to 2019 for Chile, Estonia, Iceland, Ireland and Israel.
Source: OECD Family Database, www.oecd.org/els/family/database.htm.

StatLink https://stat.link/dteyfm

Even so, traditional marriage comes with entry- and exit costs, which may be relatively high in Korea. The direct costs of marriage, but also indirect costs are affected by norms. Negative attitudes to divorce imply that the individual locks into a partner with significant exit costs. In many OECD countries, marriage is seen as a milestone in a couple's relationship without many added expectations from family or wider society compared to cohabitation. In other countries, marriage carries a number of expectations, often rooted in traditional gender stereotypes. In the case of Korea, direct costs include costs for a proposal ceremony, engagement ceremony, the wedding itself, and the cost of purchasing a home, which is seen as a necessary condition to marriage by many. Marriage in Korea is also intricately connected to the expectation of having children, even though younger generations of married couples increasingly see childbearing as optional (OECD, 2024b). Housekeeping, caring for and following up children's education are largely seen as the mother's task. The Korean marriage package is therefore for many women a significant step towards motherhood and away from career. It may also imply an expectation to submit to her husband as the head of the household. One illustration of such patriarchal values is that the share of Koreans finding it justifiable for a husband to beat his wife is higher than in most other OECD countries for which data is available (World Values Survey, 2023). Combined with negative attitudes to divorce, this may increase the barriers to family formation compared to countries where cohabitation is more acceptable and divorce less stigmatised.

Marrying and having children have traditionally been seen as duties in Korea, but these norms have been shifting rapidly among young people, who increasingly reject the idea of marriage as a duty (Figure 3.18, Panel A). Unmarried women are much more likely than unmarried men to cite the loss of freedom from having children and the desire to keep their career as important reasons for not wanting children (Panel B). Norms towards having children have also changed among those who chose to get married. The share of married women who see it as their duty to have children fell from almost 80% in 1994 to approximately 30% in 2021 (Panel C), and norms about the expected number of children have also fallen steadily over time (Panel D). The ideal number of children has fallen less, and remains above two for married women.

A typical trait of the male breadwinner-female carer model is that prime-aged men's labour supply is not very sensitive to their wage level, while married women's labour supply is largely determined by their spouse's income, and is also very sensitive to the level of their own wages. In other words, men will be fully dedicated to work and providing for their families, while women will only work out of necessity or if the financial reward is very convincing. This pattern describes Korea's past very well (Yoon, 2012b; Chang and Cheon, 2014), but considerable changes took place from the early 2000s to the mid-2010s. Jung (2019) suggests that the elasticity of married women's labour supply in response to their own wages has been decreasing since the early 2000s, falling from 1.98 during 2005-08 to 0.7 during 2013-16. The labour supply elasticity in response to spouses' income also significantly decreased after the financial crisis. Even when categorizing spouses' income into upper, middle and lower classes and calculating the elasticity to wages, the decrease in labour supply elasticity suggests a diminishing influence of wage and income effects on the work decisions of married women. This trend, where women increasingly choose to work regardless of their own and their spouses' wage levels, points towards a labour supply pattern among married women which is increasingly resembling that of men. This could reflect a change in preferences, but could also be influenced by policies supporting continuous employment for women or by the characteristics of women's jobs. With these caveats, the finding that married women's labour supply is less affected by wages and spouse's income seems to imply that the traditional norm of the man as the main breadwinner and the woman as the main caretaker in couple households is weakening among cohorts who have been in childbearing age in recent years, and that women increasingly base their labour supply decisions on their own work-family preferences. More research is needed to establish this as a fact.

**Figure 3.18. Norms towards marriage and childbirth are changing in Korea**

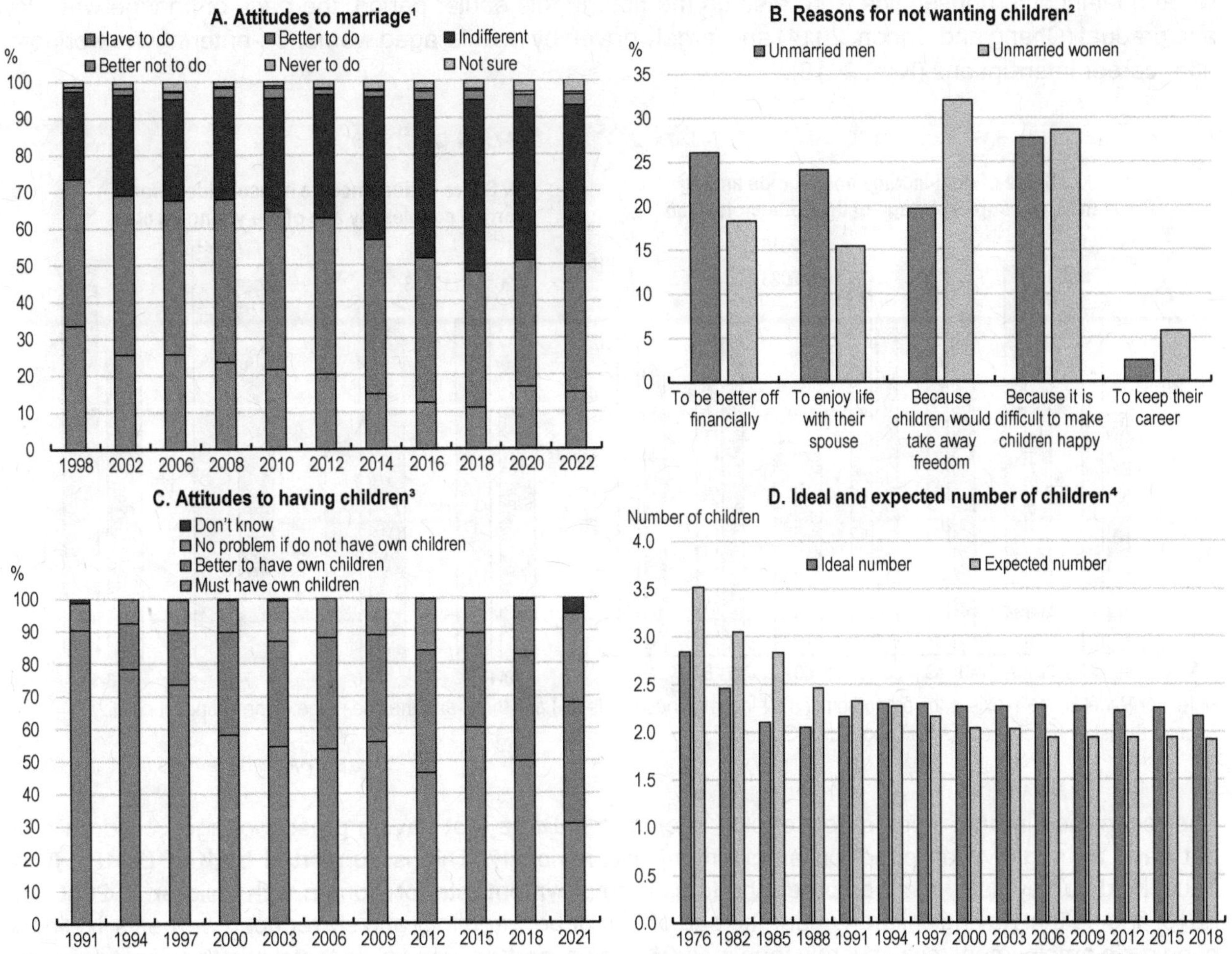


1. Distribution of responses to the question "What do you think about marriage?", total population over 15 between 1998 and 2006 and since 2008 population over 13.

2. Among people aged 20-44, 2018.

3. Distribution of responses to the question "Do you think you have to have your own child(ren)?", married women. Data for 1991, 2015 and 2018 cover married women aged 15-49 and 2021 data cover married women aged 19-49. Data for 1994-2012 cover married women aged 15-44. In 1991, "Must have" and "Better to have" are combined. In 2012, husbands could answer on behalf of their wives if their wives were absent when the survey was conducted.

4. Average ideal and expected number of children among married women.

Source: Statistics Korea; National Survey on Fertility, Family Health & Welfare in Korea; Korea Institute for Health and Social Affairs.

StatLink https://stat.link/24z51k

Women with education and high labour market status have over time become more attractive as spouses in Korea. This is reflected in the rise of the dual-income family, where women's income is increasingly an important part of the family economy. The shift in livelihood support in married-couple households from a sole male breadwinner to dual-income support is largely driven by couples in their twenties and thirties (Figure 3.19, Panel A). In 2015, 48.0% of households made up of individuals aged 15-64 had two incomes, meaning both spouses were employed. This increased to 55.7% by 2023. It is noteworthy that after rising considerably since 2015, the share of dual-income couples among those in the childbearing and childrearing ages of 15-29 and 30-39 are no longer significantly different from the average across age groups. Moreover, this appears to be directly related to a rise in the employment rate of married women with children. The percentage of dual-income households with children under 18 increased from 47.2% in 2015 to 56.8% in 2023, with a particularly notable increase for households with children aged 0-6

(Figure 3.19, Panel B). These developments stand apart from the period from the 1990s to the early 2010s, when dual-income households were also on the rise. In this earlier period, the pace of change was slow and gradual (Chang and Cheon, 2014) and largely driven by middle-aged women re-entering the workforce after career interruptions (Kim, 2015).

Figure 3.19. Share of dual-income households among married couples

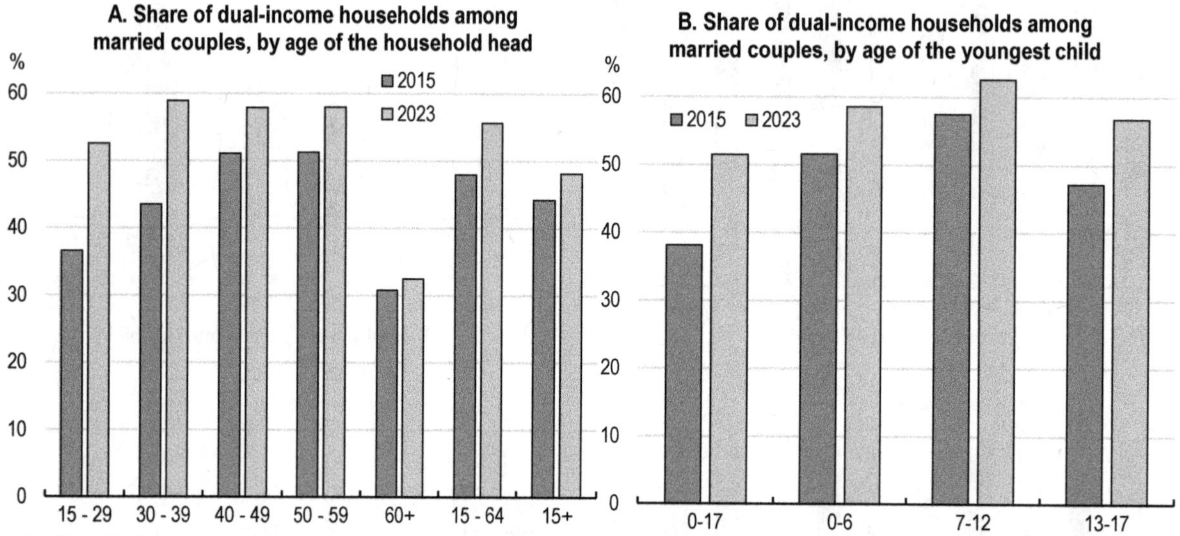


Note: For Panel B, the Y-axis is the proportion of dual-income households (%) and the X-axis the age range of the youngest child.
Source: Statistics Korea, Local Area Labor Force Survey.

StatLink https://stat.link/q7xwme

The recent rise in dual-income households seems to indicate that having preschool-aged children does not have as negative an effect on employment as previously. This is supported by Kim (2018), using household survey data. Kim compared the female employment rate for women with children in 2006 and 2016, finding that having children under the age of four or between four and six reduced women's likelihood of being in employment less severely than in 2006. However, Kim also found that while the effect of having elementary school children was not as great as having children of pre-school age, the negative employment effect of having elementary school-aged children had increased during this period.

Some gender differences remain in terms of how individual income affects fertility. While within-couple fertility increases uniformly with men's income, the relationship with women's income is U-shaped. In general, couples with low combined incomes are reluctant to have children. Couples with mid-to-high combined incomes have lower fertility the more total family income depends on the wife's income, as this increases the opportunity cost of motherhood. This opportunity cost seems to decline as the wife's income surpasses the median. This could reflect a higher ability to combine work and family for high-income women, for example through a combination of more secure employment status and having the economic means to procure childcare and other domestic services in the market (Choi et al., 2024; Nam and Kim, 2016; Ham, 2020).

## *Policies to facilitate more fertility-friendly norms*

Norms do not exist in a vacuum. They are formed as people observe the actions of friends, family, colleagues and other role models like managers in the workplace or public figures. This implies that policies and the political discourse do have roles to play. For example, policies facilitating working for mothers, as discussed in Chapter 4, will make more mothers work, and this will create role models for their children, colleagues and friends. Managers, high-level officials or politicians taking paternal leave will signal that this is indeed acceptable or even desirable. Political parties explicitly targeting gender-balanced representation in elected positions, central and local government can create a signal to other political parties and to society at large that this is desirable. Governments can also affect norms by information campaigns and through the public discourse. The most direct way to seek to move norms is by legislation (or decree), which indeed codifies standards of acceptable behaviour in society.

*Legal protections against discrimination and for cohabiting couples*

Strong legal protections, sanctions and enforcement against discrimination and requirements to report and publish related data, for example on gender wage gaps, are likely to affect business practices as mentioned above. Similarly, giving cohabiting parents the same legal rights as married couples would send a signal that cohabitation should be seen as socially acceptable, and thereby lower barriers to family formation. Some OECD countries require cohabiting parents to either marry or register their union if they want their children to benefit from legal protections and rights that resemble those provided for a family with married parents. Civil or registered partnerships exist in two thirds of OECD countries, typically giving equal legal rights to married couples. This right is reserved for same-sex couples in a number of countries, including Czechia, Finland, Germany, Hungary, Italy, Slovenia and the United Kingdom. Moreover, in some countries including Canada, Mexico, Spain, Switzerland and the United States, access to civil partnership registration depends on the region, which has the final responsibility to create such a status (Miho and Thévenon, 2020).

Almost all OECD countries extend certain family rights to "de facto" families with cohabiting partners. This status is obtained by for example living together for a specified length of time, living together and having children together or more subjective criteria, like having "family bonds" or a "stable emotional and economic community". The rights obtained by these cohabiting families are usually limited compared to those granted to married couples. Generally, countries give parental leave to both parents regardless of marital status, but in some countries these rights are conditional on some criteria, including the duration of cohabitation. Germany, Hungary and Poland require that the leave-taker is the legal parent of the child. De facto cohabitation usually gives weaker inheritance rights and other protections in the event of death of one partner. Belgium, the Czech Republic, Greece, Hungary, Poland, and Portugal do not extend joint property rights equal to those of married couples to cohabiters, Sweden limits this right to a specific type of property, while France, Norway and Italy grant such rights in the case of a cohabitation contract. Finland, the Netherlands, Iceland, and Norway extend such rights if the cohabiter can argue that they contributed to the acquisition of the property. Cohabiting survivors may also have limited rights to survivors' pensions, and they may have weaker tenant protection compared to married couples. Taxation also differs by the formal status of a couple. For example, some countries, including Australia, the Netherlands, Portugal, Slovenia and Sweden, grant couples who cohabit informally the same tax advantages as married couples. In others, including Belgium and Greece, they are taxed as single persons unless they have a child together. De facto unions may also carry some disadvantages compared to the case where each partner is treated as a single person. Informally cohabiting couples with children from previous relationships are for example less taxed across the OECD if they are taxed as single parents than if they were married or recognised as cohabiting (Miho and Thévenon, 2020).

Under the Korean Civil Code, only relationships arising from marriage between man and woman, blood ties, and adoption are acknowledged as constituting a family. However, Korean courts typically recognise de facto marriage (사실혼) if: the couple has either publicised, announced, or otherwise outwardly shown that their relationship is akin to a marriage; the couple had a formal public wedding ceremony; or the couple lived together like a married couple. This legal recognition gives cohabiting couples legal rights equivalent to those of married couples, except for a couple of areas such as inheritance rights. Consequently, the surviving partner of a cohabiting couple in a de facto marriage risks abruptly losing her or his place of residence if the partner dies, subject to the decisions made by blood-related family members who inherit the property. Although cohabiting partners in a de facto marriage can legally apply for parental leave, obtaining it can be challenging in practice. Mothers may be categorised as single parents once they have a child, because when children are born to cohabiting couples in a de facto marriage, the children are not automatically recognised as having a legal father. The biological father must undergo a legal procedure to establish formal recognition as the father of the child. Same-sex couples experience all the difficulties mentioned above, but in addition they cannot be recognised as legal guardians in medical institutions, limiting their ability to sign consent forms for their partner's surgery or hospitalisation and they may be ineligible to obtain health insurance as a dependent family member. The share of the population aged 13 and above who find cohabitation without marriage acceptable has increased, reaching 65% in 2022, with the share for young people (aged 19-34) at 81% (Statistics Korea, 2022). Based on this social consensus, further steps towards equal treatment of alternative family constellations could give couples an opportunity to form a family in incremental steps without incurring the immediate costs and expectations attached to marriage (Yang et al., 2024). Cohabiting can also provide at least a short-term financial relief for a couples' housing burden (KWDI, 2021).

### *Leading by example in the public sector and politics*

The public sector is a major employer and can directly facilitate a better balance between work and family life for its employees and thereby lead by example. Work practices and policies with high relevance for Korea include the absence of gender discrimination in pay, family-friendly working hours, flexibility of work hours, possibilities to telework and encouraging parental leave for both genders. The public sector has been leading by example over time, with the result that working in government in Korea is attractive relative to the private sector for women who want to balance family and career. Nonetheless, many civil servants remain subject to a punishing working culture with long hours and a lack of flexibility in practice. Civil servants are not defined as employees, and thereby not subject to labour law. The 52-hour work week reform for example does not apply to them, and their rights to participate in strikes or demonstrations are limited. It is quite common in OECD countries that civil servants have employment modalities that differ from minimum standards in labour law. This can affect pay, job security, performance evaluation and access to training, among others (OECD, 2019a). As labour reforms like the 52-hour reform improve the work-life balance in the private sector, the public sector needs to put in additional efforts to continue to lead by example.

A more gender-equal representation in politics creates role-models and is likely to lead to policies more adapted to the needs and interests of both genders, including policies facilitating both women and men combining career and family. Political parties' nomination process for elected office is a key mechanism to balance gender representation in politics, as illustrated in the case of Norway, where the share of women Members of Parliament increased fairly quickly from below 10% in the 1969 elections to close to 35% in 1985. This steep improvement in female representation was largely attributed to a change in political parties' nomination processes. When two small parties adopted gender quotas in 1975, this challenged the Labour Party (Norway's largest party at the time) to increasingly nominate women in winnable spots. From the 1985 election the Labour Party also implemented a gender quota. These quotas were implemented not as a necessary evil, but partly as it was seen as "the right thing to do" as women make up half of the electorate, and partly as it was seen as an important element of a winning political strategy. The adopted quotas put pressure on other parties to increase female representation, and some of the other parties implemented their own quotas later.

254 out of 300 seats in the Korean Parliament are elected from single-seat constituencies, and 46 by proportional representation. Single-seat constituencies may make it harder to increase women's representation compared to the Norwegian case of proportional representation from each electoral region. In the search for the "best" candidate, the pool of male candidates with distinguished careers is likely larger than that of women in Korea, and gender stereotypes may further favour male candidates. However, there should not be a lack of qualified women in any of Korea's regions if political parties decided to increase their efforts to secure gender balance.

### *Honorific language*

Norms about how people use formal language in addressing each other is a manifestation of Korean's relatively strong norms towards deference to authority and the hierarchy, and may contribute to uphold such norms with a number of possible consequences relevant to fertility. For example, it may contribute to long hours, seniority pay and career progression, which contribute to lower fertility as discussed above. Korea's norm towards polite speech ("honorific language", or *Jondaemal*) is almost unique among the OECD membership and tends to mark an individual's place in the hierarchy following Confucian tradition and military hierarchy culture in a society where men are obliged to serve in the military. Honorific language is used for those who are older or in a higher social position. Those two categories typically coincide, but it can create awkwardness when they do not. In the Korean debate, the link between formal speech and seniority-based careers, hierarchical organization and fear of putting forward ideas or speaking up against superiors is frequently drawn, even though causal evidence of a direct link to honorific language is lacking due to a dearth of research. Ko and Han (2019) showed that hierarchical culture is positively associated with the tendency to keep silent in a company. Kim and Park (2022) also found that the hierarchical culture is negatively correlated with personal performance.

Formal speech conventions exist across the OECD, but have weakened considerably over time and largely disappeared from practical use in a number of OECD countries. Only Japan has a similar tradition of honorifics (*keigo*). Countries like Germany and France commonly use the formal form in the workplace, when dealing with the authorities, with the elderly or with strangers (*vous* instead of *tu* in France, *Sie* instead of *du* in Germany, in both countries replaceable with first name in casual speech and Mr/Ms followed by family name in formal form). Spain has similar polite forms (*usted* instead of *tu*), but they are less and less frequently used. In a number of OECD countries, including the Nordics, formal form exists, but is seldom used. You was traditionally the formal way to address people in the English language, but is now the universal form with some exceptions like Sir/Madam or royal titles. Norwegian language has a formal form (*de* instead of *du*), but formal speech is in practice almost exclusively reserved for addressing members of the royal family.

In most countries, the move towards addressing people more informally and less hierarchically has been gradual and not much influenced by policy. However, the political discourse and role models have played important roles, as illustrated by the so-called *du* reform in Sweden, popularising the first-person singular *du* as the universal form of address in Sweden in the late 1960s. Before the reform, formal speech in Sweden had many similarities to Korea today, with a complex and sometimes confusing set of conventions in place to address people correctly. The *du* reform was not a top-down reform, but rather a gradual evolution, sped up by front-running newspapers and role models. It was seen as a watershed moment when the then head of the National Board of Health and Welfare announced that he would address everyone as *du* in a speech to his staff in 1967.

Many Korean firms have implemented new naming conventions in attempts to encourage good ideas, promote talent and make decision-making better, nimbler and more horizontal. In CJ Group, employees have been calling each other "sir" instead of using titles since year 2000. Kakao, one of South Korea's largest Internet companies, decided in 2014 that all employees would go by English nicknames, with many companies in the digital field implementing similar policies. Following initial attempts to introduce horizontal forms of address in 2017, Samsung Electronics recently banned the use of job titles and asked employees to announce their preferred nicknames internally, ranging from English names to initials to their given name (followed by "nim", which roughly translates to Mr./Ms.).

Ultimately, naming conventions in themselves should not be expected to affect company performance unless they are part of wider changes. Indeed, new naming conventions are perceived as more successful in cases where they were accompanied by efforts to move towards performance-based pay and career progression, and a move towards a more horizontal organisational structure by reducing the number of executive levels. Some companies, for example KT and Hanwha group, reverted to previous naming conventions after a period of time. In these cases, changing names was done in isolation and created a degree of confusion, while potential benefits were not realised as the work structure stayed the same. Others, like online platform Naver, found that reducing the hierarchy to two levels led to blurring of responsibilities, and re-introduced a third level.

## References


Adema, W., C. Clarke and O. Thévenon (2020), “Family policies and family outcomes in OECD countries”, *The Palgrave Handbook of Family Policy*, Palgrave Macmillan, Cham.

Alderotti, G., D. Vignoli, M. Baccini and A. Matysiak (2021), “Employment Instability and Fertility in Europe: A Meta-Analysis”, *Demography*, Vol. 58/3.

Anderson, T. (2018), “Shadow education and the quality-quantity tradeoff in the 21st century”, *Population Association of America*.

Bar, M., M. Hazan, O. Leukhina, D. Weiss and H. Zoabi (2018), "Why did rich families increase their fertility? Inequality and marketization of childcare", *Journal of Economic Growth*, Springer, Vol. 23(4).

Becker, U. and H. Schwartz (eds.) (2005), *Employment 'Miracles': A Critical Comparison of the Dutch, Scandinavian, Swiss, Australian and Irish Cases versus Germany and the US*, Amsterdam University Press, Amsterdam.

Blum, S., A. Koslowski, A. Macht and P. Moss (2018), *14th International Review of Leave Policies and Related Research 2018*.

Bray, M. (2021), “Shadow education in Europe: growing prevalence, underlying forces, and policy implications”, *ECNU Review of Education*, Vol. 4/3, pp. 442-475.

BOK (2021), *Financial Stability Report (December 2021),* Bank of Korea (in Korean).

Cha, Y. (2010), “Reinforcing separate spheres: The effect of spousal overwork on the employment of men and women in dual-earner households”, *American Sociological Review*, Vol. 75.

Chang, J. (2020), “A Study of cohort comparison on job stability of young women”, *Korea Social Policy Review*, Vol. 27/4 (in Korean).

Chang, J. and B. Cheon (2014), “Female labour supply and its impacts on household level income inequality”, *Korean Journal of Labor Studies*, Vol. 20/2 (in Korean).

Cho, D. and J. Han (2024), “Women’s career interruptions and the declining fertility rate in South Korea”, *KDI Focus 2024*, Vol.132, Korea Development Institute.

Cho, Y., J. Li, and S. Chaudhuri (2020), “Women entrepreneurs in Asia: Eight country studies”, *Advances in Developing Human Resources*, Vol. 22/2.

Choi, I. and S. Lee (2022), “Types and affecting factors of job quality changes in women during pregnancy and the parenting period: precarious work and career breaks”, *Women's Studies*, Vol. 113/2 (in Korean).

Choi, S. (2021), “The impact of education levels and paths on labor market outcomes in South Korea: focusing on vocational high school graduates”, *Social Sciences & Humanities Open*, Vol. 4, No. 1.

Choi, S., E. Kwak and S. Jeong (2020), *Childbirth and Female Employment*, Korea Labor Institute (in Korean).

Choi, S. and K. Chang (2004), “The modern reconstruction of the division of labour: Focusing on Korean women's career breaks during family formation period”, *Journal of Social Studies*, Vol. 4 (in Korean).

Choi, S., S. Ham, Y. Yang and J. Pareliussen (2024), “Women's employment and fertility in South Korea: a review of recent research”, *OECD Economics Department Working Papers*, No. 1825, OECD Publishing, Paris.

Choi, S. et al. (2022), *Work together and care together? An evaluation of how children affect parents' labor supply in Korea*, Korea Labour Institute.

Cowper-Coles, M. et al. (2021), "Bridging the gap? An analysis of gender pay gap reporting in six countries", *King's Global Institute for Women's Leadership.*

Delventhal, M., J. Fernández-Villaverde and N. Guner (2021), "Demographic transitions across time and space", *NBER Working Papers*, No. 29840, National Bureau of Economic Research.

Doepke, M., A. Hannusch, F. Kindermann and M. Tertilt (2022), "The economics of fertility: A new era", *NBER Working Papers*, No. 29948, National Bureau of Economic Research.

Doepke, M. and F. Kindermann (2019), "Bargaining over babies: Theory, evidence, and policy implications", *American Economic Review*, Vol. 109/9.

EC (2024), *European Credit Transfer and Accumulation System (ECTS)*, European Commission (accessed in February 2024).

Edaily (2023), *Workplace Gender Discrimination, 99% 'Corrective Measures' Only,* Edaily (in Korean).

Eichhorst, W. and P. Marx (2019), "How stable is labour market dualism? Reforms of employment protection in nine European countries", *IZA Discussion Paper Series*, No. 12309, IZA Institute of Labour Economics.

EU-OSHA (2023), *Regulating Telework in a Post-COVID-19 Europe: Recent Developments*, European Agency for Safety and Health at Work.

Eurofound (2017), *Working Time and Work-life Balance.*

EPRS (2020), "The right to disconnect", *EPRS Briefing*, European Parliamentary Research Service.

Fagan, C. (2009), "Working time in the UK – developments and debates", *JILPT Report*, No.7, The Japan Institute for Labour Policy and Training.

Federation of Korean Industries (2023), *7.48 million Workers Who Want to Work Flexibly but Can't... Twice the Number of People Using It.*

Fluchtmann, J., V. van Veen and W. Adema (2023), "Fertility, employment and family policy: A cross-country panel analysis", *OECD Social, Employment and Migration Working Papers*, No. 299, OECD Publishing, Paris.

Galinsky, E., K. Sakai and T. Wigton (2011), "Workplace flexibility: From research to action", *Future of Children*, Vol. 21/2.

Galor, O. (2005), "The demographic transition and the emergence of sustained economic growth", *Journal of the European Economic Association*, Vol. 3/3.

Guill, K., O. Lüdtke and J. Schwanenberg (2020), "A two-level study of predictors of private tutoring attendance at the beginning of secondary schooling in Germany", *British Educational Research Journal*, Vol. 46/2, pp. 437-457.

Ham, S. (2020), "Rich parent, poor parent: differences in the parenthood effect on income across the wage distribution", *Health and Social Welfare Review*, Vol. 40/2 (in Korean).

Han, J. (2022), "College majors in limited supply: the case of private universities in Korea", *Korean Economic Review*, Vol. 38/3, pp. 381-414.

Hazan, M. and H. Zoabi (2015), "Do highly educated women choose smaller families?", *Economic Journal*, Royal Economic Society, Vol. 125(587).

Human Rights Commission (2018), *Survey on Discrimination Against Pregnancy, Childbirth, and Parental Leave, National Human Rights Commission of Korea* (in Korean).

IHREC (2024), *Equality laws in Ireland*, Irish Human Rights and Equality Commission.

ILO (2023), "*Equality of opportunity and treatment*", International Labour Organisation.

Inglehart, R. and C. Welzel (2005), *Modernization, Cultural Change, and Democracy: The Human Development Sequence*, Cambridge University Press.

Jones, R. (2020), *Policies to Stabilise Housing Prices in Korea*, Korea Economic Institute.

Jung, S. (2023), "*A study on the career retention of women during childbirth and rearing period*", The Journal of Women and Economics, Vol. 20/1 (in Korean).

Jung, S. (2019), "*Part-time work and non-voluntary part-time employment*", Monthly Labor Review, March (in Korean).

Kang, D. (2022), *Impact of Housing Price Fluctuations on Marriage and Birth rates and Policy Implications*, Korea Institute of Public Finance (in Korean).

Kang, Y. (2007), "*The changes of labour market and work-family articulation after the 1960s industrialisation*", Issues in Feminism, Vol. 7/2 (in Korean).

KEDI (2022), *Educational Public Opinion Poll, Korean Educational Development Institute* (in Korean).

KIHASA (2022), *2022 National Work-Life Balance Survey*, Korea Institute for Health and Social Affairs (in Korean).

KIHASA (2019), *Analysis of the Prolonged Ultra-Low Birthrate and the Outlook*, Korea Institute for Health and Social Affairs (in Korean).

Kim, A. and Y. Hahn (2022), "*The motherhood effect on labour market outcomes: evidence from South Korea*", Asian-Pacific Economic Literature, Vol.36/2.

Kim, C. and B. Oh (2019), "*No gender discrimination before career disruption? Gender earnings gap at the early stage of work career among college graduates in South Korea*", Korean Journal of Sociology, Vol. 53/1 (in Korean).

Kim, Y. and J. Park (2022), "T*he effect of organizational culture types on individual performance: Mediating effect of communication and moderating effect of organizational trust*", The Journal of Korean Career·Entrepreneurship & Business Association, Vol. 6/3 (in Korean).

Kim, E. and K. Park (2019), "*Life course of Korean women: conflictual gender differentiation and enforced classification*", Economy and Society, Vol. 122 (in Korean).

Kim, E., W.J. Wang and M.J. Kim (2021), "*Determinants of perceived accessibility of maternity leave and childcare leave in South Korea*", *International Journal of Environmental Research and Public Health*,18(19).

Kim, H. (2017), *The Role of Education in Social Capital and Policy Directions*, Korea Development Institute.

Kim, I. (2017), *The Effects of Work-Family Balance Policies in Korea and Policy Implications*, Korea Development Institute.

Kim, J., S. Jung and W. Noh (2021), *Changes in the Structure of the Korean Women's Labor Market since 2000*, Korean Women's Development Institute (in Korean).

Kim, N. (2017), "*The wage gap among generations and between genders and implications thereof*", *Ewha Journal of Gender and Law*, Vol. 9/2 (in Korean).

Kim, N., S. Park and D. Shin (2015), “Effects of substitutability between mother's child care and market care service on life-cycle labour supply and fertility behaviour”, *Kukje Kyungje Yongu*, Vol.21/2 (in Korean).

Kim, S. (2015), “Who has taken the lead in the transition to dual earner model? Age, period, cohort analysis”, *The Journal of Korean Women's Studies*, Vol. 31/4 (in Korean).

KLI (2024), *Quarterly Journal of Labor Policy, Vol. 24/1,* Korea Labour Institute (in Korean).

KLI (2023a), *Monthly Labour Review, October*, Korea Labour Institute.

KLI (2023b), Proposals to Improve Alternative Dispute Resolution Functions of the Labor Committee, Korea Labour Institute (in Korean).

Ko, E. and Y. Han (2019) “The effects of hierarchical organizational structure and performance-based human resource system on climate of silence and selfish silence behaviour”, *Korean Journal of Industrial and Organizational Psychology*, Vol.32/4 (in Korean).

KOSIS (2023), *Housing price to income ratio*, Korean Statistical Information Service.

KRIHS (2023), *KRIHS Issue report, No. 78*, Korea Research Institute for Human Settlements.

Kwak, E. (2022), “The impact of paid childcare leave on fertility decisions”, *Korean Journal of Labor Economics*, Vol. 45/3 (in Korean).

KWDI (2021), *Study on Improvement Measures for Employment Discrimination Corrective System*, Korean Women's Develoment Institute (in Korean).

KWDI (2018), *Survey on the Discrimination in Pregnancy, Childbirth, Parental Leave of Workers, 2018*, Korean Women's Develoment Institute (in Korean).

Kwon, H. (2016), “Flexible work arrangements and work-life balance in Korea from a comparative perspective: What reduces their effectiveness?”, *Journal of CEO and Management Studies*, Vol. 19/1 (in Korean).

Lee, C. (2012), “A decomposition of the decline in the total fertility rate in Korea: effects of changes in marriage and marital fertility”, Korea Journal of Population Studies, Vol. 35/3 (in Korean).

Lee, J. and Y. Koh (2023), “University rankings and lifetime income inequality”, *Economic Research*, Vol. 71/2.

Lesthaeghe, R. (2014), “The second demographic transition: A concise overview of its development”, *Proceedings of the National Academy of Sciences of the United States of America*, Vol. 111/51.

Levy, J. (1999), “Vice into virtue? Progressive politics and welfare reform in continental Europe”, *Politics and Society*, Vol. 27/2.

Mcdonald, P. and A. Belanger (2016), “A comparison of fertility in Canada and Australia, 1926-2011”, *Canadian Studies in Population*, Vol. 43/1-2.

MCST (2023), *2023 Worker Annual Leave Survey*, Ministry of Culture, Sports and Tourism (in Korean).

Miho, A. and O. Thévenon (2020), “Treating all children equally? Why policies should adapt to evolving family living arrangements”, *OECD Social, Employment and Migration Working Papers*, No. 240, OECD Publishing, Paris.

Minea-Pic, A. (2023), "Catching up on lost learning opportunities: research and policy evidence on key learning recovery strategies", *OECD Education Working Papers*, No. 292, OECD Publishing, Paris.

Min, H. (2012), “Mothers' employment experience surrounding a first childbirth in South Korea: an application of group-based trajectory model”, *Korean Journal of Sociology*, Vol. 46/2 (in Korean).

Ministry of Education (2024), *Survey on the private education cost for primary and secondary students in 2023*, Ministry of Education of Korea (in Korean).

Ministry of Education (2022), *Regulatory Reform and Evaluation System Overhaul to Expand the Autonomous Operation of Universities*, Ministry of Education in Korea (in Korean).

MOE and KRIVET (2023), *Survey on the Current State of College Career Education*, Ministry of Education and Korea Research Institute for Professional Education and Training (in Korean).

MOLIT (2024), *Housing Supply Ratio*, Ministry of Land, Infrastructure and Transport (in Korean).

Muffels, R. and T. Wilthagen (2013), "Flexicurity: A new paradigm for the analysis of labour markets and policies challenging the trade-off between flexibility and security", *Sociology Compass*, Vol. 7/2.

Nam K. and D. Kim (2016), "Analysis of the determinants of women' marriage and fertility", *The Journal of Women and Economics*, Vol. 13/2 (in Korean).

Noja, G. (2018), "Flexicurity models and productivity interference in C.E.E. countries. New approach based on cluster and spatial analysis", *Economic Research-Ekonomska Istrazivanja*, Vol. 31/1.

Noja, G. and M. Cristea (2018), "Working conditions and flexicurity measures as key drivers of economic growth: Empirical evidence for Europe", *Ekonomicky Casopis*, Vol. 66/7.

OECD (2024a), *Education at a Glance 2024: OECD Indicators*, OECD Publishing, Paris.

OECD (2024b), *OECD Economic Surveys: Korea 2024*, OECD Publishing, Paris.

OECD (2024c), *Society at a Glance 2024: OECD Social Indicators*, OECD Publishing, Paris.

OECD (2023a), *Education at a Glance 2023: OECD Indicators*, OECD Publishing, Paris.

OECD (2023b), *Health at a Glance 2023: OECD indicators*, OECD Publishing, Paris.

OECD (2023c), *OECD Better Life Index*

OECD (2023d), *OECD Economic Surveys: Spain 2023*, OECD Publishing, Paris.

OECD (2023e), OECD employment database: share of female managers.

OECD (2023f), *PISA 2022 Results (Volume II): Learning During – and From – Disruption*, OECD Publishing, Paris.

OECD (2023g), *Reporting Gender Pay Gaps in OECD Countries: Guidance for Pay Transparency Implementation, Monitoring and Reform*, OECD Publishing, Paris.

OECD (2022), *OECD Economic Surveys: Korea 2022*, OECD Publishing, Paris

OECD (2021a), *Education at a Glance 2021: OECD indicators,* OECD publishing, Paris.

OECD (2021b), *Inclusive Growth Review of Korea: Creating Opportunities for All*, OECD Publishing, Paris.

OECD (2021c), OECD regions and cities statistics (accessed in November 2024).

OECD (2019a), *Government at a Glance 2019*, OECD Publishing, Paris.

OECD (2019b), *Investing in Youth: Korea*, OECD Publishing, Paris.

OECD (2019c), Rejuvenating Korea: Policies for a Changing Society, OECD Publishing, Paris.

OECD (2019d), *The Governance of Land Use in Korea*, OECD Publishing, Paris.

OECD (2018), *OECD Economic Surveys: Korea 2018*, OECD Publishing, Paris.

OECD (2017), OECD Employment Outlook 2017, OECD Publishing, Paris.

OECD (2016), LMF2.6: Time spent travelling to and from work, OECD Family Database.

OECD (2013), *The 2012 Labour Market Reform in Spain*, OECD Publishing, Paris.

OECD (2009), *OECD Economic Surveys: France 2009*, OECD Publishing, Paris.

Oh, E. and S. Kim (2021), "Utilization of maternity protection policy during childbirth and child-rearing period and its impact on women's career interruption", *The Journal of Asian Women*, Vol. 60/1 (in Korean).

OHRH (2018), First Criminal Conviction under Belgium's Anti-sexism Act, Oxford Human Rights Hub.

Pareliussen, J. (2022), "How labour market outcomes reflect age, gender and skills in Korea", *OECD Economics Department Working Papers*, No. 1739, OECD Publishing, Paris.

Park, Y., C. Kang and Y. Koh (2018), *Research on University Regulation and Private Education*, Korea Development Institute (in Korean).

PCASPP (2023), *Low Birthrate Perception Survey*, Presidential Committee of Ageing Society and Population Policy (in Korean).

Rajgelj, U. (2007), "Does family policy affect decisions to become a parent? Case examples", Anthropological Notebooks, Vol. 13/2.

Saram-In (2022), Survey on Gender Preference When Hiring (in Korean).

Shim, J. and H. Kim (2020), "Impacts of the 52-hour Workweek Policy on Employment and Labor Productivity of Listed Firms Using the Difference-in-differences Method", Productivity Review, Vol. 34/4.

Shin, K. and E. Lee (2021), "The necessity and dilemma of flexible working arrangements from the gender perspective", *Family and Culture*, Vol. 33/4 (in Korean).

Song, J. (2014), *Inequality in the Workplace: Labor Market Reform in Japan and Korea*, Cornell University Press.

Statistics Korea (2024a), *Ecomically Active Population by Gender and Age* (in Korean)

Statistics Korea (2024b), *Employment Survey by Region in the First Half of 2024: Employment Status of Married Women* (in Korean).

Statistics Korea (2024c), *Supplementary Surveys of Economically Active Population by Work Type* (in Korean).

Statistics Korea (2022), *Supplementary Surveys of Economically Active Population by Work Type* (in Korean).

Tonkikh, N., A. Pesha and T. Markova (2019), "The Impact of Teleworking on the Quality of Women's Parental Labour and Fertility Behaviour: Russian Case 2019", *34th IBIMA Conference, 13-14 November 2019*, International Business Information Management Association.

World Values Survey 7 (2023), World Values Survey.

Xu, J. and S. Lee (2023), "Problems with complex college admissions policies and overloaded after-school private education on middle-and high-school students' mental health in South Korea", *Journal of Global Health Reports*, Vol. 7.

Yang, Y., H. Hwang and J. Pareliussen (2024), "Korea's unborn future: lessons from OECD experience", *OECD Economics Department Working Papers*, No. 1824, OECD Publishing, Paris.

Yoo, I., and J. Lee (2020), "The effects of marriage and childbearing on labour market outcomes and subjective well-being among women", *Korean Journal of Labor Economics*, Vol. 43/4 (in Korean).

Yoo, J. (2017), "An analysis of the gender wage gap in the youth generation", *Journal of Korean Women's Studies*, Vol. 33/1 (in Korean).

Yoon, J. (2012), "An analysis of changes in family labour supply since the financial crisis", *The Journal of Women and Economics*, Vol. 9/1 (in Korean).

Yun, S. and K. Kim (2014), "The effects of the price ceiling regulation on the new apartment price on characteristics of housing in Korea", International Conference on Economics, Education and Humanities.

Zaidi, B. and P. Morgan (2017), "The second demographic transition theory: A review and appraisal", *Annual Review of Sociology*, Vol. 43.

# 4 Family policies are a piece of the puzzle, not a cure-all

Yoonyoung Yang, Economics Department of the OECD
Jon Pareliussen, Economics Department of the OECD
Sunyoung Choi, Korea Institute for Health and Social Affairs
Sunyu Ham, Korea Institute for Health and Social Affairs
Hyunjeong Hwang, Economics Department of the OECD

Family policies, including early childcare and education, paid parental leave and financial benefits, can make it easier to combine work and family and thereby reduce the opportunity cost of having and raising children. Korea has scaled up family policies considerably and compares well with other OECD countries on many indicators. Even so, the policies have not been sufficient to make work and motherhood compatible in general. Resulting fertility gains have therefore in the big picture been marginal and mostly come at the expense of female employment. The effects of policy interventions vary based on factors like women's education and labour market position, access to support programmes like quality childcare, and childcare support from relatives. Some gaps remain to bring childcare fully in line with working parents' needs. Parental leave eligibility is restricted and take-up low for a number of reasons including low replacement rates and weak legal protection against discrimination compared to OECD best practice.

Family policies, including early childhood education and care, paid parental leave and family benefits, can reduce the direct cost and limit the loss of lifetime earnings from having and raising children (referred to as the opportunity cost of childrearing in Chapter 3). Policies such as publicly financed childcare and paid parental leave are designed to make it easier to combine work and parenthood, but any cash transfer or subsidised service provided in-kind will increase a household's disposable income. As is the case with a spouse's income, this income effect enables parents (usually mothers) to stay at home, and the overall effect will depend on individual situations and preferences. To illustrate the point with an extreme example, a stay-at-home mother who already has her child enrolled in childcare while it is payable will not start working if it becomes free. On the contrary, the savings on childcare expenses could enable her to stay at home longer than what would otherwise be the case. Likewise, mothers prone to enrol their children and increase their labour supply if childcare became cheaper would only do so if childcare was available, conveniently located and fulfilled the parent's quality requirements. These mechanisms can help explain why such policies are not always as impactful as expected and why the effects vary based on individual circumstances and cross-country differences in for example labour market institutions and gender norms, as discussed in Chapter 3.

OECD countries follow different pathways in building their packages of family policies. Nordic countries spend a considerable amount on providing public services for families with children. Some countries, such as Hungary and the Czech Republic, focus more on providing families with financial support through family cash benefits and tax breaks. Other countries put greater emphasis on targeted benefits directed at specific groups, such as single-parent families or families on low incomes. France combines generous cash and tax benefits with active spending on family services. Others, including Japan, Türkiye, the United States and some countries in Southern Europe, have lower family spending than the OECD average (Figure 4.1, Panel A). Despite these differences, family policies have shifted in many OECD countries in recent years to encourage a more gender-equal division of labour by boosting public support for early childhood education and care and promoting paid leave for both parents.

Korea has introduced or strengthened a number of family policies in recent years. Public spending on family benefits increased from 0.7% of GDP in 2010 to 1.5% in 2020, and is estimated to have increased further by about 0.1-0.2% of GDP since then. The enrolment rate in childcare facilities has increased significantly with higher public investment in preschool childcare. Income loss from parental leave gave the right to employment insurance from 2001 and the parental leave benefit for dual-income parents has been increased since 2022 conditional on both parents using parental leave (OECD, 2024a). The eligibility for child allowances has been expanded to children up to the age of eight (previously five), and the allowance amount for infants under two years has been significantly increased.

However, notable gaps persist and there is scope to prioritise the use of public funds to maximise their effect. Despite a remarkable increase in family spending, the total fertility rate has continued to decline, indicating a potential misalignment between public spending and actual needs (Figure 4.2). Usage rates of paid parental leave are the third lowest in the OECD, after Ireland and Japan. Some gaps exist between the level of service parents need from childcare and what is actually given, and there is room to further increase quality to converge to high-performing OECD peers. The largest share of the budget was allocated to housing, which is a much less direct way of supporting fertility than parental leave policies, the category receiving the smallest portion of Korea's fertility budget despite survey results and research underscoring their importance in addressing the low fertility rate. Moreover, the share of the budget allocated to overall policies aimed at enhancing work-life balance has declined in recent years (NABO, 2023). Public spending on family benefits is still lower than the OECD average of 2.3% (Figure 4.1, Panel A). Korea's low family spending is partly due to the relatively low number of children, but spending per child (as a share of GDP per capita) is also lower than the OECD average (Panel B).

**Figure 4.1. Family spending varies in size and composition**

2019 or latest

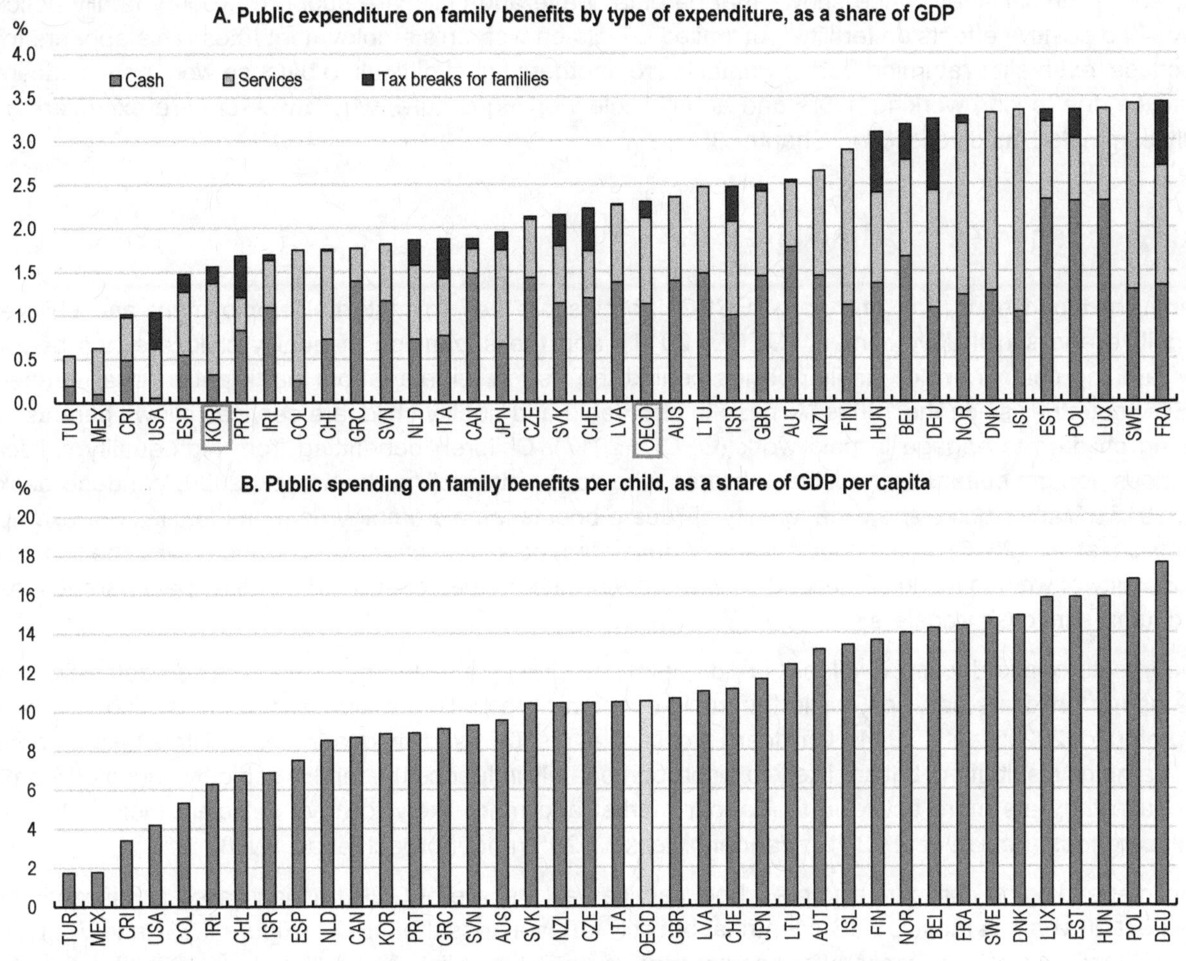


Source: OECD, Social Expenditure Database, OECD National Accounts Database and own calculations

StatLink https://stat.link/dc6gvi

**Figure 4.2. There is a possible mismatch between public spending and needs to boost fertility**

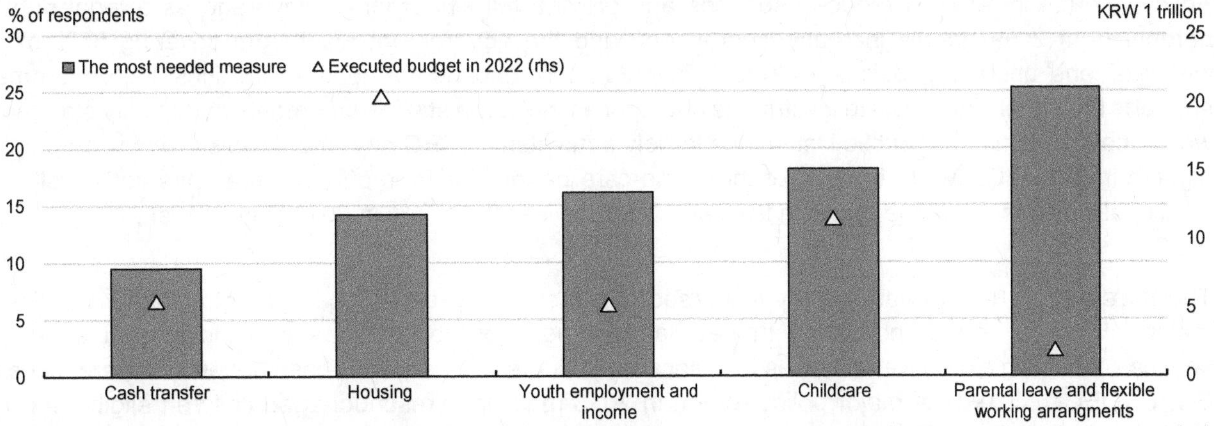


Note: Bars represent the result of the government's survey on the most needed measures to boost the fertility rate. The survey targeted 1,200 citizens aged 18 to 79 residing nationwide in Korea. The triangles represent the executed budget to boost fertility in 2022.
Source: OECD Economic Surveys: Korea 2024.

Research findings suggest that these gaps in family policies, working culture and gender norms are mutually reinforcing the difficulties of combining career and family in Korea (Seo and Kim, 2016; Yang et al., 2021). Empirical evidence shows that parental leave and childcare support, two key family policies, have had positive effects on fertility, but limited effects on women's employment rates. This appears to be because, even after returning from parental leave, mothers find it difficult to balance work and childcare in practice due to long working hours and an inflexible working culture, where workers are expected to be fully committed, as discussed in Chapter 3.

## Early childhood education and care

Early childhood education and care (ECEC) policies are key to maternal employment and children's cognitive and social development (OECD, 2011), and the expansion of quality childcare has been an overarching component of family policies behind the rise in female labour participation in a number of OECD countries since the 1960s. Access to affordable and quality childcare services allows parents with young children to engage in paid work (OECD, 2017). Children benefitting from high-quality childcare services perform better in school than children who do not attend (Vandenbroeck, 2020; Vandenbroeck et al., 2018). Many studies show that quality childcare boosts female employment and fertility. For example, Greulich et al. (2016) found that childcare development at the country level increases the individual probability of women having a second child more than other types of support, such as paid parental leave and lump-sum cash transfers.

The trifecta of affordability, availability and quality, all directly affected by policy, are key determinants of the use of childcare services, while the socio-economic status and attitudes of parents also play a role (Eurofound, 2020; Janta, 2014). Childcare provision and subsidised childcare fees facilitate take-up across the earnings distribution, but are likely to disproportionately influence the fertility of highly educated women, because they are more active in the labour market and more likely to have sufficient income to cover childcare fees (Baizan et al., 2016; Vandenbroeck, 2020; Vandenbroeck et al., 2018).

Public spending on childcare and preschool services as a share of GDP has increased significantly over the past 20 years in most OECD countries, but still varies across the OECD (Figure 4.3, Panel A). Nordic countries, Belgium and France offer comprehensive, largely publicly funded childcare and allocate a high share of family-related spending to public childcare. Sweden and Denmark have spent the most per child on childcare services since the early 1990s (Sobotka et al., 2019). Another example is Norway, where public expenditure on childcare almost doubled between 1998 and 2012, when it reached 1.4% of GDP. Policy reforms initiated to reduce user fees and provide full kindergarten coverage as a legal right to parents from 2009 greatly increased enrolment, and the government went from covering 55% of the kindergartens' operating costs in 2000 to 85% in 2012. To expand the qualified facilities, the government supports both public and private institutions and applies the same staff requirements and quality standards, which makes private and public institutions largely equivalent. ECEC enrolment rates are now among the highest in the OECD while the use of the home-care benefit which is offered as an alternative fell from 75% of all children aged one to two in the early 2000s to less than 25% in 2011 (Engel et al., 2015; OECD, 2023a).

The Korean government has sharply increased public spending on childcare by introducing a series of major reforms aimed at increasing the availability and affordability of early childcare and education services, including extensive subsidies to childcare providers and generous cash benefits for parents using ECEC (OECD, 2019d). A major policy reform in 2013 made all preschool-aged children eligible for free childcare regardless of parental income, accompanied with the introduction of a parental home-care allowance for parents opting to care for their child at home (Home Childcare Allowance). Measured as a share of GDP, Korea's spending on ECEC is still lower than the Nordic countries, but spending per child as a share of GDP per capita is approximately 20%, which is third-highest in the OECD and on par with the Nordics (Figure 4.3, Panel B). Even so, the current childcare system falls short of meeting the needs of working parents, with approximately 30% of mothers citing a lack of suitable childcare options as a reason for career interruption (MOHW, 2022). This reflects quality differences between different categories of suppliers, a scarcity of the high-quality childcare options in high demand, gaps in the service offer after school hours, and a mismatch between parents' long and inflexible working hours and the shorter opening hours at childcare centres.

**Figure 4.3. Public early childhood education and care spending has increased considerably in Korea**

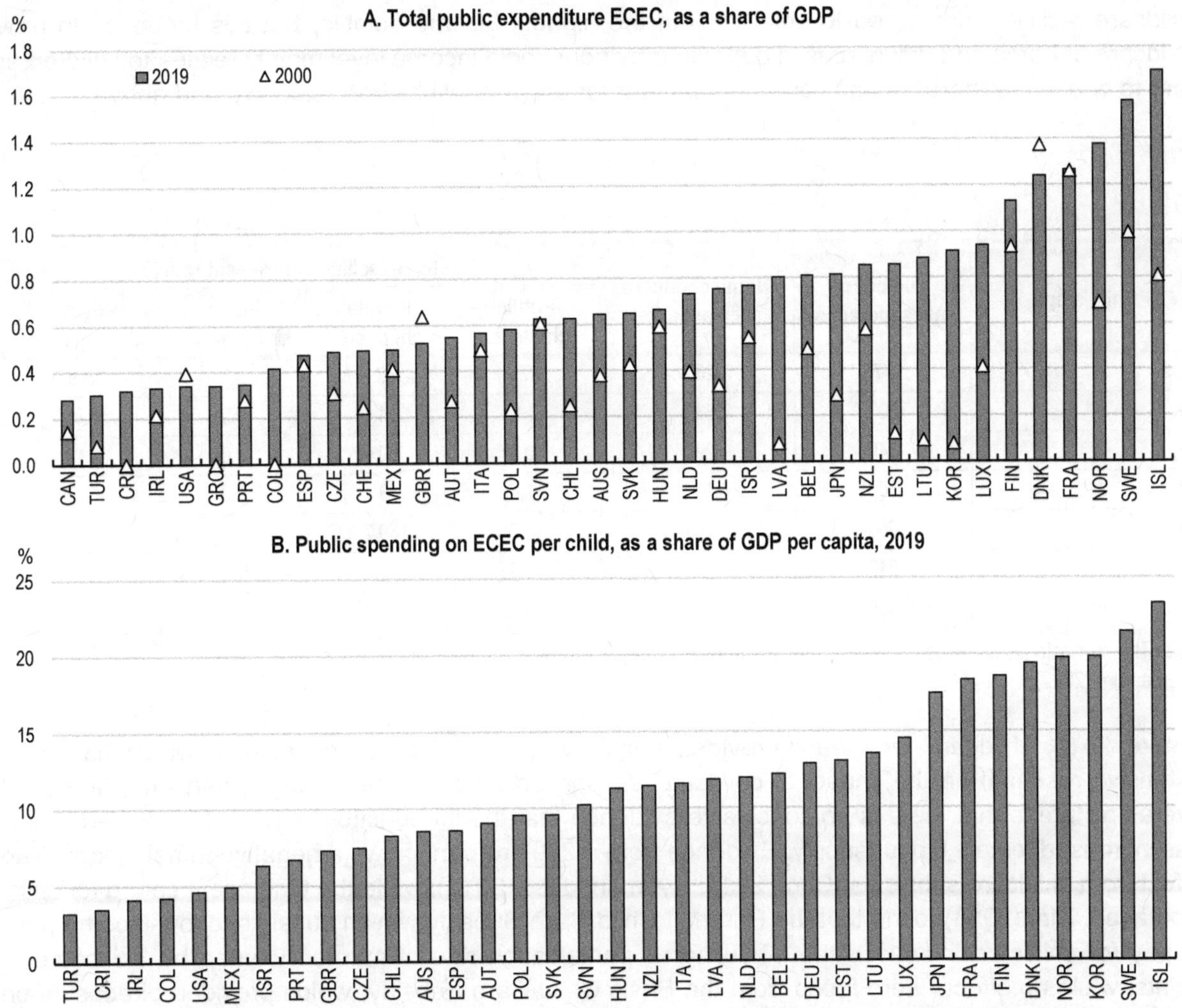


Note: Public expenditure on early childhood education and care covers all public spending towards formal day-care services (e.g. day care centres, generally aimed at children aged 0 to 2, inclusive) and pre-primary education services (including kindergartens and day-care centres which usually provide an educational content as well as traditional care for children aged from 3 to 5, inclusive). In some countries local governments play a key role in financing and providing childcare services. Such spending is comprehensively recorded in Nordic countries, but in some other (often federal) countries it may not be fully captured by the OECD social expenditure data.
Source: OECD Family Database, OECD National Accounts Database and own calculations.

StatLink https://stat.link/cgtva2

Lee (2016) provides tentative evidence of an increase in both the labour force participation and the number of hours worked by mothers between 2010 and 2013, when the universal free childcare policy began. However, because of the simultaneous introduction of universal free childcare and the homecare allowance, it has been difficult to establish empirically the effect of childcare policies on labour supply. Common to the two policies is that any monetary or in-kind transfer increases families' disposable income, and this income effect will reduce female labour supply when seen in isolation. Apart from this, these two alternatives give parents diametrically opposite incentives. Childcare support is an indirect subsidy of women's labour participation, while a parental home-care allowance increases non-labour income for households conditional on caring for your own child, thereby directly subsidising staying at home to care for children (Cukrowska-Torzewska, 2017).

The uptake of childcare and home care allowances varies by the age of the child and parents' income quintile. The rate of receiving the allowance for children aged zero is overwhelmingly high at 83.8%, but it drops significantly to 29.2% at age one and decreases to less than 10% from age three onwards (Table 4.1). According to Noh (2016), 12.2% of the households in the lowest income quintile do not use childcare facilities, compared to only 3.5% in the highest income quintile, but this tendency to provide childcare at home and differences in behaviour by household income level mainly relates to children aged zero to one, while there was no consistent pattern for pre-school children aged two and above.

### Table 4.1. Household income, childcare allowance and use of childcare facilities

2018

| Child's age | Number of cases (persons) | Home childcare allowance (%) | Childcare facilities enrolment rate (%) | | | |
|---|---|---|---|---|---|---|
| | | | Public childcare | Private childcare | Public kindergarten | Private kindergarten |
| 0-5 | 3775 | 26.8 | 10.1 | 36.2 | 8.0 | 18.9 |
| 0 | 803 | 83.8 | 2.1 | 14.1 | 0.0 | 0.0 |
| 1 | 540 | 29.2 | 10.9 | 60.0 | 0.0 | 0.0 |
| 2 | 568 | 14.0 | 17.6 | 68.1 | 0.2 | 0.1 |
| 3 | 650 | 8.8 | 11.7 | 39.7 | 9.1 | 30.7 |
| 4 | 549 | 6.0 | 11.8 | 24.1 | 18.0 | 40.2 |
| 5 | 665 | 8.6 | 8.8 | 22.0 | 19.9 | 40.7 |

Note: The percentages are weighted values, and the number of cases represents the actual number of respondents.
Source: Kim (2022).

Before 2013, childcare fees were provided primarily for low-income households, which has allowed extensive research on the impact of childcare support on employment among low-income groups. The overall picture is that there is no conclusive evidence that the introduction of publicly financed childcare has increased female labour supply. Evidence from a 2007 reform shows a negative female labour supply effect from childcare subsidies (Choi, 2011; Byun and Heo, 2014), while the time spent caring for children increased. Kim (2018) found that the Parental Child Care Subsidy, which subsidised low-income parents to pay for childcare increased the labour force participation rate of married women by 3.5 percentage points, while no effects were found from the Basic Child Care Subsidy, which provided direct support to childcare facilities for infants based on the number of children in the facility. Neither of the subsidies had a significant impact on the weekly working hours of married women who participated in the labour market.

Kim (2022) suggests that for public funding of childcare to have a positive labour supply effect, a change in caregiver is required. If children are already attending childcare institutions, paying for childcare merely reduces household expenses, creating an income effect without necessarily increasing the incentive to participate in the labour market. Kim found that there was no increase in the labour participation rate among the group providing childcare at home – the exact group the policy had targeted. Instead, Kim's results show a decrease in working hours and labour participation among employed women.

The dominance of the income effect of childcare subsidies should be seen in the context of the quality and availability of subsidised childcare options. Min and Lee (2020) pointed out that the policy of childcare fee support does not guarantee access to quality childcare services. By exploiting regional differences in childcare availability they found that childcare subsidies encouraged women with more than one child in areas with good access to childcare facilities to maintain a career. According to their results, the subsidy did not affect career maintenance among mothers with one child in a dual-income household, or incite mothers who had not previously worked to enter employment. However, the findings suggest the reason many studies have been unable to detect a positive influence on career maintenance from childcare subsidies could be linked to childcare facilities being too few and geographically mismatched to demand or of insufficient quality.

Min and Lee (2020) also found evidence that childcare subsidies increased fertility, conditional on the availability of quality childcare. In areas with a high supply of childcare facilities or public daycare centres, the birth rates among women aged 30 to 49 increased after free childcare was introduced. Lee (2022) used National Health Insurance big data to explore whether the policy had different impacts on childbirth depending on the supply of public childcare facilities by city, county and district. The findings indicated that the higher the possibility of enrolling in public daycare centres, the higher the birth rate. This effect was stronger at higher income levels up to, but not including, the top 20%. Both studies indicate that the success of childcare subsidies as a policy tool to increase birth rates is directly related to the availability of adequate childcare services, both in terms of quality and quantity.

### *Availability*

Availability of childcare is crucial to reconcile work and family. In order to do so, the service should start immediately after the end of parental leave and meet parents' and children's diverse needs, such as the age of children accepted and opening hours adapted to work hours (Sobotka et al., 2019). Gaps in the service on offer, such as the limited availability of affordable after-school care, make it difficult for parents (usually mothers) to continue to work full-time.

The enrolment rate in early childhood education and care can be used as an indicator of availability. Despite increasing over time in most countries, enrolment of children aged zero to two is generally lower than that of children aged three to five, while cross-country variation in participation rates of very young children is also higher. Participation rates of children aged zero to two were 60% or above in the Netherlands, where services are often used on a part-time basis, while some countries have participation rates below 10% (Figure 4.4, Panel A).

However, as highlighted in Mills et al. (2014), it is necessary to look beyond enrolment rates to determine if childcare supports work-life balance and parental employment to its full potential. If formal childcare is provided for only a few hours per week, it is unlikely to lead to full-time employment. As an example, the EU Barcelona targets cover both participation and intensity of ECEC use in member states. The participation rate target is 50% for children under the age of three and 96% for children aged three to pre-school by 2030, and the associated criteria for satisfying intensity of participation are at least 25 hours per week for zero- to two-year-olds and 35 hours per week for those aged three or above (European Commission, 2022). In most EU countries, zero- to two-year-olds in early childhood education and care use it for more than 25 hours per week, with an average of 32 hours (OECD, 2024b).

Enrolment and intensity of participating in ECEC are both relatively high in Korea, but this may still not be sufficient to meet the needs of working parents, given long and inflexible working hours. The enrolment rate for children aged zero to two jumped from 38.2% in 2010 to 64.2% in 2021, the second highest level and the fastest increase in the OECD. More than half of OECD countries, including Korea, have enrolment rates of 90% or above for children aged three to five (Panel B). Korean childcare users (zero to five year-olds) use it for an average of 37 hours per week, which is higher than the EU average and the Barcelona target (Ministry of Health and Welfare of Korea, 2022). This likely reflects that in countries like Korea, where working hours are long and inflexible, more hours of childcare are needed to facilitate full-time employment. The standard opening hours are from 9:00 AM to 4:00 PM. Extended childcare teachers can provide services from 4:00 PM to 7:30 PM, with the flexibility to adjust hours in agreement with parents or the operating committee. However, these extended hours are not widely offered as the usual practice for parents is to pick up their children from childcare at 4:00 PM. Working parents, who are often in minority among parents, often experience feelings of guilt when they deviate from this norm, and are concerned about their children being alone in the facilities because there are not enough children for the after-hours programmes (KICCE, 2022). Consequently, many working parents resort to alternative out-of-school arrangements, such as relying on parents, relatives or private babysitters (Yang et al., 2024). As a comparison, in France, where working hours are comparatively shorter, centre-based ECEC facilities typically operate between 8:00 AM and 7:00 PM (EC, 2023). The government plans to extend basic childcare hours to 5:00 PM. Further progress in this direction would make it easier to combine family with full-time employment. This would also send a signal to parents, shaping their perceptions and norms regarding pick-up times.

### Figure 4.4. Korea's enrolment rate in early childhood education and care services is high

Share of children enrolled in early childhood education and care services[1], 0- to 5-year-olds

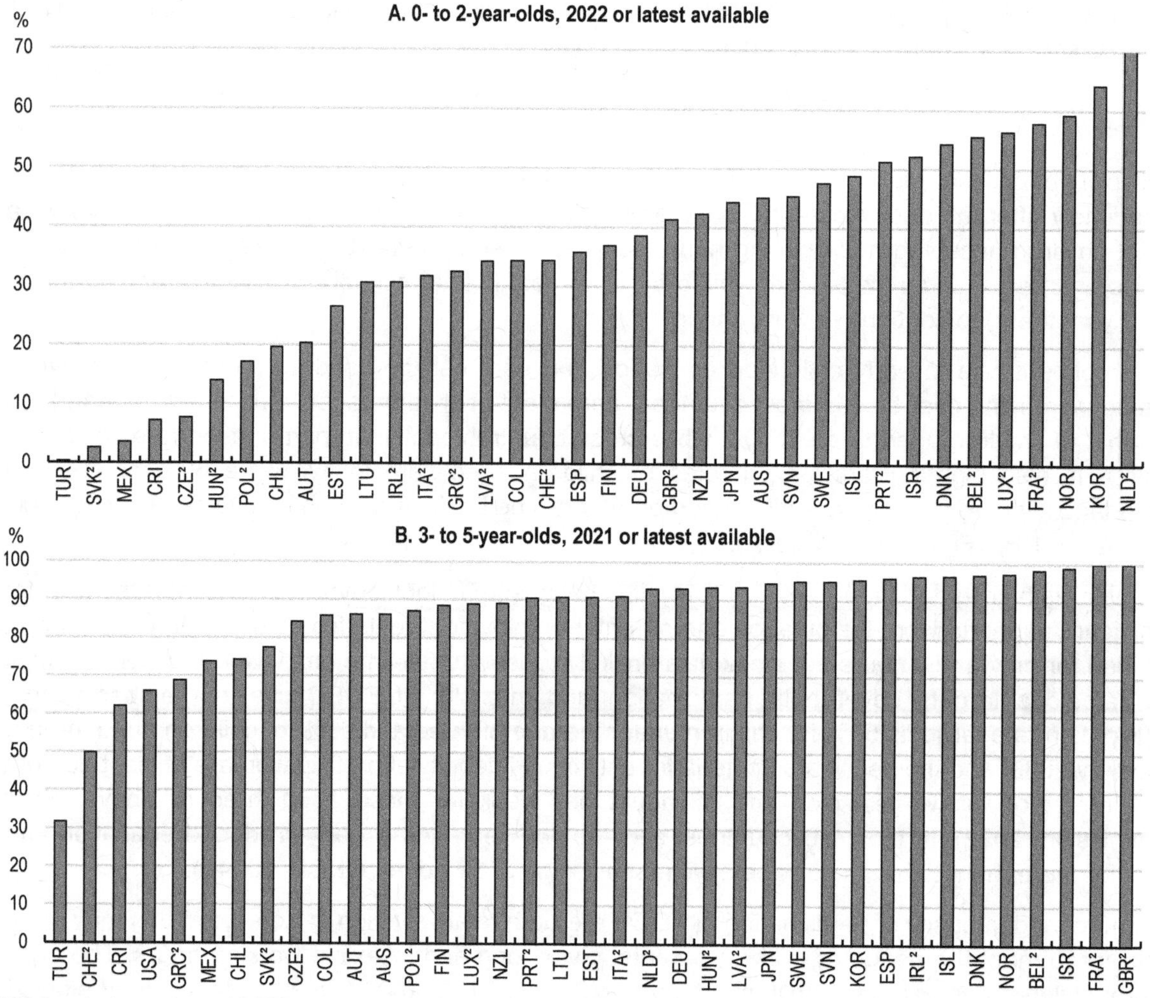


1. ISCED 0 and other registered ECEC services) for 0- to 2-year-olds and ISCED 2011 level 0 or primary education (ISCED 2011 level 1) for 3- to 5-year-olds.
2. Data for Belgium, the Czech Republic, France, Greece, Hungary, Ireland, Italy, Latvia, Luxembourg, the Netherlands, Poland, the Slovak Republic and the United Kingdom are OECD estimates based on information from EU-SILC. Data refer to children using centre-based services (e.g. nurseries or day care centres and pre-schools, both public and private), organised family day care, and care services provided by (paid) professional childminders, regardless of whether or not the service is registered or ISCED-recognised.
Source: OECD Family Database.

StatLink https://stat.link/vfyq1k

Another option to enhance accessibility is to promote employer-supported childcare. Employers can either provide on-site childcare services, partner with other employers for the provision of inter-company nurseries, or collaborate with private childcare providers or the local community (OECD, 2022d). Such childcare services offer some advantages to both companies and employees. For instance, employees can benefit from adapted opening hours and the ease and tranquillity of having their child nearby. Employers can benefit from higher productivity, employee loyalty, recruitment and talent retention (OECD, 2022d). In Europe, many large private employers provide their employees with emergency back-up care (UNICEF, 2020).

The benefits of workplace childcare are greater in countries like Korea where telework is uncommon. Employer-based childcare is consequently one of the most popular childcare options in Korea, but it is only available to a small share of parents (OECD, 2024a). Since 2012, the establishment of workplace childcare facilities has been mandatory for large companies with over 500 full-time employees or 300 female full-time workers in Korea. As a result, most large companies (93.1%) have workplace childcare facilities (MOHW, 2024). However, the large firms under the mandate account for only 0.02% of total employers with more than five employees. (MSS, 2024). As a result, the share of workplace childcare has been persistently low at less than 5% of total childcare facilities. A few OECD countries make workplace childcare mandatory with a lower threshold. For instance, it is mandatory for companies with more than 50 full-time employees in Chile and for companies with more than 150 women workers in Türkiye (World Bank, 2019; Turkish Labor law, 2017).

Even though expanding the availability of workplace childcare seems beneficial, simply lowering the firm size threshold to oblige more firms to offer it is probably not a good solution. Financing and providing childcare to the benefit of parents and the wider society should at the outset not be the responsibility of private sector firms who happen to have parents among their employees, regardless of firm size. Larger firms may able to shoulder this burden and some may see it in their interest to offer childcare to attract talent, but lowering the threshold for mandatory workplace childcare facilities may inadvertently burden businesses in general, resulting in unintended consequences such as increased gender discrimination and reduced employment opportunities for workers with parenting responsibilities.

Addressing obstacles faced by firms when establishing childcare would help expand workplace childcare services for companies who see this as beneficial. Currently, workplace childcare centres must meet all installation standards set forth in the Infant Care Act, such as establishing them on the first floor (up to fifth floor under certain conditions). This can be particularly problematic in Seoul where leasing costs for lower floors are high. Indeed, some firms in Seoul gave up setting up childcare for this reason (Asia Economy Daily, 2017). The requirements should be carefully reviewed, and streamlining the process or introducing a fast-track approval system should be considered. Government support focuses on installation costs (up to 60% for large enterprises and 90% for SMEs) (MOEL, 2024b). Employers are required to pay at least 50% of total operating costs. Currently, the burden of operating costs prevents many employers from establishing workplace childcare (KICCE, 2023). Greater support for operating costs, particularly when employers collaboratively establish childcare facilities, could help address concerns about low enrolment as well as cost burdens.

Public interventions can encourage companies to offer and maintain childcare services. In the United Kingdom, employers that set up an in-company nursery facility are exempt from the payment of tax and national insurance on the value of the nursery, provided the service complies with certain conditions (UK Government, 2022). In France, corporates that contribute to childcare costs can have 76.5% of costs reimbursed through tax credits and deductions. In Spain, the company can benefit from corporate tax relief for building childcare facilities and providing childcare services for their employees (OECD, 2020c).

The need for childcare continues when children enter primary school. A full-time working week is not directly compatible with school hours, and working families must find care solutions before and after school hours and during school holidays. This makes out-of-school hours care an essential element to reconcile work and family (OECD, 2007). Many OECD countries provide formal out-of-school services before and after school, which include homework support, recreational activities, sport and creative events to foster child development and to provide a protected environment (OECD, 2011). The use of out-of-school hours varies across European OECD member countries. France offers childcare services specialising in childcare for children of various ages and needs, including services for children under three years or school age. The Nordics continue to provide childcare services for schoolchildren (Nordic Health and Welfare Statistics, 2024). Hungary also makes extensive use of out-of-school services (OECD, 2016a). Korea's use of out-of-school hours is relatively high compared to most EU countries, except for some Nordic countries (Figure 4.5). However, it should be noted that in some countries, such as Germany, France, Austria, and Italy, extracurricular activities are included in the regular school day, resulting in a longer school day of six to eight hours (Parente and Nakano, 2020).

### Figure 4.5. Participation in out-of-school-hours services is high in Korea

Share of 6- to 11-year-olds using centre-based out-of-school-hours (before and/or after school) services during a usual week, 2019 or latest

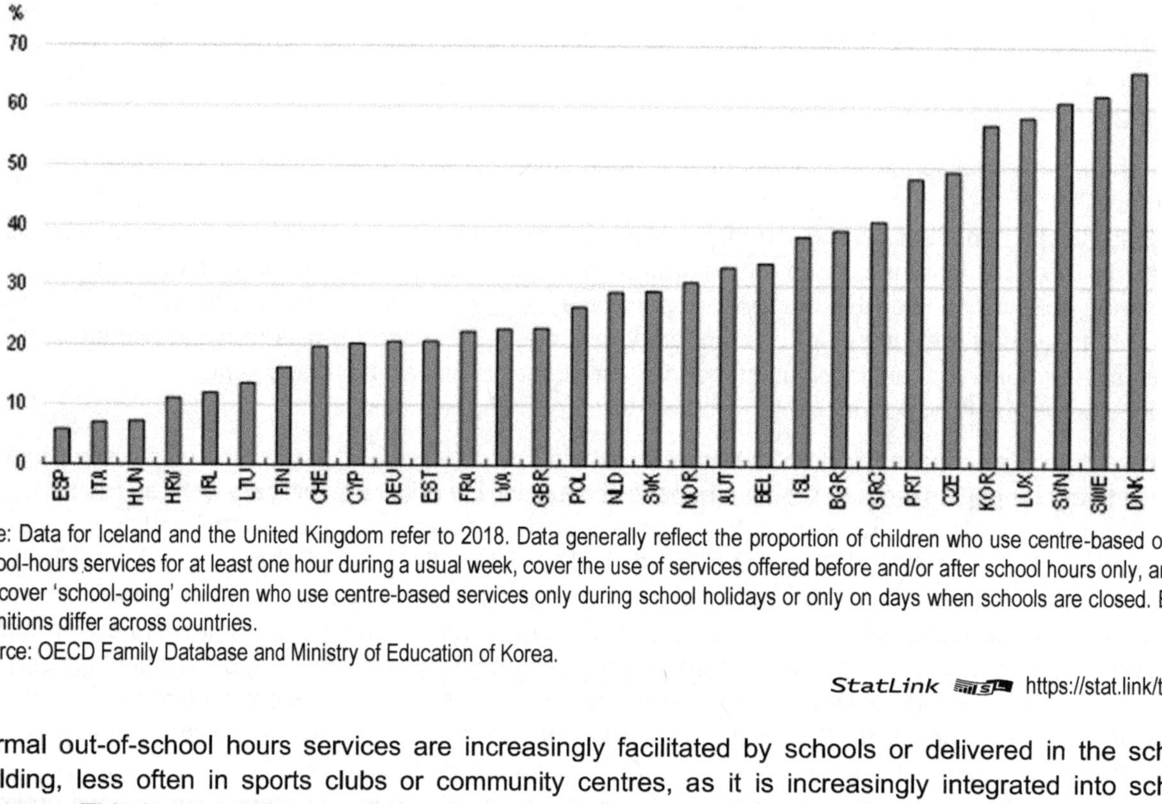


Note: Data for Iceland and the United Kingdom refer to 2018. Data generally reflect the proportion of children who use centre-based out-of-school-hours services for at least one hour during a usual week, cover the use of services offered before and/or after school hours only, and do not cover 'school-going' children who use centre-based services only during school holidays or only on days when schools are closed. Exact definitions differ across countries.

Source: OECD Family Database and Ministry of Education of Korea.

StatLink https://stat.link/trub5f

Formal out-of-school hours services are increasingly facilitated by schools or delivered in the school building, less often in sports clubs or community centres, as it is increasingly integrated into school systems. This is especially the case in countries such as Denmark and Sweden, where out-of-school services are well developed. Some countries such as Portugal, Greece and Austria also introduced all-day school systems linking out-of-school services more closely with regular school schedules (Eurofound, 2020).

In Korea, where school ends before 2:00 PM in the lower primary grades, a shortage of quality day-care services for young school-age children pushes mothers to exit employment or take parental leave (Choi et al., 2022). Han (2021) found that Korean mothers of elementary school students who use out-of-school care have a 7.8% higher labour supply than mothers who do not use out-of-school care. The government has extended the operating hours to 8:00 PM for first to fourth-grade primary school pupils from September 2024 (OECD, 2024a).

### *Affordability*

Childcare costs can weaken employment incentives for parents. Given that women remain the main caregivers, childcare costs are a greater constraint for women whose earnings tend to be lower than men's (André et al., 2023). On average, across OECD countries, the net cost of childcare (out-of-pocket childcare fees minus any benefit payment or tax relief directly related to childcare use) for a two-earner family with two children aged two and three in full-time centre-based care is under 14% of average earnings (Figure 4.6). Net childcare costs are low in countries where gross childcare fees are already relatively low, including Austria, Estonia, Germany, Iceland, Latvia, Lithuania, Norway, Spain and Sweden and in countries like Greece, Hungary, Italy, and Portugal, where childcare fees are largely offset by considerable state financial support. Korea's net childcare cost is one of the lowest in the OECD, due to fairly low fees which are compensated by government support. Informal childcare costs such as private babysitters are not covered by this measure of childcare fee, while such costs are considerable in Korea.

Figure 4.6. Net childcare costs are relatively low in Korea

Net childcare costs for a two-earner two-child family, 2021

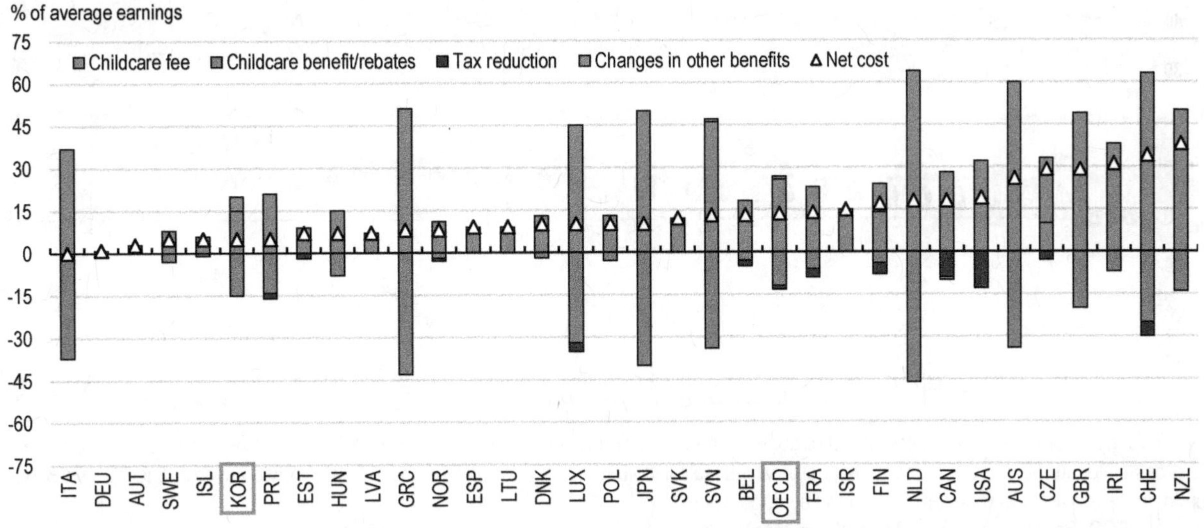


Note: Data refer to 2021 for all countries except Australia, Canada, Israel, Korea and Switzerland where they refer to 2020 and New Zealand where they refer to 2018. Data reflect the costs of full-time care in a typical childcare centre for a two-earner two-child family, where both parents are in full-time employment and the children are aged 2 and 3. Gross earnings for the two earners in the family are set equal to 100% of average earnings for the first earner, and 67% of average earnings for the second earner. Full-time care is defined as care for at least 40 hours per week. Average earnings refers to the gross wage earnings paid to average workers, before deductions of any kind (e.g. withholding tax, income tax, private or social security contributions and union dues). See the OECD Tax and Benefit Systems website (http://www.oecd.org/els/soc/benefits-and-wages.htm) for more detail on the methods and assumptions used and information on the policies modelled for each country.

Source: OECD Family Database.

StatLink https://stat.link/swaugq

Affordable childcare is vital notably for poor and sole-parent families who often face major time and money constraints. Access to affordable formal childcare helps parents in these families to participate in paid work, reduces poverty risks and supports child development. Childcare costs partly contribute to inequalities in the use of childcare services. Many countries therefore have support programmes in place to reduce the costs for low-income families. Such support usually includes fee reductions, cash benefits, or tax relief for childcare costs (OECD, 2020b). For example, countries with large-scale publicly funded childcare, such as Denmark, Iceland, Norway, and Sweden, charge lower or no fees for low-income families. Some countries such as Belgium, Denmark, Greece and Norway provide additional financial assistance and in France, Germany and Italy, priority access to services is guaranteed for large or single-parent families (OECD, 2020b; Eurydice, 2019).

Even so, high-income families are more frequent users of childcare services than low-income ones. In European OECD countries, low-income families with children under the age of three use childcare services about one-third less than higher-income families (OECD, 2016b). For example, in the United Kingdom and Ireland, where childcare costs for low-income families reach almost 30% of household income, participation rates for low-income families are less than half that of higher-income families (OECD, 2020b). On average, across OECD countries, a low-paid single mother who takes up full-time work loses almost two-thirds of her in-work earnings to childcare costs, taxes, and the loss of social benefits (OECD, 2020b). Since the net cost of childcare is low regardless of family situation in Korea, families pay a low share of earnings for childcare costs in international comparison, even though the cost remains more burdensome for low-income families (Figure 4.7).

Figure 4.7. Net childcare costs for low-income families are higher than for average earners

Net childcare costs, share of net household income, 2022

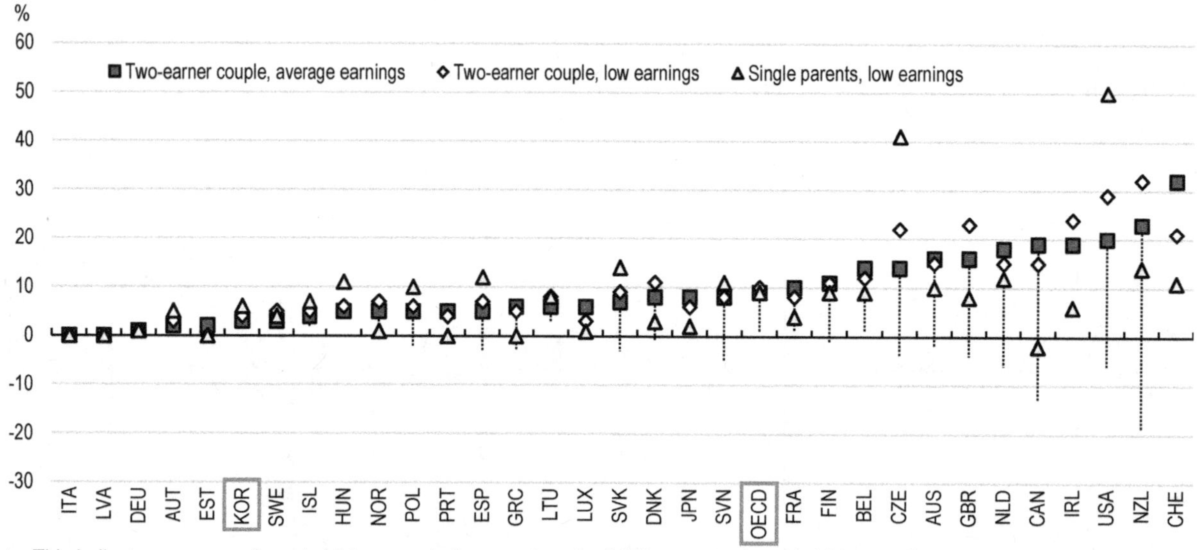


Note: This indicator measures the net childcare costs for parents using full-time centre-based childcare, after any benefits designed to reduce the gross childcare fees. Net childcare costs are calculated for both couples and lone parents assuming two children aged 2 and 3. In low-earning couples, both parents earn 67% of the average wage.
Source: OECD, Benefit, Taxes and Wages (Database).

StatLink https://stat.link/mhfsl2

## *Quality*

Quality is the last key ingredient of a good childcare system. Quality care policies historically have focused on safeguarding the children such as making standards on buildings, materials, or staff-to-child ratios. However, more attention is now paid to the educational and emotional interactions that childcare and teaching staff provide for the children and their relations with parents, which is called process quality (Vandenbroeck, 2020; OECD, 2021; La Paro et al., 2014). In a survey by the Korean government, the most desired childcare policy for parents was "improving the quality of childcare services" at 22.1% in 2022 (MOHW, 2023).

ECEC governance systems across the OECD are broadly divided between integrated and split systems. In a split system, responsibility for childcare (zero to three) and pre-primary education (three to six) is usually separated, whereas in an integrated system, it is unified and usually the responsibility of the Ministry of Education (Cadima, 2020; OECD, 2019a). In 2019, about half of OECD countries had an integrated ECEC system, and an increasing number of countries recently moved towards an integrated system (OECD, 2019a). The benefits of an integrated system have been highlighted as having more coherent policy and greater continuity in key areas such as access, regulation, funding, and staffing regimes, as well as greater effectiveness in terms of consistency and quality of care (Cadima, 2020; Kaga et al., 2010). An integrated system can also contribute to higher quality of care by providing age-appropriate education and being delivered by highly qualified staff (Eurydice, 2019). Many OECD countries such as Italy, Germany and Finland, have adopted standardised quality assessment tools and an integrated monitoring system to improve the quality of childcare facilities (OECD, 2024a). In some countries including China, Portugal and the United States, there are quality differences between public and private institutions due to country-specific differences in governance regimes and different choices in investment and human resources management (OECD, 2019c). In countries where more qualified staff are employed in public institutions, public preschool centres appear to score higher than their private counterparts in process quality (OECD, 2019c; Coley et al., 2016; Hu et al., 2016; Slot et al., 2015). However, this difference was not found in Spanish ECEC centres, where private institutions subsidised by public funds scored lower than public centres on infrastructure quality, but better in meeting children's needs (Sandstrom, 2012), and the quality of public and private kindergartens is equivalent in Norway's unified system.

Korea currently has a split early childcare and education system where childcare centres are subject to lower quality standards and different levels of quality and control than private kindergartens (OECD, 2016b). For example, staff qualification requirements are higher in kindergartens than in childcare facilities and kindergartens face stringent debt limits. Private childcare facilities are allowed to have debt up to 50% of total investments, whereas private kindergartens are required to have zero debt. According to a government survey, most childcare experts believe that the 50% debt ratio in childcare facilities is high, leading to lower quality of services, as it may force facilities to prioritise revenue generation for debt servicing, resulting in cost-cutting measures such as staffing, resources, and maintenance (MOHW, 2017).

The quality differences among childcare centres have led to a clear ranking in parents' preferences, which are tilted in favour of workplace childcare, public childcare and against private childcare centres (Figure 4.8). 77% of children attending early childhood education and care are in private institutions in Korea, which is higher than the OECD average of 32% in 2020. In 2012-13, the government abolished the income threshold for childcare subsidies paid to parents and started paying the tuition for all children, including in private childcare centres. This led to a surge in demand for childcare. In response, the government encouraged the private sector to supply childcare through subsidies and deregulation (KIHASA, 2013). The rapid expansion of private childcare facilities through easing criteria has raised concerns about a potential decline in quality. From June 2019, the Assessment and Accreditation system has been mandatory and applied to all day-care centres. However, few poor-quality childcare facilities are actually forced out of the market, due to a lack of enforcement measures (KICCE, 2019; KIHASA, 2013).

**Figure 4.8. Public and workplace childcare facilities show higher satisfaction levels but are in short supply**

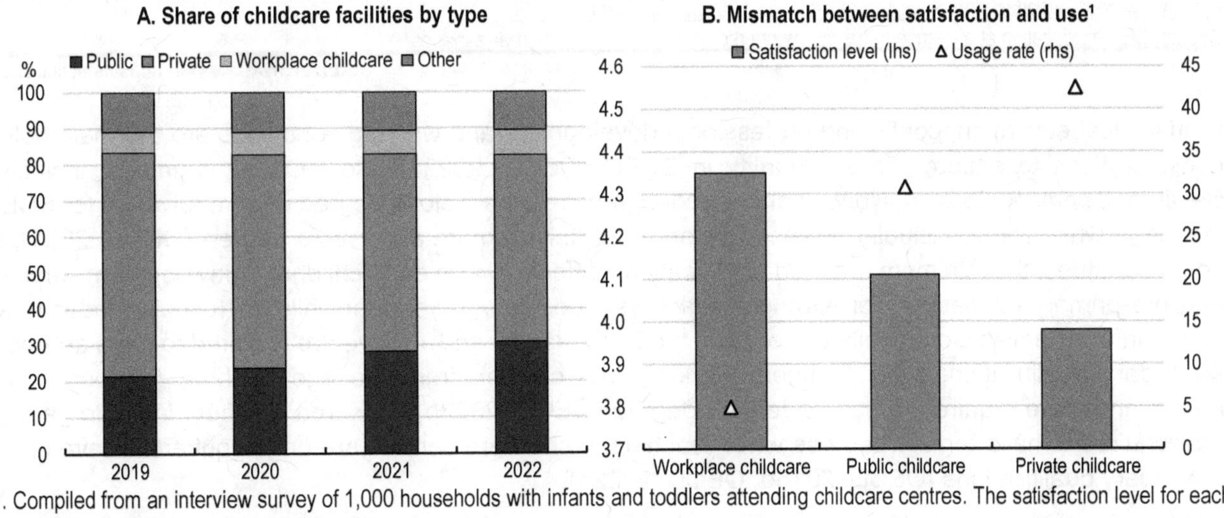


1. Compiled from an interview survey of 1,000 households with infants and toddlers attending childcare centres. The satisfaction level for each type of childcare centre ranges from 0 to 5.
Source: OECD Economic Surveys: Korea 2024.

Eliminating these quality differences and raising quality to the level demanded by parents would imply unifying regulation and governance of childcare and kindergartens, and raising standards for childcare to the level currently applicable to kindergartens. The government is planning to go in this direction and unify the management bodies of childcare centres and kindergartens under the Ministry of Education.

One often-used and easily available indicator of the quality of childcare services is the number of children per staff (Figure 4.9). The weight of evidence favours the conclusion that the child-to-staff ratio in ECEC is significantly associated with quality (Huntsman, 2008). Many OECD countries have a child-to-staff ratio between 10 and 15, while some countries such as Sweden and Iceland, are below 10. Countries such as France, Mexico and Colombia have high ratios over 20. Korea's child-to-teaching staff ratio is slightly below the OECD average, while the child-to-contact staff ratio, including teachers and teaching aides, is higher than average.

### Figure 4.9. Korea's child-to-staff ratio is higher than the OECD average

Average ratios of pupils to teaching staff and to all contact staff (teachers and teaching aides) in pre-primary education (ISCED 02) services (public and private), based on full-time equivalents, 2021

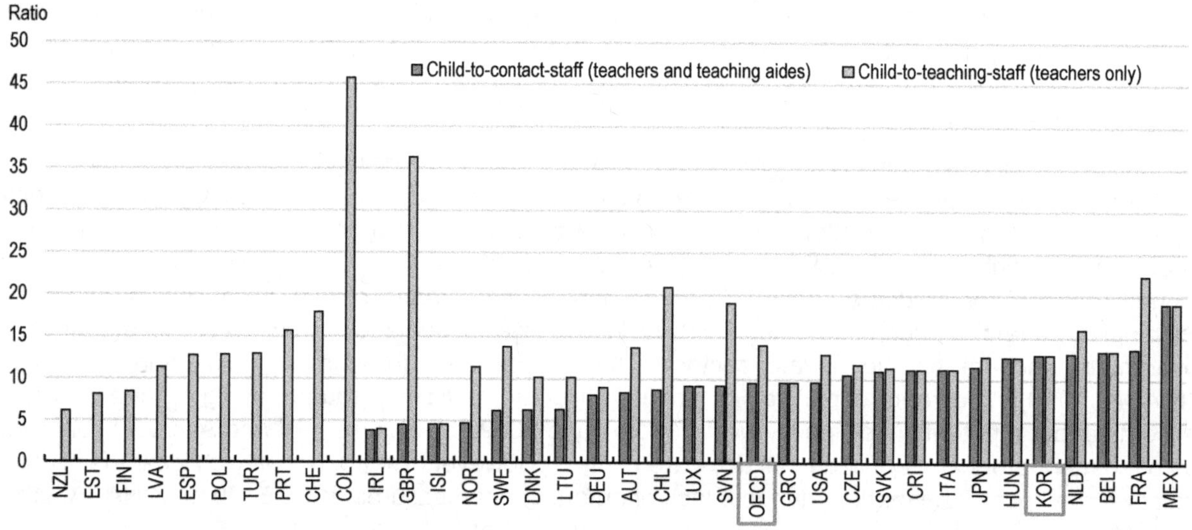


Note: The figures should be interpreted with some caution because the indicator compares the teacher/student ratios in countries with ""education-only" and "integrated education and daycare" programmes. In some countries, the staff requirements in these two types of provision are very different. Data for Japan do not cover day care centres and integrated centres for early childhood education and care. (http://www.oecd.org/education/education-at-a-glance-19991487.htm/?refcode=20190209ig).
Source: OECD Education at a Glance, https://www.oecd.org/education/education-at-a-glance/

StatLink https://stat.link/j0ldy9

Staff's initial education, continuing professional development and working conditions are the main policy considerations to ensure process quality in ECEC (OECD, 2022a). Most OECD countries, including Belgium, Denmark, Estonia, Norway and Sweden, require a bachelor's degree or an equivalent for ECEC teachers, while some, including France, Iceland and Italy, require a master's degree (OECD, 2021). In some countries, the minimum required qualifications differ between early childhood development services and pre-primary education. For example, teachers working with younger children (usually under three years) in the Flemish Community of Belgium, the Netherlands, and Türkiye are required to have an upper secondary qualification, while teachers working with children from the age of three (or four in the Netherlands) are required to have a tertiary degree (OECD, 2022b). In Korea teachers in kindergartens are required to have tertiary degrees while teachers in childcare centres are only required to have upper secondary qualifications (OECD, 2016b; OECD, 2022b).

Working conditions, including salaries, contract status, and the organisational climate, are the second pillar for building and retaining a high-quality childcare service workforce (OECD, 2020a; OECD, 2021; OECD,

2019c). In addition to salary and career progression, hours worked and time allocation are important elements of staff's working conditions and well-being (OECD, 2021). The actual qualification level of many childcare staff in European countries is lower than the qualifications required, as unfriendly working conditions hinder the recruitment and retainment of qualified personnel (OECD, 2019b). In Korea, working conditions are not frequently monitored by the government. According to a survey by Korea's Institute for Childcare and Education, most staff work overtime and are dissatisfied with their low salaries with an overall satisfaction of 3.4 on a 5-point scale (Yang, 2020).

## Parental leave

Parental leave entitlements include maternity (or pregnancy) leave and paternity leave to be used immediately before, during and immediately after childbirth, and parental (and home-care) leave, which can be used more flexibly until the child reaches a certain age. These entitlements provide employment protection for parents absent from work to care for their young children combined with income replacement benefits. While leaves of absence might have a short-term negative impact on career progression, they are expected to have a positive effect on women's employment in the long run by maintaining attachment to the labour market and employer-employee matches (Mari and Cutuli, 2018). However, the parental leave system can have two effects on women's childbirth decisions. First, if returning to one's original place of work is guaranteed by the parental leave system, the opportunity cost created by career gaps associated with childbirth and child-rearing can be reduced. At the same time, parental leave benefits compensate for income loss, thereby enabling extended absences from work. Both effects would encourage women to have children, but their relative sizes are uncertain, and the income effect from parental leave benefits could mean that increased fertility comes at the expense of female labour supply. Studies outside of Korea have not always shown that parental leave policies have a positive impact on women's participation in the labour market, nor do such policies always encourage mothers to return to their original jobs (Budig et al., 2015; Cukrowska-Torzewska, 2017; Misra et al., 2011).

Empirical research from Korea indicates that increases in parental leave benefits encourage couples to have children. Parental leave benefits have kept rising since the system's introduction in 2001, and studies have examined the impact of these policy changes on women's childbirth decisions. Research by Kim et al. (2022) and Kwak (2022) investigated the effects of switching parental leave pay from a lump-sum to a fixed rate in 2011, using parents outside of the affected income band as a control group. Both studies found that an increase in parental leave benefits had a positive effect on the probability of having a child. Kim et al. (2022) found that the policy change increased the share of women in childbearing age becoming pregnant during a given period of time by between 2.3 and 2.5 percentage points. Kwak (2022), who used the same research design but took into account the movement between the control and treatment groups and the fact that only those enrolled in employment insurance are eligible for parental leave found a 2.1 to 2.5 percentage points increase in fertility.

Bae and Cheon (2018) found that married women in paid employment who perceived there to be a high possibility that they could use maternity and parental leave and return to their previous employer afterwards were more likely to give birth to their first child than the average. However, the effect of parental leave on the rate at which women actually return to their original workplace is generally found to be insignificant or even negative, contrary to its objective. Only about 70% remained in the same job just one month after returning from leave, falling to the mid to high 50% range after a year, despite a significant increase in the uptake rate since 2002.

Kim (2008) investigated differences between mothers who used their parental leave after maternity leave and those who did not and found that using parental leave had a negative impact on returning to their original workplace, and that longer leave duration led to lower rates of return. Kim also found that those who utilised parental leave exhibited a lower willingness to continue employment compared to those who did not. The biggest influence on women's willingness to return to their original workplace, and even on their willingness to continue employment at all, was not the workplace environment, or the use of parental leave, but rather the level of childcare support provided by the mother's family. Similarly, Lee (2009) found that those women who took up parental leave after having exhausted their maternal leave stayed with their employer for a shorter duration than those who did not, although this study did not claim causality. Lee pointed to a number of potential causes for this correlation, including individual preferences for family and negative career consequences for parental leavers upon their return. Mothers already more inclined to leave their jobs could self-select into taking up parental leave, while women who are able to and/or have stronger preferences towards combining family with continued work could self-select into other arrangements.

More recent research uses event studies to establish causality. Yoon (2019) investigated whether the post-payment system, which involves paying a portion of the parental leave payment (15% from January 2011 until July 2015, 25% thereafter) six months after employees return to their previous employer, had any impact. Yoon and Hong (2014) looked at how a 2011 shift from a lump-sum parental leave benefit to a fixed rate that entitled users to 40% of their normal salary affected workers in different income brackets. Neither study showed a significant impact on the rate at which parental leave users returned to work with their original employer. Jung and Yoon (2020) reached similar conclusions, while also looking into how quality of employment affect the probability of return to the original employer. Even though the usage rate of parental leave was higher in large corporations, the rate of return to the original workplace after parental leave was lower compared to small and medium-sized enterprises. This could indicate that large corporations provide relatively favourable conditions for using parental leave, but the competitive organisational culture and long working hours may make balancing work and childcare less feasible. Meanwhile, the study found that the likelihood of utilising the parental leave system was lower for high wage earners, but the probability that they would return to their original workplace afterwards was higher, probably because of the system's low benefit ceiling.

Qualitative studies can help understand better the barriers preventing parental leave from facilitating job retention as it was intended to, even though these results based on very limited samples cannot be interpreted as causal and representative. Yang et al. (2021) interviewed 12 parents who took parental leave, and found that women faced various challenges, for example looking after their children when they had to stay home from school. They also experienced difficulties in adapting to organisational changes that were made while they were on leave, faced uncomfortable scrutiny, and scored lower on performance evaluations. These findings are supported by Seo and Kim (2016), which focused on eight individuals who resigned after their parental leave period ended. They found that women who had originally intended to return to work resigned after experiencing disadvantages at work and a strong attachment to their offspring.

There is also research suggesting that the use of parental leave has had a positive impact on preventing career interruptions for mothers in Korea, but these studies suffer from weaknesses casting the results in doubt. For instance, the empirical design used by Oh and Kim (2021) suffers from endogeneity, and Park et al. (2018) examined the impact of the respondents' perceived availability of parental leave on job retention, rather than actual use. As such the results should be understood to indicate that workplaces where parental leave is easily available tend to have characteristics with a positive effect on women's career maintenance, rather than the one causing the other.

There is no agreement on the optimal duration of parental leave (OECD, 2011; Budig et al., 2012), and the design, length and generosity of parental leave entitlements vary widely across countries (ILO, 2014). If parental leave is too short, mothers may not be ready to return to work and instead drop out of the labour force. If it is too long, skills may deteriorate, and extended absence from paid work can make return to work difficult (Canaan et al., 2022; Misra et al., 2011). Maternity leave is generally reserved for mothers (with exceptions notably for adoption) at or around the time of childbirth. Its average duration across the OECD is 19 weeks. Most OECD member countries also provide statutory rights to paid paternity leave around the birth of the child. At 2.5 weeks on average, these entitlements are much shorter than for maternity leave. Parental leave allows fathers and mothers to take longer periods of paid employment-protected leave to care for their young children (Figure 4.10). Duration varies considerably across countries. Finland provides 148.5 weeks of combined parental and home-care leave, while some countries do not offer any parental leave at all (OECD, 2023b). Korea offers 13 weeks of maternity leave, two weeks of paternity leave, and 52 weeks of parental leave for each parent on an individual basis, for a total of 119 weeks, which is the fourth longest duration in the OECD, behind Finland, Hungary and the Slovak Republic. Korea also plans to extend the maximum duration of paid parental leave for dual-income earners by six months per parent, if both parents take parental leave for more than three months each.

**Figure 4.10. Paid leave entitlements differ across the OECD**

Total number of weeks of parental leave, including maternity and paternity leave, 2023

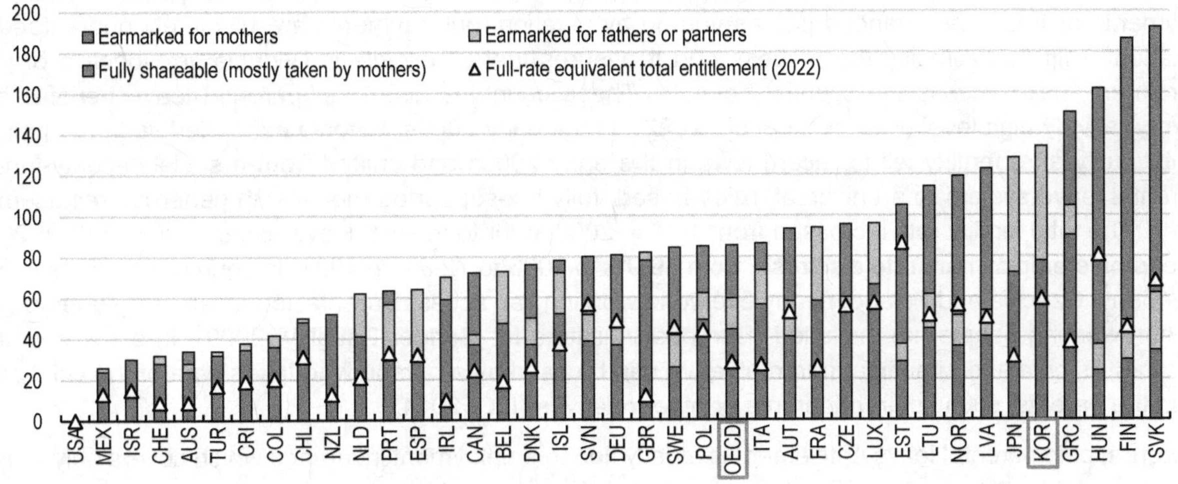


Note: Information refers to paid maternity, paternity, parental and home-care leave entitlements to care for young children in place as of April 2023. Data reflect entitlements at the national or federal level only. Because payment rates vary across countries and types of leave, entitlements are presented in both "duration in weeks" and "full-rate equivalent", the length of the paid leave in weeks if it was paid at 100% of previous earnings, calculated for an individual on 100% of national average earnings.
Source: OECD Family Database.

StatLink https://stat.link/yigxzr

Maternity, paternity, and parental leave compensation is available in most OECD countries to support parents during the time spent out of work. There are large differences between the systems in individual OECD countries, but a general pattern is that maternity and paternity leaves are well-paid, while parental leave has a lower replacement rate. Most OECD countries provide benefits that replace somewhere between one-third and two-thirds of previous earnings for paid parental leave. Some European member countries, such as Sweden, Finland, Poland, and Denmark, compensate at least 66% of previous monthly pay for parental leave, while countries like Ireland, Israel, Malta, Netherlands, Spain, and the United Kingdom make no payment (European Institute for Gender Equality, 2020; Koslowski et al., 2022). The lowest replacement rates are often found in countries with the longest entitlements. This is because these longer leaves are often paid only through low flat-rate benefits and therefore replace only a small proportion of previous earnings for average earners.

Korea's full-rate equivalent total entitlement (the paid leave in weeks if it was paid at 100% of previous earnings) is among the highest in the OECD Figure 4.10). Korea's replacement rate is 80%, which is similar to Sweden, Norway, and Iceland. However, the payment ceiling, at KRW 1.5 million (or at the end of November 2024, the exchange rate was KRW 1 394 per 1 USD ) per month (higher if both parents take leave, as explained below), is around 46% of the average wage (as of 2022), lower than in countries such as Sweden (95% of the average wage), Norway (124%), and France (82%) (Koslowski et al., 2022). From

2025, the government plans to raise the ceiling to KRW 2.5 million for the first three months of parental leave, KRW 2 million for the next three months, and 1.6 million for the last six months (see below).

Parental leave is often unavailable for certain categories of workers, such as the self-employed, non-standard (short-term, part-time), or informal workers (ILO, 2014). In EU countries, ineligibility rates are often high, notably for young workers and those with lower education, with workers in agriculture, forestry and fishery and in service and sales least likely to be eligible (European Institute for Gender Equality, 2020).

Some countries take a rules-based approach, rather than the insurance membership-based approach. Countries such as Croatia, Finland and Sweden allow all working women and men to access parental leave regardless of employment status, length of employment or type of job. In these countries, only basic conditions are imposed such as working in the country. There may be a social insurance fund making the payments or it may be financed pay-as-you-go by taxation, but payments are ultimately guaranteed by taxation. This may simplify the process and it ensures that all eligible individuals, irrespective of prior enrolment, have access to essential benefits. These countries also offer parental leave benefits at a comparatively high level (Koslowski et al., 2022). In the early 2000s, Estonia expanded its family policies ambitiously after fertility fell to record lows in the early 2000s and shifted from a social security-funded parental leave system to a universal, rules-based, fully tax-supported model with generous replacement rates. The total fertility rate increased from 1.37 in 2003, prior to the first leave expansion, to 1.61 in 2021. The female employment rate also rose, from 59.9% in 2003 to 72.3% in 2021. In countries such as Latvia, Germany, Czechia and Poland, nearly everyone working can access parental leave, and only unemployed or non-working people are excluded (European Institute for Gender Equality, 2020). In some countries such as Estonia and Lithuania, parental leave can be used by a person who takes care of the child other than the parents, such as grandparents or other relatives (ILO, 2014).

In Korea, paid parental leave entitlement is mostly tied to employment insurance which covers only around half of the total workforce (or 77% of wage earners). Employment insurance in Korea funds parental leave benefits as well as unemployment benefits. To receive the parental leave payment, employees must have been insured for at least 180 days prior to the commencement of parental leave and take at least 30 consecutive days of leave. Employment insurance is not compulsory for self-employed and some platform workers. Some workers choose not to subscribe to employment insurance despite a legal obligation to do so. This leaves many non-regular workers, characterised by inherent job instability and vulnerability, ineligible for parental leave. A provision allowing employers to deny parental leave to workers with less than six months of continuous service creates an additional barrier that disproportionately affects non-regular workers who tend to have shorter periods of continuous employment (OECD, 2024a). Strict eligibility conditions combined with low uptake among those who are eligible results in one of the lowest shares of parents in the OECD taking parental leave in Korea, and the share is particularly low among men (OECD, 2022c).

Expanding paid parental leave coverage to the entire workforce is a priority to address the current disparity. One viable approach involves extending employment insurance coverage to all workers. Another approach could be shifting from the current membership-based approach to a rules-based approach for parental leave eligibility. Either way, increasing parental leave payments would require additional funding, given the escalating deficits in the employment insurance fund (Figure 4.11, Panel A). An estimate suggests that expanding parental leave entitlements to the entire workforce would require an additional 22% of the current total parental leave benefits expenditure under existing parameters (KIHASA, 2022a). When the parental leave benefit system was introduced in 2001, it was decided to fund it primarily through employment insurance, with any financial gaps being covered by general taxation through annual budget allocations. Since 2001, however, only a fraction of the total parental leave benefit payouts have been covered by general taxation (Figure 4.11, Panel B). With an upward trend in both take-up rates and benefit levels, the share of parental leave benefit payouts in the employment insurance fund has grown. Without additional funding, this can jeopardise the primary role of employment insurance in safeguarding those who are unemployed (NABO, 2023).

Figure 4.11. Only a small share of parental leave payments are funded by general taxation

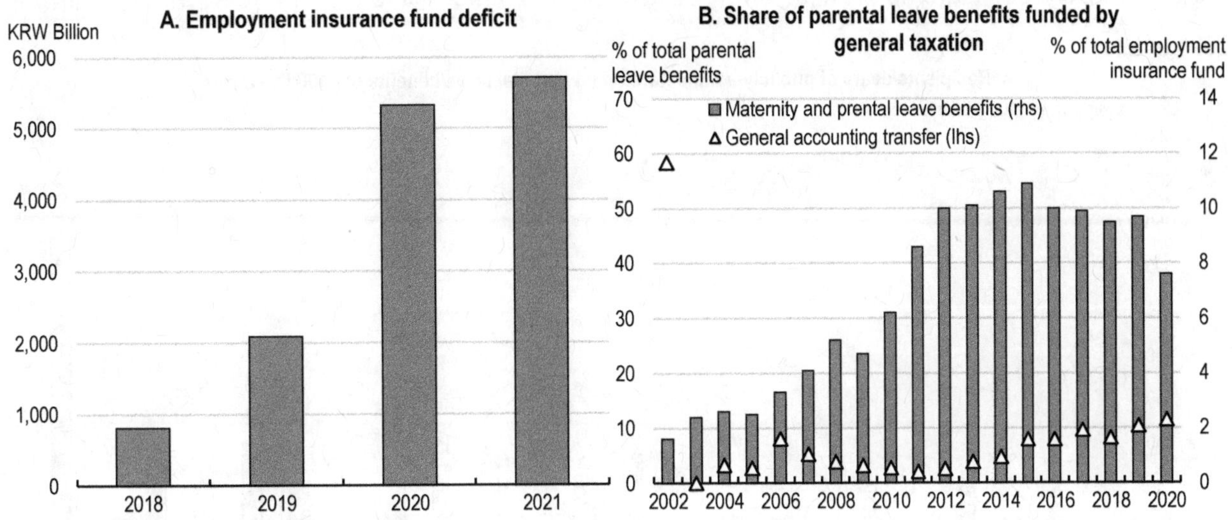


Source: OECD Economic Surveys: Korea 2024.

In most OECD countries, including Korea, fathers take considerably less parental leave than mothers (Figure 4.12, Panel B). In countries like Luxembourg, Iceland and Sweden, fathers account for almost 50% of all parental leave users, while in countries like Australia, New Zealand, Poland and Czechia, fathers hardly take any parental leave. Studies have shown that when fathers take paternity leave and are more involved in the care of young children, it positively impacts mothers' employment, reduces the gender pay gap, and stimulates children's development (Bartova and Keizer, 2020).

Another potential reason to want to reduce the gender imbalance in uptake, is that the expansion of parental leave could in intensify statistical discrimination against women in hiring, as argued by Mandel and Semyonov (2005). This does not seem to be the case in Korea. Using data 2005 to 2019, Kim (2022) showed that the introduction of the parental leave system in workplaces significantly increased the proportion of female workers within the company, in particular a substantial increase in the number of non-managerial, entry-level female employees. These findings suggest that companies adopting the parental leave system may have shifted to a more favourable stance on the employment of women. The introduction of the parental leave system could also have led to a decrease in female turnover and affected corporate preferences. However, the study said nothing about how parental leave use affects the gender wage gap, which is likely also affected by gender gaps in parental leave-taking, as discussed in Chapter 3.

There are strong correlations between gender equality, the generosity of parental leave and female employment rates. In EU countries where the gender gap in employment is small, the gap in parental leave eligibility is also small. Sweden and Finland have the highest gender equality in the European Union with universal parental leave rights (European Institute for Gender Equality, 2020). Many sociocultural factors can discourage fathers' uptake of parental leave regardless of the type of family leave provided. This includes gender norms and stereotypes that lead to gendered expectations, work practices and policies.

To enhance fathers' take-up of paid leave, many OECD countries have introduced "fathers-only" paid leave entitlements that cannot be transferred to mothers and are lost if not taken by the father. In many Nordic countries, these quotas take the form of gender-neutral specified portions of an overall parental leave period allocated exclusively for each parent. These are often referred to as "father quotas". Other countries, such as Korea, take the idea of reserved quotas to its logical conclusion and provide paid parental leave as an individual, non-transferable, gender-equal benefit (Adema et al., 2020). Certain countries, such as Germany, offer "fathers bonuses" in which a couple may be eligible for additional weeks of paid leave if both parents utilise a certain quantity of shareable leave. Evidence suggests that the introduction of fathers-only parental leave has increased the use of parental leave by fathers. In Sweden, for example, both the number of fathers taking leave and the duration of their leaves increased after the introduction of the father quota (Duvander and Johansson, 2012).

### Figure 4.12. Korean parents are less likely to use their parental leave than in most OECD countries

2021 or latest

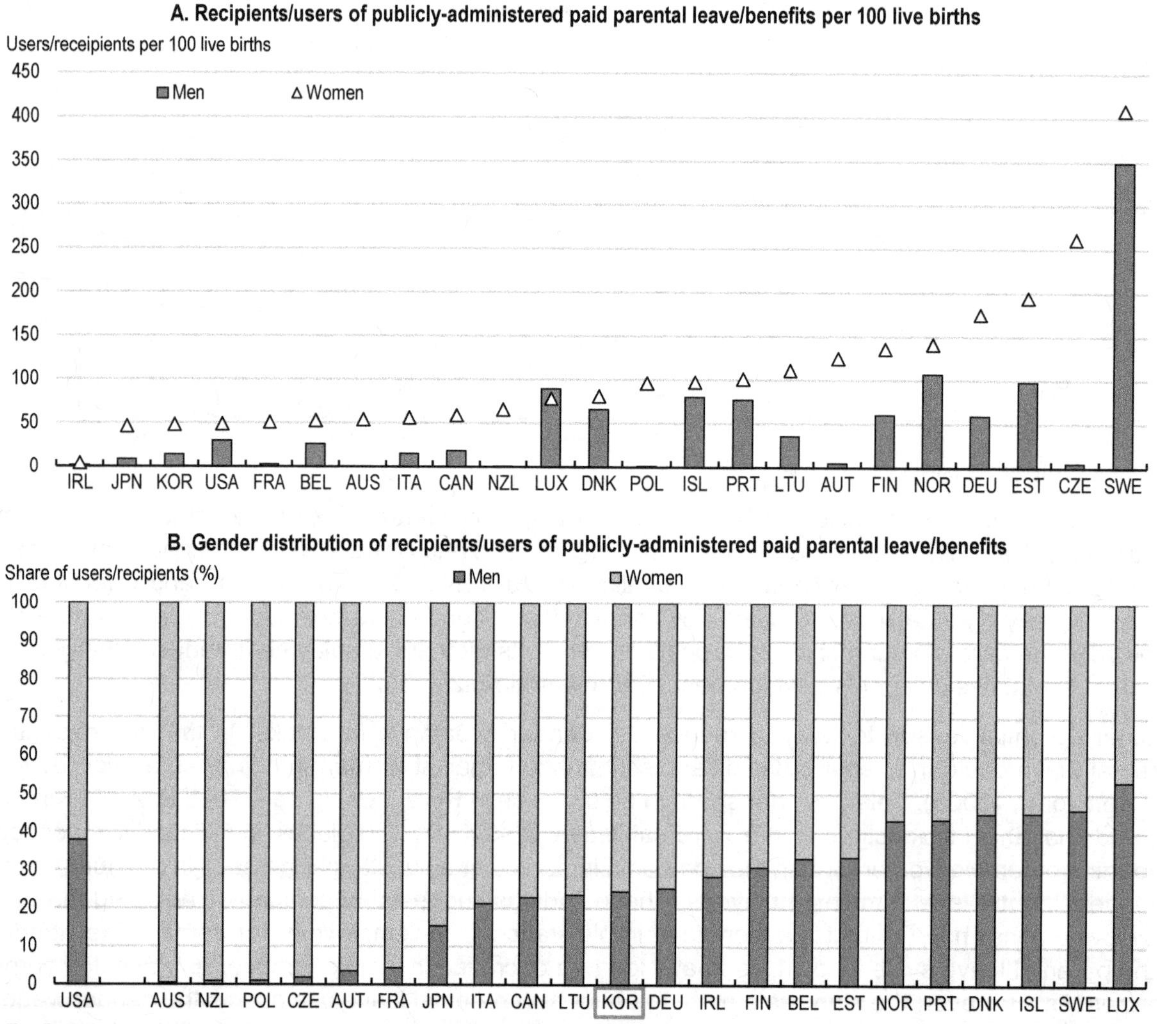


Note: For Panel A, paid parental leave recipient rates exceeding 100 reflects both high take-up and the ability of parents to take leave over several years and/or in multiple blocks. Data refer to 2021 for the Czech Republic, Estonia, Finland, Germany, Ireland, Japan, Norway and Poland. Data refer to 2020 for Austria, Belgium, Canada, Denmark, Korea, Lithuania, Luxembourg, Portugal and Sweden. Data refer to 2018 for Iceland and Italy, to 2017 for Australia and New Zealand, to 2016 for France and to a pooled average between 2016 and 2020 for the United States.
Source: OECD Economic Surveys: Korea 2024.

The benefit level is the other determinant of fathers' use of parental leave, given that the highest salary in many families is earned by the man (Karu and Tremblay, 2018). A high replacement rate is linked to a greater leave uptake by all parents, notably by fathers (Boll et al., 2014). For instance, 74% of Spanish fathers took at least some of their 4.4 weeks of fully paid paternity leave, while uptake was very low for the following parental leave without compensation (Blum et al., 2018). From 2024, if both parents use parental leave, the Korean government increased the replacement rate to 100% of previous earnings for the first six months of leave and raised the ceilings from KRW 2-3 million to 2-4.5 million based on the duration of the leave (MOEL, 2024a).

Flexibility, which enables parents to choose when and how to use their leave entitlements and the associated benefit level, also affects fathers' uptake of parental leave. For example, when the Austrian government allowed shorter leave options with a higher replacement rate in 2008, fathers' leave taking increased by 23%. The introduction of income-dependent benefits in 2010, increasing replacement rates, raised take-up by another 13% (Ziegler and Bamieh, 2023). Flexibility in the use of leave entitlements has several dimensions, including whether parents' individual and shared entitlements must be used consecutively, whether both parents can use their entitlements at the same time, whether parents need to use their whole entitlement in one go or whether they can break it into several time blocks or take the leave on a part-time basis (Bartova and Keizer, 2020). Korea allows parents to take a year's total parental leave in three batches until the child turns eight.

The use of parental leave in Korea is among the lowest in the OECD for both mothers and fathers (Figure 4.12). Consequently, public expenditure on parental leave benefits was the second-lowest in the OECD in 2019, although the recent expansion of benefits for working couples is expected to improve the ranking somewhat (Figure 4.13). As mentioned above, most self-employed and non-standard workers are excluded from parental leave benefits, but take-up rates are also low among those who are eligible. Only around three out of ten eligible parents exercised their paid parental leave right in 2022, although most of them were aware of the system, according to Statistics Korea. The utilisation rates are especially low among men and in small businesses (fewer than 50 employees). In 2021, the usage rate of parental leave during the year of the child's birth in small businesses (5-49 employees) was 54.1% for women and only 2.3% for men. In the same year, the corresponding rate in larger companies (over 300 employees) was 76% for women and 6% for men (Statistics Korea, 2022).

**Figure 4.13. Public expenditure on child-related leaves in Korea is among the lowest in the OECD**

Public expenditure on maternity and parental leaves per live birth, in current USD 2019 PPP, 2019

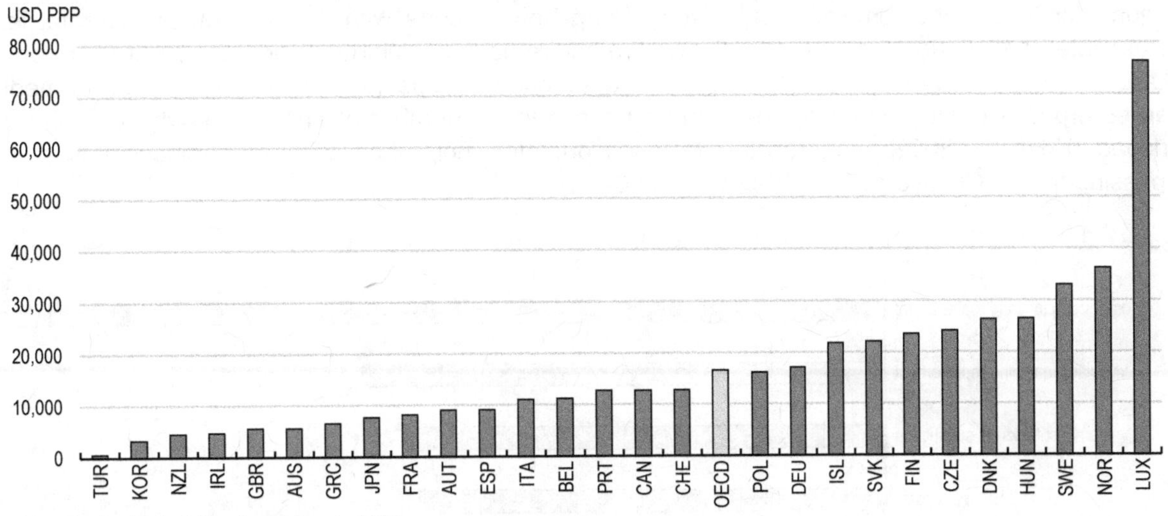


Note: Data for the United Kingdom refers to 2018.
Source: OECD Social Expenditure Database and OECD Health Statistics.

StatLink https://stat.link/w9h4eq

The low usage rate in SMEs is related to optionality in the parental leave system, where parents with children under the age of eight can either utilize parental leave or opt for a work-hour reduction system with compensation for the reduced income. The system is universal, but it is utilised differently by parents in different income brackets and employment situations. Employees of small and medium-sized enterprises (SMEs) tend to use the work-hour reduction system, whereas employees of large corporations are more likely to use the parental leave system. As of 2022, 49.4% of those using the work-hour reduction system for childcare were employed at workplaces with fewer than 30 employees, and notably, those from workplaces with 5 to 29 employees accounted for 36.8% of all users of this system. On the other hand, the proportion of parental leave benefit users from businesses with fewer than 30 employees was only 28.4%, and those from workplaces with 5 to 29 employees made up just 19.6%, which is lower than the utilization of the work-hour reduction system for childcare (Choi et al., 2024).

This suggests that the conditions for making use of the parental leave system vary depending on the workplace environment. According to the 2021 results of the Work-Family Compatibility Survey conducted by the Ministry of Employment and Labor, 92.3% of respondents from workplaces with 300 or more employees stated that there was an atmosphere where one could "apply for parental leave at any time without worry", whereas only 59.3% of those from workplaces with fewer than 10 employees and 68.3% from workplaces with 10 to 29 employees responded the same.

These findings are related to a social norm against taking parental leave, weak legal protections against gender discrimination and discrimination of leave-takers upon their return to work. For example, mothers taking maternity leave are seen as less competent at work, while those not taking leave are seen as bad parents (Morgenroth and Heilman, 2017). A government survey identified “an unfavourable workplace atmosphere or culture toward parental leave users” (31.8%) and “increased workload on colleagues” (25.2%) as the main reasons for underutilisation (MOEL, 2022).

This social pressure to avoid taking up parental leave reflects that employers often do not hire replacements. The 2021 results of the Work-Family Compatibility Survey revealed that in terms of the management difficulties caused by implementing parental leave, 28.2% of enterprises with 300 or more employees reported "no difficulties," while only 9.1% of workplaces with 5 to 9 employees and 7.7% of those with 10 to 29 employees reported the same, indicating that management difficulties vary according to the size of the enterprise. When asked about the primary management issues, 37.0% of workplaces with 5 to 9 employees cited "difficulty in finding replacement staff" as the top issue, while only 26.9% of those with 300 or more employees reported this issue (MOEL, 2022). The cost burden on employers is a primary deterrent (Figure 4.14). The absence of replacement workers generally leads to an increased workload for those who remain. In a survey asking how to cope with the gap left by parental leave, approximately half of the respondents indicated that the remaining employees bear the additional workload (MOEL, 2022). Like in other OECD countries, the situation is especially serious for small and medium-sized enterprises (SMEs) because these firms have a lower number of employees who can share the workload (KIHASA, 2022b). In Korea, SMEs account for more than 85% of domestic employment, surpassing the OECD average of 69% (OECD, 2023c).

**Figure 4.14. Cost burdens hinder employers from hiring replacements for staff on parental leave**

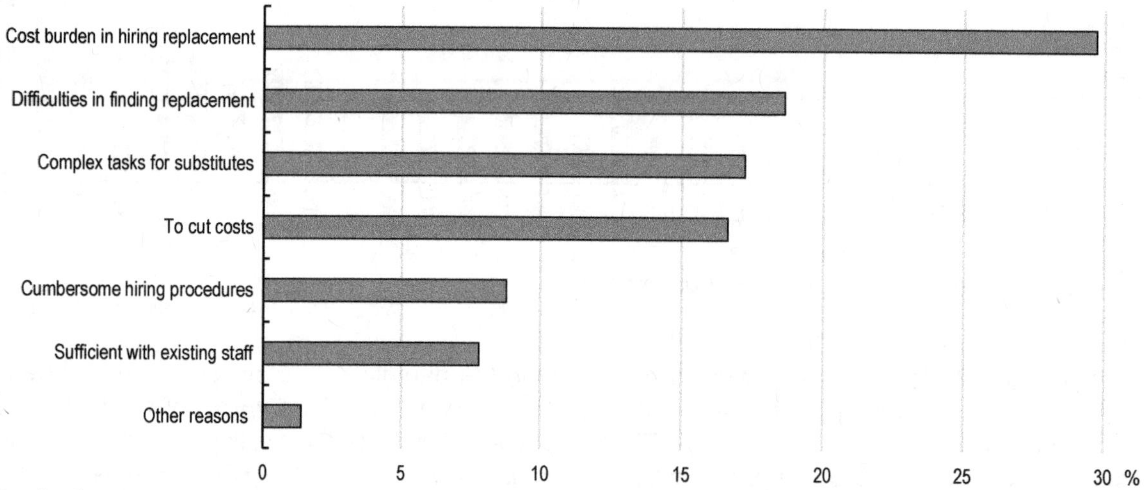


Note: Results of an online survey conducted among 506 member companies, each with exports of over $500,000 and employing more than five regular workers. The survey asked, "If your company does not hire substitute workers during an employee's parental leave, what are the reasons?".
Source: OECD Economic Surveys: Korea 2024.

Another reason why people may be discouraged from taking parental leave is that Korean employers bear a higher share of the cost of maternity, paternity and parental leave than in most OECD countries. For the first 60 days of maternity leave, employers in companies with over 500 employees are obliged to pay 100% of the ordinary earnings of leave takers (Table 4.2). If the employer hires a replacement, the employer has to pay two salaries for one position. For SMEs, the government offers maternity leave benefits for the first 60 days, but the maximum monthly amount is KRW 2.1 million which is only slightly above the monthly minimum wage (KRW 2.06 million) and employers are required to cover the gap. In addition, employers, regardless of firm size, have to continue to pay health insurance premia for parental leave takers throughout the leave period, amounting to 3.5% of gross salaries, while other social security contributions can be exempted during parental leave. The government provides financial support for replacement personnel up to KRW 800 thousand to SME employers, with an increased level of support of KRW 1.2 million per month during the take-over period (up to two months). However, this was deemed insufficient to alleviate the financial burden. For instance, when replacing employees on the minimum wage taking maternity leave for 30 days, the additional costs for SME employers were estimated at around KRW 2.01 million per month (NABO, 2023), not including the time and expenses associated with recruiting new staff and providing necessary training. SME employers now can receive a monthly allowance of KRW 2 million for the first three months and KRW 300 thousand hereafter when granting parental leave for 30 days or more, but this allowance is no longer contingent on hiring replacement staff.

**Table 4.2. Major supports for paid parental leave in 2024 in Korea**

| | Paid maternity leave | Paid paternity leave | Paid childcare leave |
|---|---|---|---|
| Eligibility | Mothers eligible for employment insurance | Fathers eligible for employment insurance | Parents eligible for employment insurance |
| Length | 90 days | 10 days | 12 months for each parent |
| Benefit level and funding source | • Large companies<br>First 60 days: 100% of previous earnings, paid by employers.<br>Remaining 30 days: The Employment Insurance funds, with a maximum monthly payment of KRW 2.1 million. Employers are not required to supplement.<br>• SMEs<br>First 60 days: The Employment Insurance funds maternity leave benefits, with a maximum monthly payment of KRW 2.1 million.<br>Employers are required to pay the difference between the regular salary and KRW 2.1 million.<br>Remaining 30 days: The Employment Insurance funds maternity leave benefits, with a maximum monthly payment of KRW 2.1 million. Employers are not required to supplement. | • Large companies<br>100% of previous earnings, paid by employers.<br>• SMEs<br>Employment insurance funds a max of KRW 401 910; employers should cover the gap with a regular salary. | 80% of previous earnings, paid by the Employment Insurance Fund (Ceilings: KRW 1.5 million).<br>If both parents use parental leaves:<br>100% of previous earnings for the first 6 months, paid by the Employment Insurance Fund.<br>Ceilings: KRW 2 million – 4.5 million<br>(First month: KRW 2 million<br>Second month: KRW 2.5 million<br>Third month: KRW 3 million<br>Fourth month: KRW 3.5 million<br>Fifth month: KRW 4 million<br>Sixth month: KRW 4.5 million) |

Note: SMEs are companies with 500 permanent employees or fewer for manufacturing industries, 300 or fewer for mining, construction, transport and warehousing, telecommunications, business facilities management, business support and rental services, professional, scientific and technical services and health and social work services, 100 or fewer for other industries, and SMEs under the SMEs Framework Act.
Source: Ministry of Employment and Labour; Ministry of Health and Welfare.

The burden of financing maternity, paternity and parental leave benefits and associated costs should in general be shared between parents and the government. Employers should be shielded from this cost, as they will tend to respond by discriminating in hiring and pay, discouraging leave taking and potentially even attempting to make pregnant workers resign. Many OECD countries, including Denmark and the United Kingdom, almost fully compensate maternity, paternity and parental leave benefits using public sources (Government of the United Kingdom, 2024; Strang et al., 2016), or compensate for the additional costs of hiring replacements during maternity leave as is the case in Italy (Clauwaert and Harger, 2000). In the United Kingdom, larger businesses can reclaim 92% of the maternity leave payments, and small employers

103% (Government of the United Kingdom, 2024). In France, employers with fewer than 50 employees receive financial support for temporary replacements during parental leave, covering up to 50% of the monthly minimum wage for each replacement (Tissot, 2024).

Enhancing workforce planning and ensuring more effective hiring of replacements can be achieved by extending the advance notice requirement for parental leave. Currently, employees seeking childcare leave must submit their application at least 30 days before the scheduled start date in Korea. This is a shorter notice period than in many OECD countries. In Sweden, for example, employees are required to give notice at least two months prior to the intended start date of childcare leave (Försäkringskassan, 2021). In Luxembourg, parental leave that follows maternity leave must be notified to the employer no later than two months before the start of the maternity leave (Government of Luxembourg, 2024).

Another challenge for workers taking parental leave is the low benefit level. The government doubled the ceiling for dual income parents in 2022 to encourage fathers to take parental leave. This increase only applied if both parents chose to take parental leave. After this reform, take-up rates among fathers increased by approximately 30% compared to the previous year (NABO, 2023). Given the positive outcomes, the government further increased the maximum by 1.5 times in January 2024 (e.g., to KRW 4.5 million or 130% of the average wage) (Table 4.2). As a result, the income loss of dual-income couples taking parental leave has been greatly reduced. For instance, if both parents, each earning an average income, take parental leave for six months at the same time, the household income reduction compared to previous earnings is now approximately 10%, down from 60% in 2021 (Figure 4.15, Panel A).

However, the general ceiling applicable when only one parent takes parental leave has seen minimal change over time (Figure 4.15, Panel B). This is an obstacle to the broader adoption of parental leave, particularly among sole leave takers. Assuming that a single-income father earns the average wage, six months of parental leave will reduce household income by more than 60% (Panel B). The government plans to raise the ceiling from KRW 1.5 million to KRW 2.5 million for the initial three months. This is a considerable improvement, but still represents only around 70% of the average wage and remains below the ceiling applied to some dual-income earners mentioned above. In most OECD countries, one ceiling around the average wage applies across all types of households and scenarios (Koslowski et al., 2022).

**Figure 4.15. Household income is reduced when taking parental leave**

Share of previous income, average earners

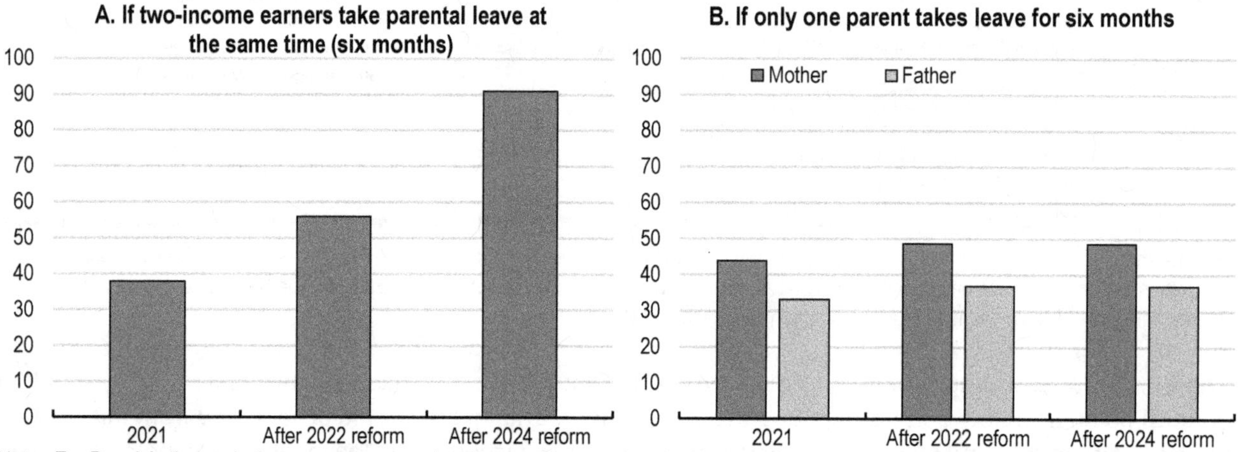


Note: For Panel A, the analysis assumes a scenario where each parent in a dual-income family earns the average salary and they concurrently take parental leave for six months. In contrast, Panel B assumes that only one parent in a single-income household takes a six-month parental leave. In both panels, the average salary for mothers and fathers is set as the average income of individuals aged 30-34 and 35-40, respectively. This choice reflects the average age at the time of childbirth, which was 33.5 for mothers and 36 for fathers in 2022.
Share of the previous household income for Panel A, and share of the previous individual income for Panel B.
Source: OECD Economic Surveys: Korea 2024.

Higher replacement rates for parental leave will lead to higher direct costs under the existing setting. Korea can limit the extra fiscal burden by giving parents the flexibility to shorten parental leaves at higher replacement rates, such as in Austria and Czechia. The introduction of such flexibility would also help increase fathers' uptake and incentivise mothers' to take leaves of shorter duration. From 2024, the Korean government extended the maximum period of parental leave per parent by another six months. The government plans to make it flexible by offering a higher benefit for the first few months and then providing support at lower levels of benefits for subsequent periods without reducing the overall duration of leave.

## Financial transfers

All OECD countries offer cash transfers or tax breaks to families with children. Family-related transfers are aimed at alleviating the direct cost of having children and creating better life conditions for children by improving families' financial conditions (Sobotka et al., 2019; OECD, 2011). It is worth noting, as discussed above, that even transfers for the purposes of childcare and parental leave do not always increase female labour supply, as the increased non-work income enables mothers to stay at home for longer if individual circumstances make this the preferred choice. By increasing non-work income without any added employment incentives, cash transfers or tax breaks to families with children may to a smaller or larger extent incentivise fertility, but they will almost without exception disincentivise female employment.

The most usual types of financial transfers are cash transfers and tax breaks. Cash transfers usually come in two types: cash benefits given on a regular basis and "baby bonuses", birth grants and other transfers paid as a lump sum. These transfers may be income-tested, and benefit levels may vary with the age or number of children. Tax breaks are typically in the form of tax credits and deductions from taxable income. Tax breaks include tax exemptions for income tax, child tax allowances reducing taxable income as a function of the number and age of children, and child tax credits. OECD countries, except for the United States, provide more cash transfers than tax support. Luxembourg, Poland, Estonia, and Belgium have cash transfers of more than 2% of GDP, while France, Hungary and Germany have high tax breaks relative to other OECD countries (Figure 4.16, Panel A). Korea's combined cash transfers and tax breaks per child are around 3% of GDP per capita. This is among the lowest in the OECD, less than half the OECD average and a third of the EU average (Panel B).

Many studies find that regular cash transfers and lump-sum grants paid around childbirth have positive but only small effects on total fertility partly because the total amount of transfers often covers only a small part of the cost of raising children. They can be comparably more beneficial to low-income or low-educated parents who have a lower alternative cost of lost earnings and are more likely to care for their children at home (OECD, 2011; Thévenon and Gauthier, 2011). For example, a study on 18 OECD countries estimated that an increase in expenditures on cash benefits as a share of GDP per capita by 1 percentage point would lead to an increase in the total fertility rate by 0.02 percentage point (Luci-Greulich et al., 2013). Spain's 2003 income tax reform increased the number of children eligible for the child tax deduction and introduced a EUR 1200 refundable tax credit for employed mothers with children up to age three. This reform was found to increase fertility by 3 per 1000 women, or 5%, compared to a no-reform baseline, with more pronounced effects for younger, less-educated women with no previous children (Azmat and González, 2009). There is some evidence pointing to increased fertility in both low- and high-income groups following the implementation of Australia's "baby bonus", a generous lump sum birth grant in place between 2004 and 2014 (Drago et al., 2011; Sinclair et al., 2012), and Quebec's Allowance for Newborn Children, a generous, non-taxable, universal grant operated between 1988 and 1997 (Malak et al., 2019; Milligan, 2005). However these schemes had a high fiscal cost, and their causal effects on fertility remain disputed (Parr and Guest, 2011; Kim, 2014).

## Figure 4.16. Public expenditures for cash transfers and tax breaks for families are low in Korea

2019 or latest

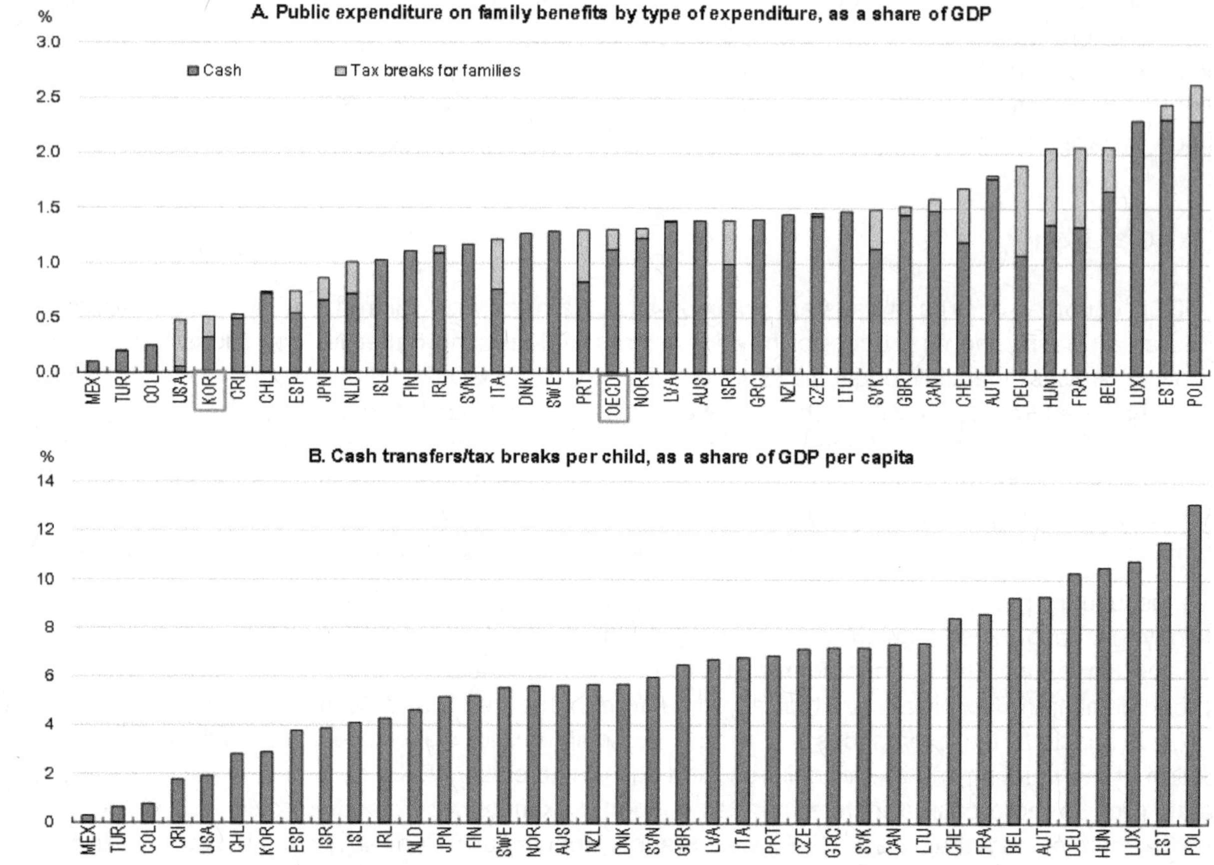


Source: OECD, Social Expenditure Database and author's calculations.

*StatLink* https://stat.link/0ohgrk

Korea provides cash allowances and tax breaks to parents (Table 4.3). The transfers mostly target parents with young children up to the age of eight. Starting in 2023, the central government introduced a cash handout for parents, offering KRW 700 000 per month for households with newborns. This amount was increased to KRW 1 million in 2024. Local governments also provide additional cash benefits to support childbirth. A study found that childcare allowances from the provincial government of Gangwon helped slow the decline in the fertility rate (Lee and Lee, 2022). There is also more anecdotal evidence that young couples move temporarily to places providing generous family support. Whether or not these local transfers have a positive effect on fertility at the national level, or if they mostly shift fertility to different places as prospective parents go "support shopping" is not clear.

What is clear is that Korea's low fertility is for the most part driven by the work-family conflict facing prospective mothers. Cash allowances or tax breaks will do nothing to ease this conflict, while they will probably induce some more women to choose family over career. However, the lost life-time income from choosing motherhood is very substantial and family benefits would need to be generous on a different scale to make up for lost income as well as women's lost opportunity to pursue their dreams and aspirations in working life. Public funds are therefore better used to invest in the quality and availability of free childcare, to improve the parental leave system, to invest in labour inspectors fighting discrimination and otherwise paving the way for labour market reforms to better balance career and family.

## Table 4.3. Major financial family supports in 2024

| | Cash allowance | | | | Tax breaks | |
|---|---|---|---|---|---|---|
| | *Maternity support* ("First meeting Voucher") | *Childcare allowance* | | *Home care allowance* | *Income tax deduction* | *Tax credit* |
| | | Parental allowance | Child allowance | | | |
| Eligibility | Children under 1 year old | Children under 2 years old | Children under 8 years old | Children not using childcare centre and not receiving parental allowance | Children under 20 years old (taxable income under KRW 1 million, but under KRW 5 million in case of only earned income) | Children 8 to 20 years old |
| Duration | One-off | 23 months | 95 months | 85 months | 20 years | 12 years |
| Benefit level | For the first child: KRW 2 million<br>From the second child: KRW 3 million | Children 0 to 11 months old: KRW 1 million per month<br>Children 12 to 23 months old: KRW 500 thousand | Children 0 to 95 months old: KRW 100 thousand per month | Children 24 to 85 months old: KRW 100 thousand | 1.5 million per year | For one child: KRW 150 thousand per year<br>For two children: KRW 350 thousand<br>For three or more children: KRW 350 thousand + KRW 300 thousand from the third child |

Source: Ministry of Health and Welfare; Ministry of Economy and Finance; NABO.

## References


Adema, W., C. Clarke and O. Thévenon (2020), “Family policies and family outcomes in OECD countries”, *The Palgrave Handbook of Family Policy*, Palgrave Macmillan, Cham.

André, C., O. Causa, E. Soldani, D. Sutherland and F. Unsal (2023), "Promoting gender equality to strengthen economic growth and resilience", *OECD Economics Department Working Papers*, No. 1776, OECD Publishing, Paris.

Asia Economy Daily (2017), “Why don’t securities firms have workplace daycare centers?”, *Asia Economy Daily* (in Korean).

Azmat, G. and L. González (2009), "Targeting fertility and female participation through the income tax", *IZA Discussion Papers*, No. 4405.

Bae, H. and J. Cheon (2018), “The effects of maternity and parental leave and childcare leave usability on childbirth: focusing on new-married women”, *Women’s Studies*, Vol. 96/1 (in Korean).

Baizan, P., B. Arpino and C. Delclòs (2016), “The effect of gender policies on fertility: The moderating role of education and normative context”, *European Journal of Population*, Vol. 32/1.

Bartova, A. and R. Keizer (2020), “How well do European child-related leave policies support the caring role of fathers?”, *The Palgrave Handbook of Family Policy*, Palgrave Macmillan, Cham.

Blum, S., A. Koslowski, A. Macht and P. Moss (2018), *14th International Review of Leave Policies and Related Research 2018.*

Boll, C., J. Leppin and N. Reich (2014), “Paternal childcare and parental leave policies: Evidence from industrialized countries”, *Review of Economics of the Household*, Vol. 12/1.

Budig, M., J. Misra and I. Boeckmann (2015), “Work–family policy trade-offs for mothers? Unpacking the cross-national variation in motherhood earnings penalties”, *Work and Occupations*, Vol. 43/2.

Byun, G. and Y. Heo (2014), “The effects of an increase in childcare subsidy on the time allocation of women: focusing on low-income and moderate-income women with pre-school children”, *Korean Journal of Social Welfare*, Vol. 66/2 (in Korean).

Cadima, J. (2020), “Literature review on early childhood education and care for children under the age of 3”, *OECD Education Working Papers*, No. 243, OECD Publishing, Paris.

Canaan, S., P. Rosenbaum, A.S. Lassen and H. Steingrimsdottir (2022), “Maternity leave and paternity leave: Evidence on the economic impact of legislative changes in high income countries”, *IZA Discussion Paper Series*, No. 15239, IZA Institute of Labour Economics.

Cartmel, J. and B. Hurst (2021), *More Than ’Just Convenient Care’: What The Research Tells Us About Equitable Access To Outside School Hours Care*, Griffith university.

Choi, S. (2011), “Childcare subsidies and the labour supply of married women”, Korean Social Security Studies, Vol. 27/2 (in Korean).

Choi, S., S. Ham, Y. Yang and J. Pareliussen (2024), “Women's employment and fertility in South Korea: a review of recent research”, *OECD Economics Department Working Papers*, No. 1825, OECD Publishing, Paris.

Choi, S. et al. (2022), *Work together and Care together?: An Evaluation of How Children Affect Parents’ Labor Supply in Korea*, Korea Labour Institute.

City of Helsinki (2023), *After-school Activities*.

Clauwaert, S. and S. Harger (2000), "Analysis of the implementation of the parental leave directive in the EU member states", *European Trade Union Institute.*

Coley, R. et al. (2016), "Comparing public, private, and informal preschool programs in a national sample of low-income children", *Early Childhood Research Quarterly*, Vol. 36.

Cukrowska-Torzewska, E. (2017), "Cross-country evidence on motherhood employment and wage gaps: the role of work-family policies and their interaction", *Social Politics: International Studies in Gender, State & Society*, Vol. 24/2.

Drago, R. et al. (2011), "Did Australia's Baby Bonus increase fertility intentions and births?", *Population Research and Policy Review*, Vol,30.

Duvander, A. and M. Johansson (2012), "What are the effects of reforms promoting fathers' parental leave use?", *Journal of European Social Policy*, Vol. 22/3.

EC (2023), *Organisation of Centre-based ECEC*, European Commission.

Engel, A., W. S. Barnet, Y. Anders and M. Taguma (2015), Early Childhood Education and Care Policy Review: Norway, OECD Publishing, Paris.

Eurydice (2019), *Key Data on Early Childhood Education and Care in Europe – 2019 Edition*, European Education and Culture Executive Agency, Publications Office of the European Union.

Eurofound (2020), *Out-of-school Care: Provision and Public Policy,* Publications Office of the European Union, Luxembourg.

European Commission (2022), *Proposal for a Council Recommendation on the Revision of the Barcelona Targets on early childhood education and care.*

European Institute for Gender Equality (2020) *Gender Equality Index 2019 – Work–life balance*, Publications Office.

Försäkringskassan (2021), *Parental leave employee.*

Government of Luxembourg (2024), *Pregnancy and maternity leave* (accessed in November 2024).

Government of the United Kingdom (2024), *Get financial help with statutory pay* (accessed in November 2024).

Greulich, A., O. Thevenon and M. Guergoat-Larivière (2016), *Securing Women's Employment: A Fertility Booster in European Countries?,* hal-01298862.

Han, S. (2021), "How to improve the primary school care system in response to increased female economic activity", *KDI Focus*, Korea Development Institute (in Korean).

Hu, B. Y., M. C. K. Mak, J. Neitzel, K. Li and X. Fan (2016), "Predictors of Chinese early childhood program quality: Implications for policies", *Children and Youth Services Review*, Vol. 70.

Huntsman, L. (2008), "Determinants of quality in child care: A review of the research evidence", New South Wales Department of Community Services, Australia.

ILO (2014), *Maternity and Paternity at Work : Law and Practice across the World*, International Labour Organisation.

Janta, B. (2014), *Caring for Children in Europe: How Childcare, Parental Leave and Flexible Working Arrangements Interact in Europe*, Rand Europe, Cambridge.

Jung, H. and J. Yoon (2020), "The use of maternity leave and return to work after childbirth: focus on the firm size and wage level", *The Journal of Women and Economics*, Vol. 16/4 (in Korean).

Jung, S. (2023), "A study on the career retention of women during childbirth and rearing period", *The Journal of Women and Economics*, Vol. 20/1 (in Korean).

Kaga, Y., J. Bennett and P. Moss (2010), *Caring and Learning Together: A Cross-national Study on the Integration of Early Childhood Care and Education Within Education*, UNESCO, Paris.

Karu, M. and D. Tremblay (2018), "Fathers on parental leave: an analysis of rights and take-up in 29 countries", *Community, Work and Family*, Vol. 21/3.

KICCE (2023), *Survey on Compliance with Mandatory Establishment of Workplace Childcare Centres,* Korea Institute of Child Care and Education (in Korean).

KICCE (2022), *Childcare Gaps in Households Utilising Childcare Centers and Kindergartens*, Korea Institute of Child Care and Education (in Korean).

KICCE (2019), "Analysis of demand and supply of daycare centres according to changes in infant and toddler population", Korea Institute of Child Care and Education (in Korean).

KIHASA (2022a), "Research on plans to reform maternity, paternity, and parental leave systems", Korea Institute for Health and Social Affairs.

KIHASA (2022b), *Monitoring and challenges of work-family reconciliation support policies,* Korea Institute for Health and Social Affairs (in Korean).

KIHASA (2013), "A study on improving the childcare delivery system through analysis of actors in childcare services", Korea Institute for Health and Social Affairs (in Korean).

Kim, D. H. (2022), "The effect of the introduction of parental leave on employment of female workers", *Quarterly Journal of Labour Policy,* Vol. 22/1 (in Korean).

Kim, D. I. (2022), "Child-care subsidy and mothers' labour supply", *Korean Journal of Labor Economics,* Vol. 45/2 (in Korean).

Kim, E. (2022), "Home childcare allowance users vs. daycare users", *Gender Statistics Information System Report (22-3),* Korea Women's Development Institute (in Korean).

Kim, H. (2018), "A panel data analysis on child care subsidies and married women's labour supply in Korea", *The Journal of Women and Economics*, Vol. 15/1 (in Korean).

Kim, J. (2008), "An empirical study on parental leave and job continuity among female workers", *Social Welfare Policy*, Vol.33 (in Korean).

Kim, K., S.H. Lee and T.J. Halliday (2022), "Paid childcare leave, fertility, and female labour supply in South Korea", *IZA Discussion Paper Series*, No. 15223, IZA Institute of Labour Economics.

Kim, Y. (2014), "Lifetime impact of cash transfer on fertility", *Canadian Studies in Population*, Vol.41/1-2.

KITA (2024), *Recommendations for establishing a family-friendly birth and parenting culture within companies*, Korea International Trade Association (in Korean).

Koslowski, A., S. Blum, I. Dobrotić, G. Kaufman and P. Moss (Ed.) et al. (2022), *18th International Review of Leave Policies and Related Research 2022*.

Kwak, E. (2022), "The impact of paid childcare leave on fertility decisions", *Korean Journal of Labor Economics,* Vol. 45/3 (in Korean).

La Paro, K., A. Williamson and B. Hatfield (2014), "Assessing quality in toddler classrooms using the CLASS-Toddler and the ITERS-R", *Early Education and Development*, Vol. 25/6.

Lee, C. (2022), "An analysis of heterogeneity in the effects of pronatal policies: effects of cash and childcare supports by income group", *The Korean Economic Forum*, Vol. 15/3 (in Korean).

Lee, C. and S. Lee (2022), "Effect of cash benefit on marital fertility: evidence from the Basic Child Care Allowance in Gangwon Province", *The Korean Journal of Economic Studies*, Vol. 70/2 (in Korean).

Lee, S. (2016), "The effect of childcare subsidy expansion on labour supply of mothers", *Korean Welfare Panel Academic Conference*, Vol. 9 (in Korean).

Lee, S. (2009), "The impact of parental leave on women's employment", *Korean Society and Public Administration*, Vol. 20/1 (in Korean).

Luci-Greulich, A. and O. Thévenon (2013), "The impact of family policies on fertility trends in developed countries", *European Journal of Population*, Vol. 29.

Malak, N. M. Rahman and T.Yip (2019), "Baby bonus, anyone? Examining heterogeneous responses to a pro-natalist policy", *Journal of Population Economics*, Vol. 32.

Mandel, H. and M. Semyonov (2005), "Family policies, wage structures, and gender gaps: sources of earnings inequality in 20 countries", *American Sociological Review*, Vol. 70/6.

Mari, G. and G. Cutuli (2019), "Do parental leaves make the motherhood wage penalty worse? Assessing two decades of German reforms", *SOEP papers on Multidisciplinary Panel Data Research*, DIW Berlin, The German Socio-Economic Panel (SOEP), No. 1025.

Milligan, K. (2005), "Subsidizing the stork: new evidence of tax incentives and fertility", *The Review of Economics and Statistics*, Vol.87/3.

Mills, M., P. Präg, F. Tsang, K. Begall, J. Derbyshire, L. Kohle, C. Miani, and S. Hoorens (2014), "Use of childcare in the EU Member states and progress towards the Barcelona targets", *Short Statistical Report No. 1*, Rand Corporation.

Min, G. and C. Lee (2020), "The effects of universal childcare subsidy on female labour supply and fertility", *Korean Journal of Labor Economics*, Vol 43/4 (in Korean).

Misra, J., M. Budig and I. Boeckmann (2011), "Work-family policies and the effects of children on women's employment hours and wages", *Community, Work and Family*, Vol. 14/2.

Ministry of Health and Welfare of Korea (2022), *Childcare Centres Satisfaction Survey Results in 2022,* Press release (in Korean).

MOEL (2024a), *6+6 Parental Leave Fact Sheet,* Ministry of Employment and Labour (in Korean).

MOEL (2024b), *Women, career interruption prevention and re-employment support*, Ministry of Employment and Labour (in Korean).

MOEL (2022), *2021 Survey on the Work-family Balance*, Ministry of Employment and Labour (in Korean).

MOHW (2024), *2023 Workplace Childcare Centers Suvey*, Ministry of Health and Welfare (in Korean).

MOHW (2022), *2021 National Childcare Status Survey - Kindergarten Survey Report*, Ministry of Health and Welfare (in Korean).

MOHW (2017), *Development strategies for childcare support systems*, Ministry of Health and Welfare (in Korean).

Morgenroth, T. and M. Heilman (2017), "Should I stay or should I go? Implications of maternity leave choice for perceptions of working mothers", *Journal of Experimental Social Psychology*, Vol. 72.

MSS (2024), *Status of Korean SMEs*, Ministry of SMEs and Startups (in Korean).

NABO (2023), *Analysis and evaluation of projects in response to low fertility*, National Assembly Budget Office (in Korean).

Noh, H. (2016), "Unequal distribution of family policy in Korea", *Korean Journal of Social Welfare Studies*, Vol. 47/3 (in Korean).

Nordic Health and Welfare Statistics (2024), *Early Childhood Education and Care*

OECD (2024a), *OECD Economic Surveys: Korea 2024,* OECD Publishing, Paris.

OECD (2024b), *OECD Family Database*.

OECD (2023a), *Exploring Norway's Fertility, Work, and Family Policy Trends*, OECD Publishing, Paris.

OECD (2023b), *Joining Forces for Gender Equality: What Is Holding Us Back?,* OECD Publishing, Paris.

OECD (2023c), *OECD SME and Entrepreneurship Outlook 2023,* OECD Publishing, Paris.

OECD (2022a), "Early childhood education and care workforce development : A foundation for process quality", *OECD Education Policy Perspectives*, No. 54, OECD Publsishing, Paris.

OECD (2022b), *Education at a Glance 2022: OECD Indicators*, OECD Publishing, Paris.

OECD (2022c), *OECD Economic Surveys: Korea 2022*, OECD Publishing, Paris.

OECD (2022d), *Reducing the Gender Employment Gap in Hungary*, OECD Publishing, Paris,

OECD (2021), *Starting Strong VI: Supporting Meaningful Interactions in Early Childhood Education and Care*, OECD Publishing, Paris.

OECD (2020a), *Building a High-Quality Early Childhood Education and Care Workforce: Further Results from the Starting Strong Survey 2018, TALIS*, OECD Publishing, Paris.

OECD (2020b), "Is Childcare Affordable?", *Policy Brief on Employment, Labour and Social Affairs*, OECD, Paris.

OECD (2020c), *Technical Support to Reduce the Gender Employment Gap in the Hungarian Labour Market Report on International Practice in Policies to Close Gender Employment Gaps*, OECD Publishing, Paris.

OECD (2019a), *Education at a Glance 2019 : OECD indicators,* OECD Publishing, Paris.

OECD (2019b), *Good Practice for Good Jobs in Early Childhood Education and Care*, OECD Publishing, Paris.

OECD(2019c), *Providing Quality Early Childhood Education and Care: Results from the Starting Strong Survey 2018*, OECD Publishing, Paris.

OECD (2019d), *Rejuvenating Korea: Policies for a Changing Society*, OECD Publishing, Paris.

OECD (2017), *The Pursuit of Gender Equality: An Uphill Battle,* OECD Publishing, Paris.

OECD (2016a), *Walking the tightrope: Background brief on parents' work-life balance across the stages of childhood,* OECD Publishing, Paris.

OECD (2016b), Who Uses Childcare? Background Brief on Inequalities in the Use of Formal Early Childhood Education and Care (ECEC) among Very Young Children, OECD Publishing, Paris.

OECD (2011), *Doing Better for Families*, OECD Publishing, Paris.

OECD (2007), *Babies and Bosses: Reconciling Work and Family Life*, OECD Publishing, Paris.

Oh, E. and S. Kim (2021), "Utilization of maternity protection policy during childbirth and child-rearing period and its impact on women's career interruption", *The Journal of Asian Women*, Vol. 60/1 (in Korean).

Parente, C. and N. Nakano (2020), "Compared analysis of the school day in European Union countries", *Cadernos de Pesquisa*, Vol. 50/175.

Park, C., S. Cho and N. Kim (2018), "The effects of maternity protection schemes on women's career interruption", *Korean Social Security Studies*, Vol. 34/4 (in Korean).

Parr, N. and R. Guest (2011), "The contribution of increases in family benefits to Australia's early 21st-century fertility increase: An empirical analysis", *Demographic Research*, Vol.25.

Seo, J. and S. Kim (2016), "Study on the resignation backgrounds of female workers leaving work after parental leave", *Korean Journal of Social Welfare Studies*, Vol. 47/4 (in Korean).

Sinclair, S., J. Boymal and A. Silva (2012), "A Re-appraisal of the fertility response to the Australian baby bonus", *The Economic Record*, 88.

Slot, P., M. Lerkkanen and P. Leseman (2015), The relations between structural quality and process quality in European early childhood education and care provisions: Secondary data analyses of large scale studies in five countries, CARE.

Sobotka, T., A. Matysiak and Z. Brzozowska (2019), "Policy responses to low fertility: How effective are they?", *Technical Division Working Paper series*, No. 1, UNFPA.

Statistics Korea (2022), *2021 Parental Leave Statistics* (in Korean)

Strang, L. and M. Broeks (2016), "Maternity leave policies: trade-offs between labour market demands and health benefits for children", *Rand Health.*

Thévenon, O. and A.H. Gauthier (2011), "Family policies in developed countries: a 'fertility-booster' with side-effects". *Community, Work & Family*, *14*(2).

Tissot (2024), *Congé maternité : aide financière au remplacement* (accessed in November 2024).

Turkish Laborlaw (2017), Lactation rooms and child care units for working mothers in Turkey, Turkishlabourlaw.com.

UK Government (2022), *Employer Supported Childcare (480: Appendix 11),* Government of the United Kingdom.

UNICEF (2020), "Universal child benefits: Policy issues and options*", Briefing,* UNICEF.

Vandenbroeck, M. (2020), "Early childhood care and education policies that make a difference", *The Palgrave Handbook of Family Policy*, Springer International Publishing.

Vandenbroeck, M., K. Lenaerts and M. Beblavý (2018), Benefits of Early Childhood Education and Care and the Conditions for Obtaining Them, European Expert Network on Economics of Education.

World Bank (2019), *Women, Business and the Law 2019,* World Bank.

Yang, M. (2020), "How to improve working conditions and compensation for teachers in daycare centres", *KICCE Issue Paper 2020-12*, Korea Institute of Child Care and Education (in Korean).

Yang, Y., H. Hwang and J. Pareliussen (2024), "Korea's unborn future: lessons from OECD experience", *OECD Economics Department Working Papers*, No. 1824, OECD Publishing, Paris.

Yoon, J. (2019), “Effects of parental leave policy on returning to work with a focus on the post-leave-payment system”, *Korean Social Security Studies*, Vol. 35/2 (in Korean).

Yoon, J. and M. Hong (2014), “Effects of the paid maternity leave policy on female employment”, *Quarterly Journal of Labor Policy*, Vol. 14/4 (in Korean).

Ziegler, L. and O. Bamiehm (2023), “What drives paternity leave: Financial incentives or flexibility?”, *IZA Discussion Paper Series*, No.15890, IZA Institute of Labour Economics.

www.ingramcontent.com/pod-product-compliance
Lightning Source LLC
LaVergne TN
LVHW060453061126
851857LV00016B/1814
* 9 7 8 9 2 6 4 5 4 5 1 1 3 *